Microsoft Office XP Quick Reference

Quick Keys That Work in *All* Office Applications

Lose your mouse and use your keyboard to enter common commands in...

To	Press	To	Press	To	Press
Select entire document	Ctrl+A	Print file	Ctrl+P	Delet...	
Copy selection	Ctrl+C	Save file	Ctrl+S	Get help	F1
Insert page break	Ctrl+Enter	Copy format of selection	Ctrl+Shift+C	Check spelling	F7
Find text or format	Ctrl+F	Paste format	Ctrl+Shift+V	Look up word in thesaurus	Shift+F7
Replace text	Ctrl+H	Paste selection	Ctrl+V	Activate menu bar	F10
Insert hyperlink (on a Web page)	Ctrl+K	Cut selection	Ctrl+X	File, Save As command	F12
Create new file	Ctrl+N	Cancel last undo action	Ctrl+Y	Insert line break	Shift+Enter
Open file	Ctrl+O	Undo last action	Ctrl+Z		

Microsoft Word Keystrokes

Word has more shortcut keys than can be listed here, but these are the pick of the lot (mostly for formatting text).

To	Press	To	Press	To	Press
Change font	Ctrl+Shift+F	Uppercase/ lowercase letters	Shift+F3	Single-space lines	Ctrl+1
Change font size	Ctrl+Shift+P	Make text bold	Ctrl+B	Double-space lines	Ctrl+2
Increase font size	Ctrl+Shift+>	Underline text	Ctrl+U	Center paragraph	Ctrl+E
Decrease font size	Ctrl+Shift+<	Underline text but not spaces between words	Ctrl+Shift+W	Move selected text or graphic	F2, move insertion point, and press Enter
Remove paragraph formatting	Ctrl+Q	Make text italic	Ctrl+I		
Remove character formatting	Ctrl+Spacebar	Remove text formatting (plain text)	Ctrl+Shift+Z	Insert an AutoText entry after typing its abbreviation	F3
Open selected drop-down list	Alt+Down Arrow				

Microsoft Excel Keystrokes

When you have a lot of entries to type, you don't want to be fumbling with your mouse. Use the following keystrokes, instead.

To	Press	To	Press	To	Press
End entry you typed	Enter (or Arrow key)	End cell entry and move to next cell to the right	Tab	Flip to previous worksheet page	Ctrl+Page Up
Cancel entry you typed	Esc	Select entire column	Ctrl+Spacebar	Go to specific cell or named range	F5
Create new line in a cell	Alt+Enter	Select entire row	Shift+Spacebar	Recalculate all formulas	F9
Edit cell entry	F2	Move one screen to the right	Alt+Page Down	Paste function into a formula	Shift+F3
Edit cell comment	Shift+F2	Move one screen to the left	Alt+Page Up	Insert AutoSum formula	Alt+= (equal sign)
Fill cell entry into cells below	Ctrl+D	Flip to next worksheet page	Ctrl+Page Down	Insert date	Ctrl+; (semi-colon)
Fill cell entry into cells to the right	Ctrl+R				

cut here

D0352848

Microsoft PowerPoint Keystrokes

PowerPoint shortcut keys vary depending on the selected view. Use the following table as your guide.

Outline and Slide Views		Slide Show Controls	
To	**Press**	**To**	**Press**
Promote paragraph	Alt+Shift+Left Arrow	Display next slide	Enter
Demote paragraph	Alt+Shift+Right Arrow	Display previous slide	Backspace
Move selected paragraphs up	Alt+Shift+Up Arrow	Go to specified slide number	Slide#+Enter
Move selected paragraphs down	Alt+Shift+Down Arrow	Start or stop timed slide show	S
Show only level 1 headings	Alt+Shift+1	End slide show	Esc
Show or collapse all text and headings	Alt+Shift+A	Set new timings during rehearsal	T
Collapse text below selected heading	Alt+Shift+– (minus sign)	Use original timings during rehearsal	O
Show text below selected heading	Alt+Shift++ (plus sign)	Change mouse pointer to a pen	Ctrl+P
		Change pen back to a mouse pointer	Ctrl+A

Microsoft Access Keystrokes

Yes, even Access has its own shortcut keys.

To	Press	To	Press
Move to next field in a form or table	Tab	Delete current record	Ctrl+– (minus sign)
Move to previous field in a form or table	Shift+Tab	Save changes to the current record	Shift+Enter
Insert current date	Ctrl+;	Select column to the left of currently selected column in Datasheet view	Shift+Left Arrow
Insert current time	Ctrl+Shift+;		
Insert field's default entry	Ctrl+Alt+Spacebar	Select column to the right of currently selected column in Datasheet view	Shift+Right Arrow
Insert same value as in the previous record	Ctrl+'		
Add new record	Ctrl++ (plus sign)	Open selected drop-down list in a field	Alt+Down Arrow

Microsoft Outlook Keystrokes

You don't want to spend more time managing your life than you do living it, so use the following keystrokes to create new entries in Outlook.

To	Press	To	Press
Create new e-mail message	Ctrl+Shift+M	Create new Office document	Ctrl+Shift+H
Make new appointment	Ctrl+Shift+A	Make new folder or subfolder	Ctrl+Shift+E
Send meeting request	Ctrl+Shift+Q	Send and receive e-mail	F9
Add task to your task list	Ctrl+Shift+K	Display Address Book	Ctrl+Shift+B
Send task request	Ctrl+Shift+U	Find item	Ctrl+Shift+F
Add contact to Address Book	Ctrl+Shift+C	Reply to selected e-mail message	Ctrl+R
Record journal entry	Ctrl+Shift+J	Reply to sender and all recipients of e-mail message you received	Ctrl+Shift+R
Post note to yourself	Ctrl+Shift+N		
Post message in a newsgroup	Ctrl+Shift+S	Forward e-mail message you received	Ctrl+F

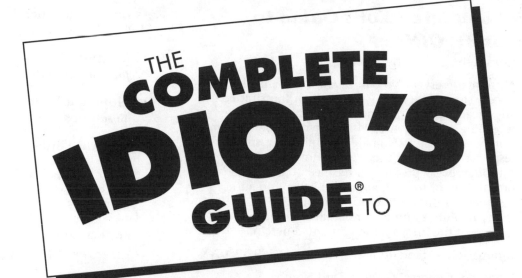

THE COMPLETE IDIOT'S GUIDE® TO

Microsoft® Office XP

by Joe Kraynak

alpha books

201 West 103rd Street
Indianapolis, IN 46290

A Pearson Education Company

The Complete Idiot's Guide to Microsoft® Office XP

International Standard Book Number: 0-7897-2507-X

Library of Congress Catalog Card Number: 20-01087724

First Printing: June 2001

03 02 01   8 7 6 5 4 3 2 1

Trademarks

Warning and Disclaimer

Associate Publisher
Greg Wiegand

Acquisitions Editor
Stephanie McComb

Development Editor
Susan Hobbs

Technical Editor
Mark Hall

Managing Editor
Thomas F. Hayes

Project Editor
Tricia S. Liebig

Copy Editor
Megan Wade

Indexer
Kelly Castell

Proofreader
Jeanne Clark

Page Layout
Ayanna Lacey

Interior Designer
Nathan Clement

Cover Designer
Michael Freeland

Illustrator
Judd Winick

Contents at a Glance

Contents

About the Author

Joe Kraynak has been writing and editing computer books and other technical stuff for more than 10 years. His long list of computer books includes *The Complete Idiot's Guide to PCs*, *The Big Basics Book of Microsoft Office*, *10 Minute Guide to Excel*, *Microsoft Internet Explorer 3 Unleashed*, and *More Easy Windows 98*. Joe graduated from Purdue University in 1984 with a master's degree in English, a bachelor's degree in Philosophy and Creative Writing, and a strong commitment to make technology more accessible to the average…er…Joe.

Dedication

To my wife, Cecie.

Acknowledgments

Special thanks to Stephanie McComb (acquisitions editor) for choosing me to write this book and for expertly dealing with contract details and all that other messy stuff; to Suz Hobbs (development editor) whose insightful comments and questions significantly enhanced this book; to Megan Wade (copy editor) for ferreting out my typos and polishing my prose; to Tricia Liebig (project editor) for shepherding this book through the production cycle; and to Mark Hall (technical editor) for thoroughly checking the instructions, figures, and explanations for clarity, and...er...mistakes.

A special round of applause goes to the illustrators and page layout crew for transforming my loose stack of files, figures, and printouts into such an attractive, bound book.

Tell Us What You Think!

As the reader of this book, *you* are our most important critic and commentator. We value your opinion and want to know what we're doing right, what we could do better, what areas you'd like to see us publish in, and any other words of wisdom you're willing to pass our way.

As an Associate Publisher for Alpha, I welcome your comments. You can fax, e-mail, or write me directly to let me know what you did or didn't like about this book—as well as what we can do to make our books stronger.

Please note that I cannot help you with technical problems related to the topic of this book, and that due to the high volume of mail I receive, I might not be able to reply to every message.

When you write, please be sure to include this book's title and author as well as your name and phone or fax number. I will carefully review your comments and share them with the author and editors who worked on the book.

Fax: 317-581-4666

E-mail: CIGfeedback@pearsoned.com

Mail: Greg Wiegand
          Alpha
          201 West 103rd Street
          Indianapolis, IN 46290 USA

Introduction: Your Office of the Future

Computers have revolutionized the traditional office. Gone are the days of manual typewriters, adding machines, ledger books, and desktop rolodexes. In the modern office, these familiar tools have been replaced with word processing applications, spreadsheets, computerized databases, and electronic address books. Even the relatively recent day planners are migrating to the PC.

And that's not all. Currently, the computer revolution is also changing the way we communicate and collaborate. Instead of printing a memo and distributing copies, we broadcast it via e-mail. Instead of publishing a report, we save it to a centralized network server or publish it on the Web. And we rarely even think about mailing an order form or brief letter; faxes and e-mail are much more efficient.

Mastering the New Age with Microsoft Office XP

To master this new age, a simple word processing or spreadsheet application is no longer sufficient. We need a new set of tools—a suite of applications that work together and conform to the way we humans really work. We need Microsoft Office XP.

Office XP introduces some innovative new features that even the Jetsons would find intriguing. With built-in support for voice commands and dictation, you can now enter commands and "type" documents without touching the keyboard. New task panes and smart tags display the most commonly used commands right alongside your document, so you don't have to hunt through a series of cascading menus. And Office XP extends the capabilities of its former versions by adding tools that make it even easier to collaborate on projects over a network, via e-mail, or on the Web.

With Office XP and the right training on how to use its components individually and together, you will be equipped not only to manage your office of the future, but to master it, as well.

Welcome to *The Complete Idiot's Guide to Microsoft Office XP*

The Complete Idiot's Guide to Microsoft Office XP is your key to success with Office XP. It explains the new versions of the Microsoft Office programs: Word, Excel, PowerPoint, Access, Outlook, and Publisher—including all the nifty things you can do with them. This book covers everything from word processing to spreadsheet number crunching, from database management to graphics, from slide shows to appointment books. And that's not all—for a limited time only, I tell you how to make the programs work together so you can tackle even bigger tasks. And you'll learn how to unleash these various tools through e-mail and on the Web.

Specifically, this book will help you do the following:

➤ Grasp the basics of Office XP (and use its help system when you get into a jam).

➤ Master the ins and outs of using Office XP to create documents of all kinds, design graphic presentations with pizzazz, make spreadsheets using formulas and functions, keep an electronic calendar, and much more.

➤ Get the most out of Office XP, by using all the applications together. Here, you will learn how to transform a Word document into a PowerPoint presentation, drop an Excel spreadsheet or graph into a Word document, or even merge a list of addresses from an Access database into a form letter created in Word.

➤ Communicate more effectively with people in your company and around the world, through e-mail. You will learn how to send messages, documents, and files right from the Office XP applications instead of using a separate e-mail program.

➤ Publish professional-looking pages on the Web. You will learn how to transform Word documents, Excel spreadsheets, and PowerPoint presentations into brilliant Web pages!

The Unconventional Conventions

To make this book even easier to use, we took it upon ourselves to follow a few conventions. Anything you need to type appears in bold, like this:

Type **this entry**

If there's any variable information to be typed in, such as your own name or a filename, it appears in italic, like this:

Type ***this number***

In addition, you'll find boxed information (similar to the following examples) scattered throughout the book to help you with terminology, boring technical background, shortcuts, and other tips. You certainly don't have to read these little boxes, although I did work hard putting them together for you. If you want to understand more about a topic, you might find these boxes helpful. But in case you don't, they're tucked out of the way so you can quickly skip them.

Whoa!

Before you click that button or press that key, check out the Whoa! sidebar for precautionary notes. Chances are that I've made that same mistake myself. Let me tell you how to avoid the same blunder...or recover, if you already made the mistake.

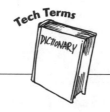

TechTerms

In the computer industry, jargon and cryptic acronyms rule the roost. When a computer term baffles you or an acronym annoys you, look to the TechTerms sidebar for a plain English translation.

Insider Tip

When you've been working with Office for as long as I have, you learn better ways to perform common tasks, and you pick up a few tricks for avoiding the most common pitfalls. Check out the Insider Tip sidebars, where I pass along some of my favorite tricks.

Web Work

Office XP is built for the Web. When we're about to wander from your desktop out to the Web and experiment with Office XP's powerful Web features, the Web Work! sidebar lets you know what to expect.

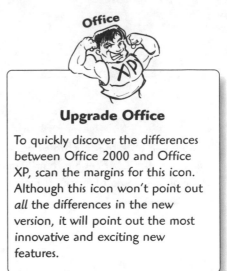

Upgrade Office

To quickly discover the differences between Office 2000 and Office XP, scan the margins for this icon. Although this icon won't point out *all* the differences in the new version, it will point out the most innovative and exciting new features.

The Least You Need to Know

At the end of every chapter in this second edition, you'll find a section called "The Least You Need to Know," which lists the tasks you should be able to perform after completing the chapter. Read through this section as a quick review before tackling any more new material.

Part 1
Microsoft Office XP Over Easy

When you first drive a new car off the dealer's lot, you usually don't know that much about it. The salesperson takes three minutes out of his busy life to show you how to turn on the lights and the windshield wipers, scan for radio stations, and set your cruise control. It takes a couple weeks to figure out all the little things, such as how to turn on the air conditioner, open the glove compartment, and keep your airbag from acting as a lethal weapon.

It's the same with your new version of Office. You need to know what's new about it, why it places that extra toolbar on your desktop, how to use its new speech recognition features, and how to navigate its help system when you back yourself into a corner. This part teaches you all that and a little more so that you can sit behind the wheel of Office XP with complete confidence.

Chapter 1

Up and Running with Office XP

In This Chapter

➤ Running the Office XP applications

➤ Using and configuring the Office Shortcut bar

➤ Saving and opening files

➤ Learning some fancy mouse moves

You're no idiot. You've probably poked around in several Windows applications, and you have a general idea of how they work. You are quite capable of opening pull-down menus and clicking buttons, and you didn't shell out 20 bucks to be told what you already know. So I'm not going to give you the step-by-boring-step tutorial of how to use Windows or Windows applications. Instead, this chapter provides you with a brief overview of how to run the various Office XP applications, as well as some tips that can help you perform the basics a little more quickly.

Firing Up Your Office Applications

The Office installation places icons for the Office XP applications on the Windows Start, Programs menu. Just open the **Start** menu, rest the mouse pointer on **Programs**, and then click the name of the application you want to run. You also can run some of the applications by using the Microsoft Office Shortcut bar (explained in the following section).

My Office Looks Different!

As you work through the chapters of this book, you might notice that the screens shown here don't match your screens or features I discuss are not available on your menus. If a feature is unavailable, run the Office installation again, as explained on the inside back cover of this book, and install the feature. If your screen looks a little different, don't fret; Office is set up to hide options you rarely use and make those options you use frequently more easily accessible. You'll learn how to access all options as you proceed.

Do-It-Yourself Office Shortcut

If you use a particular Office XP application frequently, consider placing a shortcut to it on the Windows desktop. Close or minimize all open program windows, so the desktop is clear. Open the **Start**, **Programs** menu, and then use your right mouse button to drag the Office application's icon to a blank area on the Windows desktop. Release the mouse button and click **Create Shortcut(s) Here**.

Scooting Up to the Shortcut Bar

Microsoft Office comes with its very own toolbar, called the *Shortcut bar*, which typically pops up on the right side or top of the Windows desktop whenever you start Windows. The Shortcut bar contains buttons for creating new documents, composing e-mail messages, setting appointments, and performing other common Office tasks.

If the Shortcut bar does not appear, you can turn it on: Select **Start**, **Programs**, **Microsoft Office Tools**, **Microsoft Office Shortcut Bar**. The first time you choose to display the Shortcut bar, the Office setup might prompt you to install it from the installation CD; insert the Office CD and follow the onscreen instructions to install it. The Microsoft Office Shortcut Bar dialog box asks whether or not you want the

Shortcut bar to run automatically on startup. Click the desired button—**Yes** or **No**. Figure 1.1 shows the Shortcut bar in action. The list following the figure describes the buttons. Later in this chapter, I'll show you how to move the bar.

I Have No Microsoft Office Shortcut Bar Option!

If you open the **Start**, **Programs**, **Microsoft Office Tools** menu, and no Microsoft Office Shortcut Bar option is available, it might not be installed to run on first use. Insert the Office Installation CD and use **My Computer** to run the setup or installation program from the CD. Select the option to add or remove features, and then click the plus sign next to **Microsoft Office Tools**. Click the **X** button next to Microsoft Office Shortcut Bar and click **Run from My Computer**. Click the **Update** button to complete the installation.

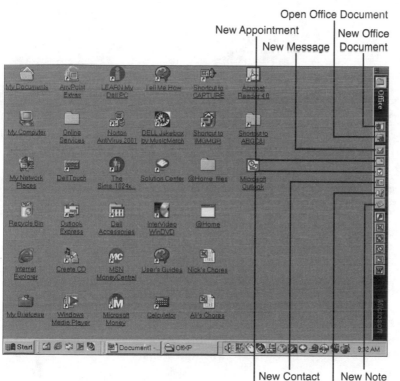

Figure 1.1

The Shortcut bar is your one-stop shop for everything Office XP.

New Office Document. Enables you to create a document using a template. The application that runs depends on the type of document you choose to create—for instance, if you choose a presentation template, PowerPoint runs.

 Open Office Document. Enables you to open and start editing a document that already has been created and stored on your computer or on the network. By default, Office looks in the C:\My Documents folder for Office documents.

 New Message. Displays a window you can use to create and send an e-mail message.

New Appointment. Enables you to add an appointment to your schedule in Outlook. Outlook can display a reminder before the scheduled date and time, as explained in Chapter 23, "Keeping Track of Dates, Mates, and Things to Do."

 New Task. Displays a dialog box that enables you to add a task to your to-do list (as if you didn't have enough to do). Again, this button runs Outlook.

New Contact. Enables you to add a person's name, address, phone number, e-mail address, and all sorts of other information to your address book in Outlook.

New Journal Entry. Prompts you to enter information about something you have done during the day, about an e-mail message you sent or received, or about anything else you want to record in Outlook.

New Note. Places an electronic "sticky note" on your screen, compliments of Outlook.

ScreenTip Tip

When you rest the mouse pointer on a button in the Shortcut bar or in any toolbar, a box pops up displaying the name of the button. This is called a *ScreenTip*. To change the name of a button in the Shortcut bar, right-click the button and select **Rename**. To turn off a button, right-click it and select **Hide Button**.

Activating Other Shortcut Bars

The Shortcut bar initially displays the Office toolbar, which contains buttons primarily for Outlook tasks. You can turn on other toolbars to enable quick access to other files and programs on your computer. To turn a toolbar on or off, right-click a blank area of the Shortcut bar and select any of the following toolbars:

➤ **Office**—Displays the icons described in the previous section. This toolbar is the only toolbar displayed when you first run the Microsoft Office Shortcut bar.

➤ **QuickShelf**—Turns on a toolbar that displays shortcuts for Microsoft Bookshelf reference material, assuming Bookshelf was installed on your computer before you installed Office. Bookshelf includes a dictionary, a thesaurus, an encyclopedia, a book of quotations, and an almanac.

➤ **Favorites**—Displays icons for Web pages you added to your list of favorites in Internet Explorer (assuming you cruise the Web with Internet Explorer).

➤ **Programs**—Turns on the toolbar equivalent of the Windows Start, Programs menu.

➤ **Accessories**—Displays icons for applications on the Start, Programs, Accessories submenu.

➤ **Desktop**—Turns on a toolbar that displays the shortcuts that appear on your Windows desktop.

Whenever you turn on a toolbar, an icon for that bar appears in the Shortcut bar and the toolbar's buttons appear. Only one toolbar's buttons are shown at a time. You can display the buttons of another toolbar (assuming you turned it on earlier) by clicking its icon (shown in Figure 1.2).

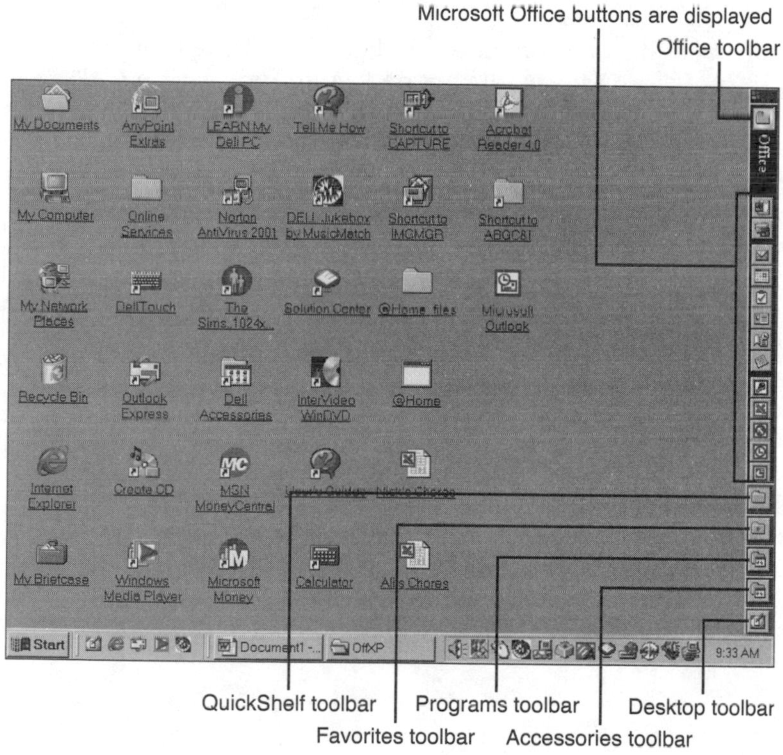

Microsoft Office buttons are displayed
Office toolbar

QuickShelf toolbar
Favorites toolbar
Programs toolbar
Accessories toolbar
Desktop toolbar

Figure 1.2

If you need more buttons, give your toolbar a swift click.

Customizing the Shortcut Bar

The first thing you might want to know about the Shortcut bar is how to move it. Drag any blank area of the Shortcut bar to the desired position on your screen: left, right, top, bottom, or (to make it most intrusive) smack dab in the middle. To turn off the Shortcut bar, right-click its title bar (at the top or left end of the Shortcut bar) and click **Exit**.

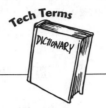

Dockable Toolbars

Toolbars are considered dockable if you can drag them from one position to another. If you drag a dockable toolbar from its dock onto a free area (say over your document), the toolbar is said to float. When you drag and drop the toolbar onto an area of the window where it will click into place, it is said to be *docked*.

If you have a genuine affection for the Shortcut bar and decide to leave it on, you can customize it in all sorts of ways. My favorite option is Auto Hide, which tucks the Shortcut bar out of the way as you work in an application. To turn on Auto Hide, right-click a blank area of the Shortcut bar and click **Auto Hide**. Whenever you need the Shortcut bar, slide the mouse pointer over to the right side of the screen (or wherever you moved the bar) to display it. If Auto Hide is grayed out (inactive), Auto Fit in Title Bar Area is on; see the following Insider Tip.

For additional customization options, right-click a blank area of the Shortcut bar and click **Customize**. The View tab appears up front, displaying options for changing the appearance and behavior of the Shortcut bar. I'm not going to bore you with all the details. Just be sure that if you have more than one toolbar turned on, you select the toolbar you want to customize from the Toolbar drop-down list before you start changing settings.

Before we move on, check out the Buttons tab. It contains a list of buttons you can turn on or off. A check in the box next to a button indicates that the button is turned on. You can add icons for commonly used files or folders by clicking the **Add File** or **Add Folder** button. You also can move buttons by clicking the button and then clicking the **move up** or **move down** arrow (or simply Alt+drag a button on the Shortcut bar to the desired location).

Let's Get Fancy

Do you see that wasted space in your Office application's title bar? You can squeeze the Shortcut bar in there. In the Customize dialog box, on the View tab, under Options, turn on **Auto Fit into Title Bar Area** and click **OK**. Now you can drag the Shortcut bar into the title bar of your Office application when the window is maximized. If the window is not maximized, the Shortcut bar appears at the top of the Windows desktop.

Getting Help in Dialog Boxes

Dialog boxes are typically packed with cryptic options. To determine what an option does, right-click its name and select **What's This?**, or click the question mark icon in the upper-right corner of the dialog box and click the option's name. A small text box appears describing the option.

Meeting Office Face to Face

Although each Office application has its own unique look, highly dependent on its function, they all share some common qualities. So, you need to learn some basic maneuvers, no matter which Office application you're using. The following sections show you just how to get started.

Picking Commands from Menus

In the previous version of Office—Office 2000—Microsoft streamlined the Office menus and toolbars and gave them some intelligence. The toolbars and menus initially list only the most commonly used commands and display a double-headed arrow for expanding the menus or toolbars. Click the double-headed arrow to view additional commands or options, as shown in Figure 1.3. As you work, your Office

Figure 1.4

The new Office task panes place the most common options one click away.

Click the Close button to hide the pane.
Point and click to select the desired option.

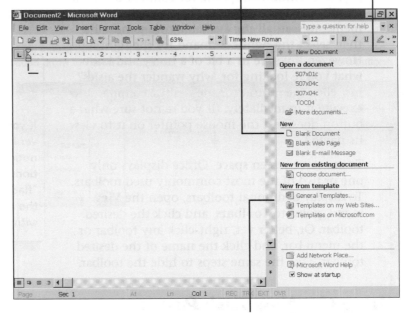

Drag the border to resize the pane.

Figure 1.5

Smart tags pop up onscreen to provide additional options.

Smart tag

Options

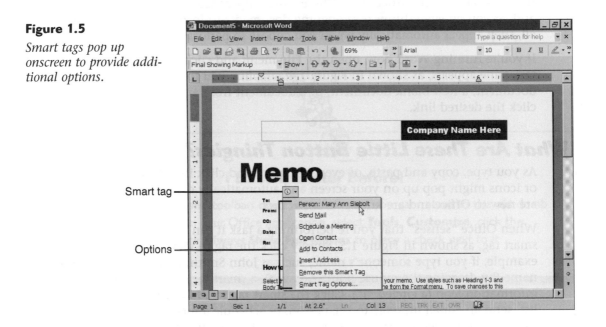

Saving, Naming, and Opening the Files You Create

Whichever Office application you use, the first thing you need to know is how to create, save, and open files.

 To create a new file in most of the Office applications, click the **New** button or open the **File** menu and select **New**. The New button slaps a new document window on your screen, no questions asked. File, New opens the New Document task pane, which enables you to choose a template (a prefab document, such as a business letter) with which to start. (You'll learn more about templates in later chapters.)

To save a file in any of the Office applications, open the **File** menu and select **Save** (or click the **Save** button on the toolbar). The first time you save a file, the application prompts you to name it and specify where you want it stored. Select the folder in which you want to store the file, as shown in Figure 1.6. Type a name for the file in the **File Name** text box. (Don't type a period or a filename extension; the application adds the correct extension.)

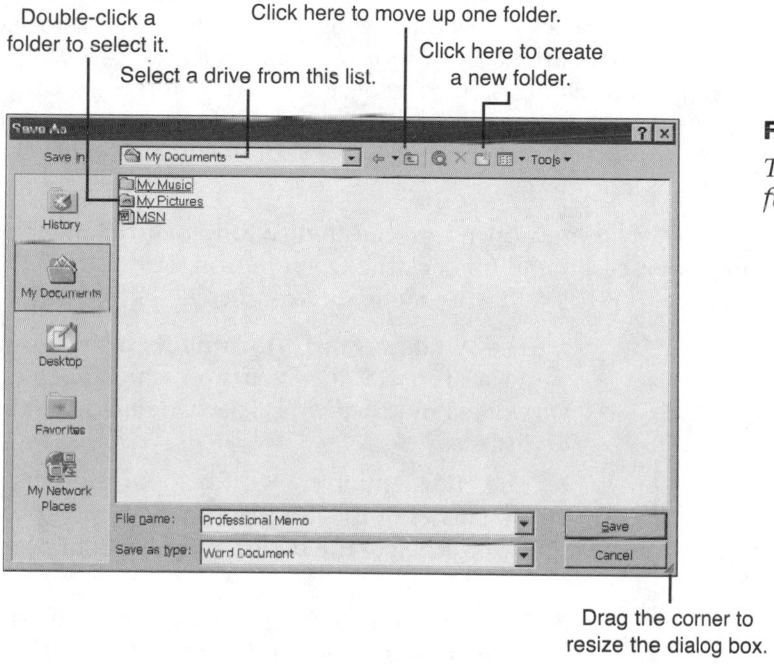

Double-click a folder to select it.

Click here to move up one folder.

Select a drive from this list.

Click here to create a new folder.

Figure 1.6

The first time you save a file, you must name it.

Drag the corner to resize the dialog box.

You should save your file every ten minutes or so to protect your work in the event of a power outage or system crash. After you name a file, saving your changes is easy: Just click the **Save** button. Your application remembers the name and location of the file and saves it automatically.

The Save Options

By default (unless you changed it), all Office applications save files to the My Documents folder and look to that folder whenever you enter the Open command. To use a different folder as the default folder for one of the Office applications, open the Office application's **Tools** menu and select **Options**. Click the **File Locations** tab, click **Documents**, click the **Modify** button, and select the desired folder.

To further protect your document as you work on it, be sure the Save AutoRecover Info option is turned on. Open the Office application's **Tools** menu and select **Options**. Click the **Save** tab, and be sure **Save AutoRecover Info** is checked. Use the **Every ____ Minutes** spin box to specify how often you want AutoRecover information saved. If your computer locks up after you've made some changes to your document, but before you saved your changes, AutoRecover can help you recover the document with the changes, which otherwise would be lost. Note that AutoRecover does not replace the Save command; you must still save your document before closing it or exiting the Office application.

To work on an existing file, you must open it in the application you used to create it. You can enter the **File, Open** command (or click the **Open** button) and use the Open dialog box to select the file, but the following methods are easier:

Resizable Dialog Boxes

In Office XP, the Save and Open dialog boxes are resizable, enabling you to bring many more files into view at one time. To resize a dialog box, simply drag the lower-right corner of the box.

➤ The Windows **Start**, **Documents** menu contains a list of the 15 documents on which you've worked most recently. Select the file from this list.

➤ The **File** menu in the Office application displays the names of the last few files on which you worked. Select the file from the bottom of the File menu.

➤ Click the **Open Office Document** button in the Shortcut bar, and then locate and double-click the name of the file you want to open.

➤ If you edit the document on a regular basis, drag its icon from My Computer or Windows Explorer onto the Microsoft Office Shortcut bar or the Windows desktop. To open the document, click its icon.

Some Not–So–Basic Mouse Moves

Newer baby books now list mouse skills as a stage of human development that falls somewhere between walking and holding down a full-time job. "Click," "double-click," and "drag" are standard words in any grade schooler's vocabulary. Some new mouse moves, however, might confuse even a well-educated adult:

➤ **Right-click pop-up menus**—Sometimes the quickest way to act on existing text (or any other object in a document, including graphics) is to select it and then right-click the selected text or object to display a menu. Pop-up menus (also known as *context menus*) are great because they present options that are used only for the selected text or object.

➤ **Right-dragging**—When you right-drag, a pop-up menu appears when you release the mouse button. This menu usually provides options for moving the selected object, pasting a copy of it, or creating a *hyperlink* to it.

➤ **Free-wheeling**—If you have an Intellimouse (a mouse with a wheel between the left and right mouse buttons), click the wheel and then spin it to scroll up or down. Hold down the wheel and slide the mouse forward or backward to scroll more smoothly. (Try this in your Web browser, too!)

Hyperlink

Hyperlinks are specially formatted icons or bits of text that point to other files. These files can be stored on your hard drive, the network drive, or the Internet. When you click a hyperlink, Windows finds and runs the application needed to play the file and opens the file in that application. (See Chapter 26, "Creating and Publishing Your Own Web Pages," for more information about links.)

➤ **Scraps**—You can drag selected text onto a blank area of the Windows desktop to create a *scrap*. You can then drag the scrap into a document to paste it into that document.

➤ **Funky selection moves**—Everyone knows that you can drag over text to select it. Most applications, however, offer additional ways to select with the mouse. In Word, for example, you can double-click a word to select it or triple-click inside a paragraph to select it. (I point out these special selection techniques in the chapters that deal with the individual applications.)

➤ **Selection boxes**—If you paste pictures or other objects on a page, most applications enable you to select two or more objects by dragging a box around them.

The Least You Need to Know

Well, you just survived Office orientation day. Time to go home, kick off your shoes, and veg out. But before you do, be sure you have a handle on the basics:

➤ To run any Office application, open the **Start**, **Programs** menu and click the application's name.

➤ To display the Microsoft Office Shortcut bar, click **Start**, **Programs**, **Microsoft Office Tools**, **Microsoft Office Shortcut Bar**.

➤ To view all the options on a menu, click the menu's name, and then click the double-headed arrow at the bottom of the menu.

➤ To bypass the menu system, click the toolbar button for the desired command.

➤ To save a document, click the **Save** button, name the file, and select the disk and folder in which you want the file saved.

➤ To open a document on which you recently worked, open the **File** menu in the application you used to create the document, and then click the document's name at the bottom of the menu.

➤ You can right-click a button bar, menu, selected text, pictures, and almost any data or object onscreen to view a context menu containing commands that apply only to that object.

Chapter 2

Help!!! Getting Some Office Assistance

In This Chapter

➤ Typing a question, getting an answer

➤ Touring Office with your very own personal Office Assistant

➤ Finding a topic in the table of contents

➤ Searching an onscreen index of Help topics

➤ Getting answers and Office updates on the Web

Online help systems: You love 'em or you hate 'em. Either they're impossible to find and navigate, or they're like some overzealous philanthropist who just won't leave you alone.

In Office 97, Microsoft found a middle ground with the Office Assistant, an animated character who answers your questions and then scurries out of your way as you perform the task. In Office XP, Microsoft has fine-tuned the help system to make it even less intrusive and yet more convenient. In this chapter, you learn how to get the help you need in Office and on the Web.

Help Is Just a Click Away

Getting help in any program is fairly easy—you press the F1 key or open the Help menu and select the type of help you want. Well, Microsoft just made it even easier. In the upper-right corner of every Office application window is the Ask a Question text box, just waiting for you to type a question. Click in the box, type your question, and press **Enter**, as shown in Figure 2.1.

➤ **Closed book icon**—This icon next to a topic means a more detailed list of topics is contained within this topic area. Double-click the book icon (or the plus sign next to the book icon) to expand the list of topics.

➤ **Opened book icon**—This icon next to a topic means the topic is selected. You can close the book and collapse the list of subtopics by double-clicking the book icon again (or by clicking the minus sign next to the icon).

➤ **Question mark icon**—This icon next to a topic means detailed text is available to view about the topic. Click the topic or icon to display specific information in the pane on the right.

To change the relative size of the panes, drag the bar that separates the panes to the left or right. To completely hide the left pane and provide additional room for displaying information, click the **Hide** button in the toolbar. To display the Help window and your document side by side, click the **Auto Tile** button in the toolbar.

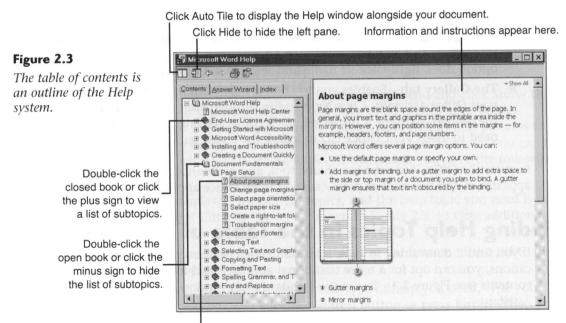

Figure 2.3

The table of contents is an outline of the Help system.

Click Auto Tile to display the Help window alongside your document.

Click Hide to hide the left pane.

Information and instructions appear here.

Double-click the closed book or click the plus sign to view a list of subtopics.

Double-click the open book or click the minus sign to hide the list of subtopics.

Click a topic to display specific information.

In addition to displaying information and step-by-step instructions, the right pane also might contain highlighted text, called *links*, which point to related information or call up a definition box. Click the link to display additional information. To go back to the previous help screen, click the **Back** button. If the instructions contain a **Show Me** button, click the button to make the help system perform the task for you.

What's This?

Earlier in this chapter, you learned how to get help in a dialog box by right-clicking an option and clicking **What's This?**. You can obtain similar help for any toolbar button or other control in your application's window. Open the **Help** menu and select **What's This?** (or press **Shift+F1**), and a question mark attaches itself to the mouse pointer. Now click the button or other control for which you want help. A box pops up describing the control. Pressing **Esc** or clicking outside the help box makes it go away.

Searching the Index for Specific Help

Most users of technical documentation rank a thorough and well-organized index as the most important part of the documentation. With that in mind, you might find the online Help index a most valuable tool. To use it, display the Office application's Help window, and then click the **Index** tab. In the **Type Keywords** text box at the top of the Index tab, type a few letters of the topic for which you're looking, as shown in Figure 2.4. As you type, the list of keywords scrolls down to show topics whose names match what you have typed so far. Double-click the desired keyword. Scroll down the **Choose a Topic** list and double-click the desired topic.

A list of topics that match what you've typed so far.

Start typing here.

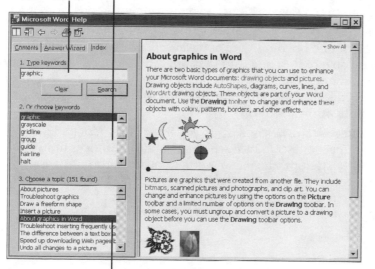

Double-click the desired topic.

Figure 2.4

You can quickly look up information using the Index.

Getting Office Help and Updates on the Web

If you can't find the help you need in the Help window, get help from Microsoft's Office Web site. Assuming you have an Internet connection, open the **Help** menu and click **Office on the Web**. This connects you to Microsoft's Web site, which contains additional information, technical assistance, free files, and other goodies.

Office Survival Skills: Recovering from Crashes

Computers have been known to lock up at inopportune times...like when you're putting the finishing touches on your annual report the night before it's due. If your computer locks up (your software doesn't respond to the keyboard or mouse), you might lose any changes you made to your document since the last time you saved it. If the crash is serious enough, you might even lose the entire document!

Fortunately, Office XP comes equipped with some safety features to help you recover data in the event of a power outage or computer crash. Microsoft refers to these features as "airbags for Office." Here's a rundown of the Office safety features:

➤ **Save on Crash**—If your system crashes when you are working on a document in Word, Excel, or PowerPoint, the application automatically saves your changes. When you restart the application, it displays a dialog box giving you the option of recovering the file.

➤ **Timed Save**—Word, Excel, PowerPoint, and Outlook automatically save your work at timed intervals. If your original file is destroyed, you can open the backup file. To check the automatic backup settings, open the **Tools** menu, click **Options**, and click the **Save** tab.

➤ **Document Recovery Task Pane**—When you restart Word, Excel, or PowerPoint after a system crash, the Document Recovery task pane automatically appears, as shown in Figure 2.5. This pane enables you to preview and compare the original, save-on-crash, and timed save versions of your documents and choose the best version.

➤ **Hang Manager**—When one of your Office applications locks up, the Hang Manager might be capable of breaking into the application and recovering your data before the application completely shuts down. To run Hang Manager, open the Windows **Start** menu, point to **Programs**, **Microsoft Office Tools**, and click **Microsoft Office Application Recovery**.

➤ **Corrupt Document Recovery**—Documents have formatting codes and other hidden codes that can become scrambled when an application locks up. Word and Excel automatically attempt to repair a corrupt document on recovery. If the document is still corrupt, enter the **File**, **Open** command to display the Open dialog box, and then click the name of the file you want to open. Click the arrow to the right of the **Open** button and click **Open and Repair**.

➤ **Office Safe Mode**—Office includes automated application troubleshooting and repair tools that help you recover control of an application on startup. If one of your Office applications fails to start, a dialog box should appear, instructing you on how to fix the problem.

Click a version to view its contents.
Click Save to save the version, if desired.

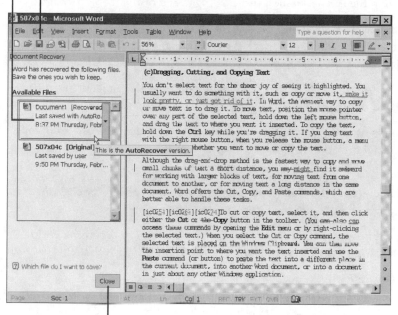

Figure 2.5

The Document Recovery task pane makes recovering from a mishap easy.

Click Close to close the saved version or delete a version you no longer need.

The Least You Need to Know

If you master an application's Help system, you can learn how to perform just about any task without having to flip through a book. (Did my publisher hear me say that?) To have a reasonable mastery of the Office help system, make sure you know the following:

➤ Enter a question in the Ask a Question text box (right end of the menu bar).

➤ If an Office Assistant starts harassing you, right-click the **Assistant** and click **Hide**. For a more permanent solution, right-click the **Assistant**, select **Options**, click **Use the Office Assistant** to remove the check mark, and then click **OK**.

➤ To beckon the Office Assistant back to the screen, open the **Help** menu and click **Show the Office Assistant**.

➤ To view a real help window, disable the Office Assistant, and then press **F1** or open the **Help** menu and click the **Microsoft Help** option for the application you're using.

➤ In the Help window, click the **Contents** tab to view a list of online "books" providing instructions on how to use the Office application features.

➤ For additional instructions, tips, Office updates, and program fixes, open the **Help** menu and click **Office on the Web** to visit the Microsoft Office Web site.

➤ If your Office application locks up, the application attempts to save your changes. The next time you start the application, follow the onscreen instructions to recover the version of the document that contains the most recent changes.

Chapter 3

Voice-Activating Your Office

In This Chapter

➤ Look, Ma, no hands—typing via dictation

➤ Making sure your computer can "hear" you

➤ Installing the Office speech recognition feature

➤ Training Office to understand your spoken words and commands

➤ Hand writing a document in Word

It's no coincidence that Office XP has built-in speech recognition and was released in the year 2001. Ever since Bill Gates saw the futuristic film *2001: A Space Odyssey*, he must have had a vision of creating a computer that could understand voice commands and take dictation. Sure, he didn't call this new version of Office "Hal" (after the talking computer in the movie), but if he weren't fighting so many legal battles already, I'm sure he would have toyed with the idea.

Be that as it may, one of the most significant additions to this version of Office is that it recognizes voice commands and can take dictation. Instead of clicking through a stack of menus and dialog boxes to get what you want, you simply *tell* your Office applications what to do, and they carry out your every command. Do you want this page printed? Say, "File, print, current page, Okay," and your printer spits out the page. Do you need to type a document while you're getting your weekly manicure? Switch to dictation mode and start talking.

In this chapter, you learn how to set up your computer to take advantage of the speech recognition features. You also learn how to train Office to recognize your voice and carry out your commands.

First, You Need a Microphone: Hardware Requirements

Although you don't need a professional recording studio to start using the speech recognition feature, you do need a fairly powerful computer equipped with a sound card and a high-quality microphone. To ensure your system is properly equipped, read through the following checklist:

This Might Take a While

Setting up your hardware and training speech recognition to recognize your voice can take more than an hour. If you're in a rush, skip this chapter and come back when you have some time.

➤ **Processor**—Pentium II 400MHz or faster. Don't try speech recognition on anything slower than a Pentium 400MHz machine. I tried running speech recognition on a computer with an AMD K6 300MHz processor with 96MB of RAM, and I could type about 10 times faster than speech recognition could take dictation.

➤ **Memory**—128MB RAM. Don't even try to run speech recognition if your system has less than 128MB RAM.

➤ **Sound card**—Most computers come equipped with a 16-bit SoundBlaster-compatible sound card or better. A 16-bit sound card is sufficient for voice commands and dictation.

➤ **Close-talk microphone**—Your Karaoke microphone might work fine for belting out a few bars of "I Did It My Way," but it's probably not the best choice for speech recognition. You need a close-talk microphone that's designed to block out background noise. Otherwise, Office won't be able to understand a word you say. If your system has a built-in microphone or a microphone that sits on your desk, you must buy a new microphone that can handle dictation.

Positioning the Microphone

Get a microphone with a headset mount and position the microphone about one inch from the corner of your mouth. Don't position the microphone directly in front of your mouth, or it will record all your heavy breathing. Try to mount the microphone in the same position each time you use it.

"Testing, One-Two-Three" (Checking Your Sound System)

Before you start talking to your computer, you should ensure your sound system is working properly. First, make sure none of your devices are muted or have their volume turned way down in Windows:

1. Double-click the **Volume** icon in the Windows taskbar (bottom-right corner of your screen, looks like a speaker). This opens the Volume Control window.

2. Open the **Options** menu and click **Properties**. The Properties dialog box appears.

3. In the **Show the Following Volume Controls** list, make sure the check box next to Microphone is checked. If the check box is blank, click it to place a check in the box. (Better yet, check all the boxes except PC Speaker.)

4. Click **OK**. This returns you to the Volume Control window, as shown in Figure 3.1.

5. At the bottom of each volume control is a Mute option. Be sure the Mute check boxes are blank, NOT checked. If a Mute check box has a check mark in it, click the check box to remove the check mark.

6. Drag the Microphone **Volume** control slider to the top to maximize the microphone volume.

7. Click the **Close (X)** button, in the upper-right corner of the Volume Control window, to close the window.

Drag the Volume slider up to maximize
your microphone volume.

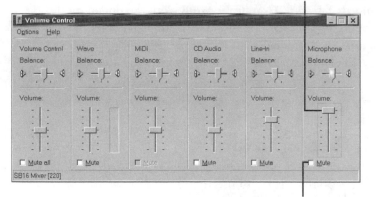

Figure 3.1

Be sure your microphone isn't muted in Windows.

The Mute check box should be blank.

Let's test your microphone to see whether it's working. Open the Windows **Start** menu, point to **Programs**, **Accessories**, **Entertainment**, and click **Sound Recorder**. This starts the Windows audio recorder. Click the **Record** button (the one with the big red dot on it) and say a few words into your microphone. Then, click the **Stop** button (the square block next to the Record button) and click the **Play** (the single pointer) button. If you hear your computer talking back to you in your own voice, your microphone is working properly.

If you don't hear your voice, check the following:

➤ Be sure your microphone and speakers are plugged in to the correct jacks on your sound card. It's easy to get the connections mixed up.

➤ If your sound card has a volume control, make sure it's cranked up.

➤ If your microphone has a power switch, make sure the switch is in the On position. (Some close-talk microphones have a switch and a volume control on the cable.)

➤ If your speakers have a power switch, make sure the switch is in the On position.

➤ If your speakers have a volume control, make sure the volume is turned up.

Troubleshooting Sound in Windows

Windows has several troubleshooters that can lead you through the process of tracking down common hardware problems. Open the **Start** menu and click **Help**. In Windows 95 or 98, click the **Contents** tab, click **Troubleshooting**, click the option for the **Windows Troubleshooters**, and click **Sound** in the list of troubleshooters. In Windows Me, click **Troubleshooting**, click **Audio-Visual Problems**, and click **Sound Troubleshooter**. Follow the instructions that appear in the right pane to track down the problem.

Installing Speech Recognition

The speech recognition component is not installed by default. Fortunately, all you need to do to initiate the installation is try to use the feature. In Word, open the **Tools** menu and click **Speech**. If you don't see the Speech option, click the double-headed arrow at the bottom of the **Tools** menu to expand the menu, and then click **Speech**.

Word displays a dialog box indicating that it cannot run the speech feature because it has not been installed and giving you the option of installing it. Click the **Yes** button to initiate the installation. If the required Office CD is not in the CD-ROM drive, another dialog box appears, telling you which CD is needed. Insert the requested CD, wait about 10 seconds, and then click **OK**. When the installation is complete, Word displays a dialog box, indicating that it will lead you through the process of setting up your microphone and training speech recognition to recognize your voice. Click **OK** and move on to the next section.

How Do I Get Rid of It?

After you install speech recognition, a language bar appears at the top of your screen. To disable the feature and hide the bar, right-click the bar and click **Close the Language Bar**. To display the bar again, open the **Tools** menu in your Office application and click **Speech**. To completely remove speech recognition from your system, run the Office setup again.

Training Office to Recognize Your Voice

To achieve success with speech recognition, you must train the speech recognition tool to recognize your voice and train yourself to speak clearly and consistently into the microphone. If you mumble through the training session, don't expect the speech recognition feature to translate your grunts into coherent text. That having been said, let's start the training session.

Assuming you just installed Speech, the Microphone Wizard should have popped up on your screen, as shown in Figure 3.2, providing instructions on how to position your microphone for best results. If the wizard is not onscreen or if you ran it and want to run it again, open the **Tools** menu in the Language bar and choose **Options**. The Speech Properties dialog box appears. Click the **Configure Microphone** button to display the Microphone Wizard. Follow the wizard's instructions to position your microphone properly and test it.

33

Figure 3.2

The Microphone Wizard shows you how to position your microphone for best results.

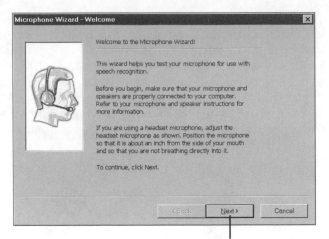

Click Next to continue.

After you complete the microphone setup, the Voice Training Wizard should appear. If the Voice Training Wizard is not onscreen, or if you already ran it and want to run it again (to fine-tune its operation), you can run it from the Language bar. Click the **Tools** button in the Language bar and click **Training**. Follow the wizard's instructions to complete the training session. The wizard displays a series of dialog boxes that require you to read sentences into your microphone, as shown in Figure 3.3. The entire session takes about 15 minutes. Here are some tips to make the training session a little more successful:

No Tools Button?!

If the Language bar is not displayed, open Word's **Tools** menu and click **Speech**. If the Language bar appears but has no Tools button, click the little down arrow on the right end of the Language bar and click **Speech Tools**.

➤ Shut yourself in a quiet room, turn off the radio, unplug the phone, and tell your roomies to leave you alone for 20 minutes.

➤ Speak in a level tone. Don't whisper, yell, or use a great deal of intonation.

➤ Read the sentences at a consistent rate of speed. Don't pause between words; the speech recognition feature can translate phrases more accurately than single words.

➤ Articulate (sound out) the words clearly, but don't go overboard. The speech recognition feature has an easier time if you say "enunciate" as you normally would rather than saying EEE-nun-seee-ate.

➤ Keep the microphone in a consistent position, no matter how much the head set tries to slide around.

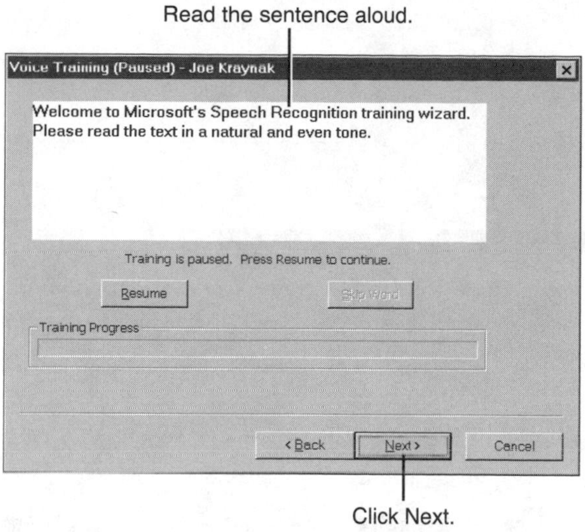

Read the sentence aloud.

Figure 3.3

The Voice Training Wizard prompts you to read aloud.

Click Next.

Tools If you share a computer with other users, a computer trained for your voice obviously will be less responsive to other voices. Fortunately, each user can train speech recognition for his or her own voice by creating a separate profile. To create a profile, perform the following steps:

1. Open the Language bar's **Tools** menu and click **Options**.
2. Under Recognition Profiles, click **New**. The Profile Wizard appears, prompting you to type your name.
3. Type your name and click **Next**. The Microphone Wizard appears, followed by the Voice Training Wizard.
4. Follow the wizard's instructions to set up your microphone and train speech recognition to identify your voice.

Tools After you have set up two or more recognition profiles, you easily can switch from one profile to another. Simply open the Language bar's **Tools** menu, point to **Current User**, and click the name of the desired user (or click **Default** to use the profile you created when you ran and trained speech recognition for the first time).

35

Finding the Speech Control Panel

When you install speech recognition, the Office installation places an icon in your Windows Control Panel for the Speech Properties dialog box. Open the **Start** menu, point to **Settings**, and click **Control Panel**. Click the **Speech** icon to view the Speech Properties dialog box.

You Speak, It Types: Dictating Your Documents

After you have trained speech recognition, the process of actually using the feature to convert your spoken words into typed text is a snap. The key is to keep an eye on the Language bar, as shown in Figure 3.4. The Language bar contains several buttons that control your microphone, let you switch between dictation and voice control modes, and let you see what the speech recognition feature "thinks" you are saying.

To start dictating text, make sure the **Microphone** button and the **Dictation** button are on (shaded light blue, instead of gray). If the Microphone button is off, both the Dictation and Voice Command buttons are hidden; click the **Microphone** button and then click the **Dictation** button. If the Microphone button is on and the Voice Command button is on, click the **Dictation** button to change to Dictation mode. Then, click in the document where you want your text to appear and start talking. Remember to speak clearly and at a steady pace. As you speak, speech recognition displays a light blue bar in your document with little dots in it, indicating that it is currently trying to convert your spoken words into text. When it has successfully translated a bit of text, the text pops up in place of the blue bar. (It can take several seconds to convert your spoken words into text. Even though you cannot immediately see what you're saying, just keep talking.)

Switch Modes with a Spoken Command

Instead of clicking a button to change from Dictation to Voice Command mode (or vice versa), just say the word. To dictate text, say "Dictation." To enter a command, say "Voice command."

If speech recognition inserts an incorrect word, right-click the word and click the correct alternative, or click **Correct** in the Language bar and click the correct word. If none of the alternative words is correct, click **More** for additional alternatives.

Click Voice Command to
issue menu commands.

Click Microphone to toggle
the microphone on or off.

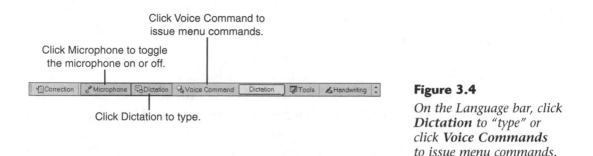

Click Dictation to type.

Figure 3.4
On the Language bar, click
Dictation *to "type" or*
click **Voice Commands**
to issue menu commands.

Noise Reduction

Try to keep your microphone as far away as possible from other electrical devices, including your computer. These devices emit EMF noise (electro-magnetic frequencies), which
can cause a low hum that might interfere with your dictation. Special noise-reduction
microphones also can help reduce background noise. You might want to stay clear of
chatty officemates, as well.

Barking Out Commands

Your new virtual secretary is very impressive when it comes to dictation, but what about carrying out simple commands, such as saving
files and printing documents? Well, let's find out. Open a document you previously
saved. Strap on your microphone, and then click the **Voice Command** button in the
Language toolbar. Say "Save." Voilà! Speech recognition passes your command along
to the current Office application, and your file is saved to disk. Double-click a word to
highlight it, and then say "Bold." Say "Italic." Pretty cool, huh? In addition, here's a
list of keyboard commands you can use in any Office application:

"Return" or "Enter" to press the Enter key

"Backspace"

"Delete"

"Space" or "Spacebar" to insert a space

"Escape" or "Cancel" to close a menu or dialog box

"Right-click," "Right-click menu," "Show right-click menu," "Context menu," or
"Show context menu" to show a context menu

"Tab"

"Control tab" to press the Ctrl+Tab keystroke

"Shift tab" to press the Shift+Tab keystroke (typically used to move back to the previous tab or to the previous option in a dialog box)

"End" or "Go end" to move the insertion point to the end of the current line

"Home" or "Go home" to move the insertion point to the beginning of the current line

"Phone home" to call your alien homeland for a quick return flight (just kidding)

"Up," "Go up," "Up arrow," or "Arrow up" to move the insertion point up one line

"Down," "Go down," "Down arrow," or "Arrow down" to move the insertion point down one line

"Left," "Go left," "Left arrow," or "Arrow left" to move the insertion point one character to the left

"Right," "Go right," "Right arrow," or "Arrow right" to move the insertion point one character to the right

"Previous page" or "Page up" to flip back one page

"Next page" or "Page down" to flip to the next page

Of course, you must be able to punctuate your text as you dictate. Punctuation is fairly intuitive. For a period, say "Period" or "Dot." For a comma, say "Comma." For a semicolon, say "Semicolon." I bet you can't guess what to say for an exclamation point... you got it, "Exclamation point."

Hundreds of commands and special characters can be accessed via dictation and voice commands in the various Office applications. To learn about these commands and characters, check out the help system.

What's with the EN Button in My Taskbar?!

If you minimize the Language bar, EN appears in the system tray (at the right end of the Windows taskbar), indicating that you're in English mode. Of course, if you're speaking Japanese, some other characters appear. Click **EN** and click **Show the Language Bar** to display the Language bar or right-click it for additional options.

Office Does Handwriting Recognition, Too

Another new Office feature for people who hate typing is handwriting recognition. That's right, instead of pecking away on a keyboard, you can scrawl away using a special stylus or even a standard mouse and have Office convert your chicken scratch into beautiful, typed text.

This feature also provides an onscreen keyboard you can use to hunt and peck with your mouse pointer or other device. This makes an excellent alternative input device.

Installing Handwriting Recognition

Handwriting recognition is not installed during a standard installation. You must run the Office installation again and choose to add the Handwriting Recognition component. Here's what you do:

1. Insert the first Office installation CD into your CD-ROM drive.
2. If a My Computer window does not open showing the CD's contents, run **My Computer** and click the icon for your CD-ROM drive.
3. Click or double-click the **Setup** icon to start the installation routine.
4. Click the **Add or Remove Features** option and click **Next**.
5. Click the plus sign next to **Office Shared Features**.
6. Click the plus sign next to **Alternative User Input**.
7. Click the icon next to **Handwriting** and click **Run from My Computer**.
8. Click **Update**.

Scrawl Away!

✍ Handwriting

After you install handwriting recognition, a new Write button pops up on your Language bar. Click the **Write** button to display a list of options for doodling onscreen. For example, click the **Write** button and click **Lined Paper** to display an onscreen notepad. If the Lined Paper window does not appear, click the **Options** button at the right end of the Language bar (the button with the down arrow on it), and then click **Microsoft Handwriting Item**. The Lined Paper button pops up in the Language bar. Click the **Lined Paper** button.

Use the Onscreen Keyboard

To display the onscreen keyboard, click the **Handwriting** button and click **On-Screen Standard Keyboard**. You can then "type" by clicking buttons on the keyboard.

T

Click the **Text** button, as shown in Figure 3.5, if it is not already on. When the mouse pointer is over the notepad, the pointer becomes a pen, allowing you to write on the pad. Use your mouse or whatever handwriting input device you have to hand write your text as you write naturally—print, write in cursive, or use a combination of the two styles.

Handwriting automatically recognizes your text and inserts it into your document whenever you write enough information that can be recognized as text, run out of room onscreen, or pause for a time after writing some text. If you write some text and the application fails to recognize it, click the **Recognize Now** button to prod it into action.

Figure 3.5

Avoid typing altogether. Hand write your text!

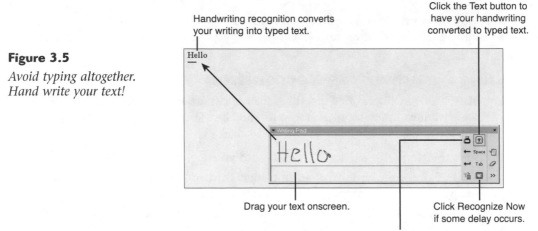

Handwriting recognition converts your writing into typed text.

Click the Text button to have your handwriting converted to typed text.

Drag your text onscreen.

Click Recognize Now if some delay occurs.

Click the Ink button to add your signature to a document.

The Least You Need to Know

After you set up speech recognition on your system and establish a rhythm with the dictation feature, you don't need to know much to take advantage of the speech recognition. However, when you're first starting out, keep the following in mind:

➤ To get started, open Word's **Tools** menu and click **Speech**.

➤ Double-click the **Speaker** icon in the Windows taskbar to determine whether your microphone is muted and to ensure that the volume is turned up.

➤ To train speech recognition for your voice, open the Language bar's **Tools** menu and click **Training**.

➤ To train speech recognition for another user, open the Language bar's **Tools** menu, click **Options**, click **New**, and follow the onscreen instructions.

➤ To type via dictation, make sure the Microphone and Dictation buttons on the Language bar are both active (shaded light blue instead of gray).

➤ To change from Dictation to Command mode, click **Voice Command** in the Language bar.

➤ After you install handwriting recognition, you can access its features via the **Write** button on the Language bar.

Part 2
Whipping Up Word Documents

Every office needs a good word processor, and Microsoft Word is one of the best. Its standard text layout tools enable you to easily set margins, indent text, and drop pictures and graphs anywhere on a page. The Table feature gives you the power to easily align chunks of text in columns and rows. And the spelling and grammar checkers provide you with a professional, online proofreader that can catch errors as you type.

In this part, you learn how to use these tools and others to crank out some high-quality documents with minimal effort.

Chapter 4

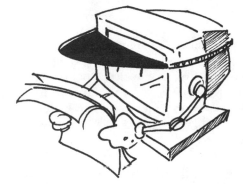

Making and Editing Word Documents

In This Chapter

➤ Using prefab documents with wizards and templates

➤ Typing, copying, and moving chunks of text

➤ Becoming a 500–word–per–minute typist with AutoText

➤ Finding and replacing bits of text

Microsoft Word has been the superhero of word processing programs for several years now, kicking sand in the face of the former giant, WordPerfect, and pummeling ambitious newcomers such as Lotus WordPro. Its powerful features have won over several generations of computer users.

Even with this power, Microsoft has not forgotten the simple word processing tasks, such as typing a letter, printing addresses on envelopes, and arranging text in columns. While beefing up Word with advanced features, Microsoft has continued to make performing these routine tasks easier.

In this chapter, you see several of these improvements in action as you learn the basics of creating and editing your documents.

Starting with the Boilerplate Special

If you're in a hurry to create a document and you don't have time to design and format your own, use one of Word's *templates* or *wizards*. A template is a ready-made document; all you have to do is add text. A wizard is a series of fill-in-the-blank dialog

Templates on the Web

If you have an Internet connection (doesn't everybody?), you can click **Templates on Microsoft.com** in the New Document task pane to access additional templates on Microsoft's Web site.

boxes that lead you through the process of creating a custom document... think of it as a publication drive-through.

Word's templates and wizards are found in the Templates dialog box, shown in Figure 4.1. To get there, open the **File** menu, select **New**, and then click the **General Templates** link in the New Document task pane. (Clicking the New button on the Standard toolbar won't open the New Document task pane; you must enter the File, New command.) The Templates dialog box contains several tabs full of wizards and templates. Click the tab for the type of document you want to create, and then double-click the desired template or wizard.

Click a template or wizard to select it, or double-click to start a new document.   Click a tab.

Figure 4.1

The Templates dialog box gives you access to document wizards and templates.

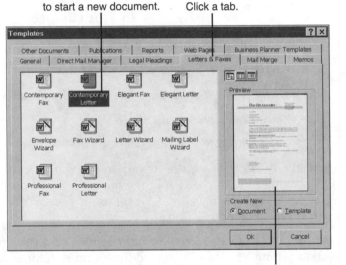

The Preview area displays the currently selected template.

What happens next depends on whether you selected a template or a wizard. If you selected a wizard, a dialog box appears, prompting you to make a selection. Simply follow the wizard's instructions, click the **Next** button until you've reached the last dialog box, and then click **Finish**. The wizard creates the document and returns you to the Word window, where you can further customize the document or print it as is.

If you selected a template, Word opens the template in its own document window, where you can start editing it. Many templates have placeholders that indicate the type of information you must enter (see Figure 4.2). For example, if you use a letter template, [Click here and type recipient's address] appears next to the greeting. Do whatever the placeholder instructs. (Whether you use a wizard or template to create your document, Word creates a new document, which you must name and save.)

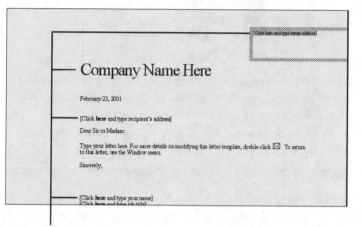

Figure 4.2

The template can't do all the work!

Placeholders tell you what to do to customize the template.

Inserting, Typing Over, and Deleting Text

If you don't know your home keys from your house keys, you should probably take a typing course. After you know how to type, typing in Word is easy—just do it. The following are a few tips that help if you're making the transition from a typewriter to a computer keyboard:

➤ Don't press **Enter** at the end of a line. Word wraps the lines for you as you type. If the text disappears off the left or right side of the window, zoom out (see "Changing Views: Zooming In and Zooming Out," later in this chapter).

➤ A blinking vertical bar, called the *insertion point*, indicates where text is inserted as you type (see Figure 4.3).

➤ A short horizontal line marks the end of the document. You can't type or insert anything below this line. (As you type, the line automatically moves down.)

No Preview?

Office installs some templates only when you choose to use them. The first time you choose a template, Word might not display it in the Preview area because it hasn't been installed. After installing the template, it appears in the Preview area when you select it.

45

Click-n-Type

Word sports a feature called *Click-n-Type* that enables you to type anywhere inside a document, providing an easy way to control the position of your text without having to press the **Enter** key. Just double-click wherever you want to insert text and start typing. (Click-n-Type works only in Print Layout view. See "Changing Views: Zooming In and Zooming Out," later in this chapter.)

➤ Move the mouse pointer (shaped like an I-beam) where you want to start typing, and then click. The text you type is inserted, and any existing text moves to the right to make room for the new text.

➤ To replace text, drag over it and start typing.

➤ To delete text to the right of the insertion point, press the **Delete** (**Del**) key. To delete to the left, press the **Backspace** key.

➤ Don't use a lot of tabs to align text in columns. (Chapter 6, "Aligning Your Text with Columns and Tables," explains a much easier way.)

The insertion point shows where the text you type will appear.

Figure 4.3

Move the insertion point and start typing.

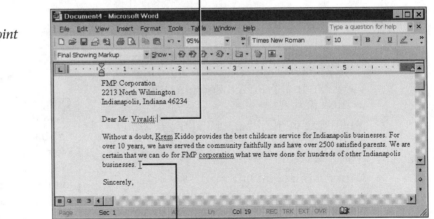

Place the I-beam pointer where you want the insertion, point and click.

What's with the Red Pen?

As you type, you might get a strange feeling that your sixth-grade English teacher is inside your computer, underlining your spelling mistakes. Whenever you type a string of characters that does not match a word in Word's spelling dictionary, Word draws a squiggly red line under the word to flag it for you so you can correct it immediately. (You can turn this feature on or off as desired. See Chapter 8, "Proofreading Your Document: Word Can Help," for details.)

You also might notice that Word automatically corrects some of your typos. For instance, if you type "teh" and press the spacebar, Word automatically inserts "the." The Office AutoCorrect feature isn't new to Office XP, but it has been redesigned to give you more control. If AutoCorrect inserts the wrong "correction," move the mouse pointer over the text and then down over the blue rectangle that appears below the first letter of the word. This is the AutoCorrect Options button. Click the button for a list of options. You can choose to revert to your original text or choose to have AutoCorrect stop correcting that text altogether. For more about AutoCorrect, see "Making Word Automatically Correct Your Typos" in Chapter 8.

Typing Has Never Been Easier!

I promised early on to teach you how to type 500 words per minute. The trick is to use AutoText. With AutoText, you can assign a term, quote, paragraph, or any other block of text to a couple of unique characters. For example, you might create an AutoText entry that inserts "Democratic National Convention" whenever you type **dnc**.

To create an AutoText entry, type the block of text for which you want to create an AutoText entry, and then drag over the text to select it. Open the **Insert** menu, point to **AutoText**, and click **New** (or just press **Alt+F3**). The Create AutoText dialog box prompts you to type a name for the entry. Type a short, unique name for the entry and click **OK**. To insert the block of text, simply type the unique name you assigned to the text and press **F3** or start typing the unique name, and when a ScreenTip appears—showing the complete entry—press the **spacebar** or the **Enter** key.

You can insert or delete AutoText entries via the AutoCorrect dialog box. To display this box, open the **Insert** menu, point to **AutoText**, and click **AutoText**. To delete an entry, select its name and click the **Delete** button.

The AutoText toolbar gives you easy access to the AutoText options. To turn on the toolbar, right-click any toolbar and select **AutoText**. This toolbar offers three buttons: click **AutoText** to display the AutoCorrect dialog box; click **All Entries** to display a list of AutoText entries you've created; click **New** to transform selected text into a new AutoText entry.

How Many Words Did I Type?

Word has always been capable of showing you the number of words in your document, but Word 10 provides quick access to the word count via the new Word Count toolbar. To turn on the new Word Count toolbar, right-click any toolbar and click **Word Count**. Click the **Recount** button in the toolbar to retally the count at any time.

Scroll, Scroll, Scroll Your Document

As you type, the screen fills up, and your text starts scrolling off the top as Word "feeds you more paper." Eventually, you need to move back up to that text to edit it or at least read it. The easiest way to move is to point and click with your mouse. To move farther, use one of the following scrollbar methods:

➤ Drag the scroll box up or down, as shown in Figure 4.4.

➤ Click an arrow at the end of the scrollbar to scroll one line in the direction of the arrow. Hold down the mouse button to scroll continuously.

➤ Click inside the scrollbar above or below the scroll box to scroll up or down one screenful of text.

➤ Click the **Previous Page** or **Next Page** button (bottom of the scrollbar) to flip one page at a time. The dot between the two page buttons gives you additional options to scroll through a document's notes, graphics, or edits. When you flip pages, the insertion point doesn't move—you must click where you want it.

Quick Jump Back

Because the insertion point doesn't move when you scroll, you can use it to quickly return to your original location in your document. When you're finished scrolling and browsing, press the left- or right-arrow key to quickly jump back to the point from which you started.

Drag the scroll box up or
down to move quickly.

Arrows

Scroll box

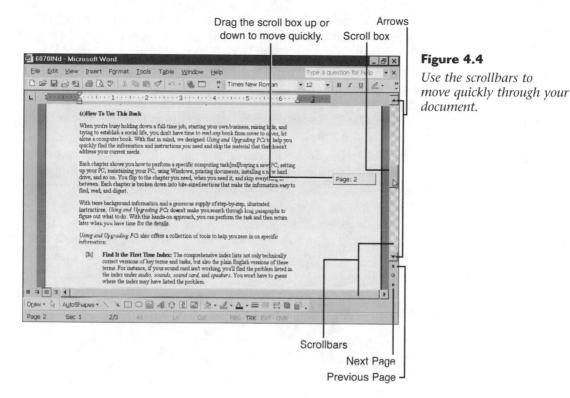

Figure 4.4

Use the scrollbars to move quickly through your document.

Scrollbars

Next Page

Previous Page

Changing Views: Zooming In and Zooming Out

99%

When you edit or format your text, you need to see what you're doing—you must be able to read the text and examine the type styles. When you're designing pages, however, you want a bird's-eye view, which shows how text is arranged on the page and how each page looks next to surrounding pages. Fortunately, Word provides a tool that enables you to zoom in and out with the click of a mouse. To zoom in or out, open the **Zoom** drop-down list in the Standard toolbar and click the desired zoom setting; choose a higher percentage to zoom in or a lower percentage to zoom out, as shown in Figure 4.5. The Page Width option automatically picks a zoom percentage that fits the text within the left and right edges of the window, so you don't need to scroll left and right to bring text into view. If the Zoom drop-down list is not displayed, click the **Toolbar Options** button at the end of the Standard toolbar. You can click inside the text box and type your own setting (zoom percentage).

Word also offers various views of a page, each of which is designed to help you perform a specific task. To change to a view, open the **View** menu and click one of the following view options (buttons for these views also are available in the lower-left corner of the document window):

Normal (**Ctrl+Alt+N**). Shows your document as one continuous document. In Normal view, Word hides complex page formatting, headers, footers, objects with wrapped text, floating graphics, and backgrounds. Scrolling is smooth because this view uses the least amount of memory.

Web Layout. Displays a document as it will appear when displayed in a Web browser. In Web Layout view, Word displays Web page backgrounds, wraps the text to fit inside a standard browser window, and positions the graphics as they will appear when viewed online.

Print Layout (**Ctrl+Alt+P**). Provides a more realistic view of how your pages will appear in print. Print Layout displays graphics, wrapping text, headers, footers, margins, and drawn objects. This uses a lot of memory, however, and can make scrolling a little jerky.

Outline (**Ctrl+Alt+O**). Enables you to quickly organize and reorganize your document by dragging headings from one location to another in the document. (If you outline a document, check out the View, Document Map feature to quickly navigate the document.)

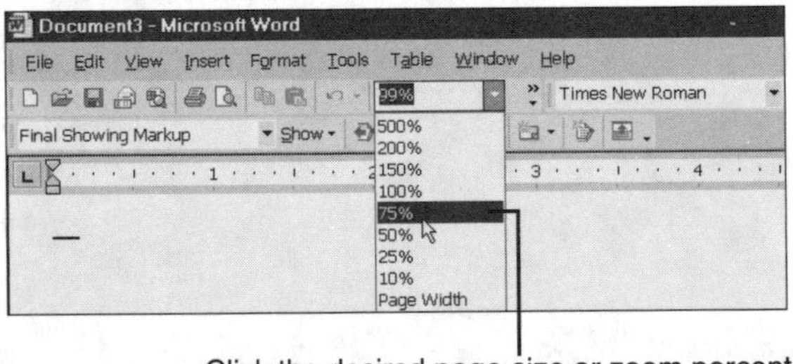

Figure 4.5

With the Zoom drop-down list, you can zoom in or out on a page.

Click the desired page size or zoom percentage.

Ten Ways to Select Text

Before you can do anything with the text you just typed, you must select it. You always can just drag over text to select it, but Word offers several quicker ways to select text. Table 4.1 outlines these techniques.

Table 4.1   Selecting Text with Your Mouse

To Select This	Do This
Single word	Double-click the word.
Sentence	Ctrl+click anywhere in the sentence.
Paragraph	Triple-click anywhere in the paragraph. Alternatively, position the pointer to the left of the paragraph until it changes to a right-pointing arrow, as shown in Figure 4.6, and then double-click.

Table 4.1   Continued

To Select This	Do This
One line of text	Position the pointer to the left of the line until it changes to a right-pointing arrow, and then click. (Drag to select additional lines.)
Several paragraphs	Position the pointer to the left of the paragraphs until it changes to a right-pointing arrow. Then double-click, hold down the mouse button on the second click, and drag up or down.
Large block of text	Click at the beginning of the text, scroll down to the end of the text, and Shift+click.
Entire document	Position the pointer to the left of any text until it changes to a right-pointing arrow. Then triple-click.
Entire document shortcut	Press **Ctrl+A**.
Extend selection	Hold down the **Shift** key while using the arrow keys, Page Up, Page Down, Home, or End.

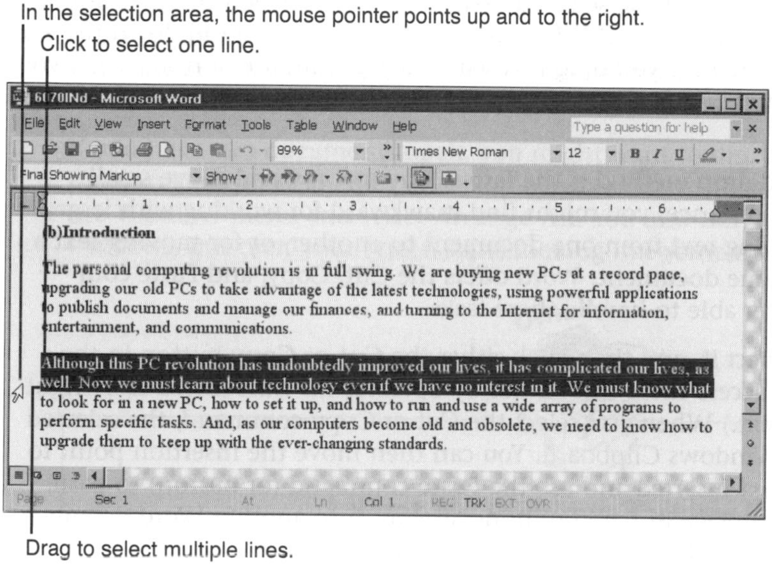

In the selection area, the mouse pointer points up and to the right.
Click to select one line.

Drag to select multiple lines.

Figure 4.6

You can quickly select blocks of text by positioning the mouse pointer in the selection area.

The Ol' Find and Replace Trick

If you have used any word processing program, you know that the program can search your document for unique words and phrases and replace those words or phrases with other text. In Word, both the Find and Replace commands are located on your Edit menu.

To search for text without replacing it, open the **Edit** menu and choose **Find**. Type the word or phrase you want to find and click **Find Next**. Word finds the specified text and highlights it. To find the next occurrence of the text, click **Find Next**. When you are finished searching, click **Cancel** to close the Find and Replace dialog box.

To have Word replace text with other text, perform the following steps:

1. Open the **Edit** menu and select **Replace**.
2. In the **Find What** text box, type the word or phrase you want to replace and type the replacement word or phrase in the **Replace With** box. (For additional replacement options, click the **More** button.)
3. To start the search and replace, click the **Find Next** button.
4. Word highlights the first occurrence of the text it finds and gives you the opportunity to replace the word or skip to the next occurrence. Click one of the following buttons to tell Word what you want to do:

   ➤ **Find Next**—Skips this text and moves to the next occurrence. (You can close the Find dialog box and use the double-headed arrow buttons below the vertical scrollbar to quickly skip to the next or previous occurrence of the word or phrase.)

   ➤ **Replace**—Replaces this text and moves to the next occurrence.

   ➤ **Replace All**—Replaces all occurrences of the specified text with the replacement text—and does not ask for your okay.

   ➤ **Cancel**—Aborts the operation.

Office

Tracking Down Misplaced Documents

You can always use the Windows **Start**, **Find** or **Start**, **Search** command to locate misplaced files on your system. Office XP now features a task pane that provides easy access to the file search feature. Open the **File** menu and click **Search** to display the Basic Search task pane (or click the **Search** button in the Standard toolbar).

Oops! Undoing Changes

If you enjoy the slash-and-burn, never-look-back approach to editing your documents, you might just decide to live with whatever changes you enter. If you're a little more hesitant, and you get that sinking feeling whenever you delete a sentence, you will feel safe knowing that Word has an Undo feature that enables you to take back any of the most recent edits you've made.

 To undo the most recent action, open the **Edit** menu and select **Undo**, or click the **Undo** button in the Standard toolbar. You can continue to click the **Undo** button to undo additional actions.

The Undo button doubles as a drop-down list that enables you to undo an entire group of actions. To view the list, click the drop-down arrow to the right of the Undo button. Then click the last action you want to undo. Be careful, Word undoes the last selected action and all actions above it in the list; you cannot pick and choose only one action from the list.

To recover from an accidental undo, use the Redo button (just to the right of Undo). It works just like the Undo button: Click the **Redo** button to restore the most recently undone action, or click the drop-down arrow to the right of the Redo button and select one or more actions from the list. (If the Redo button is not shown, click the double-headed arrow on the right end of the Standard toolbar and then click the **Redo** button.)

The Least You Need to Know

If you know how to type, you know just about all you need to be able to create documents in Word. A few tips, however, can make your life easier by giving you more control over the onscreen page. At this point, you should be able to perform the following tricks:

➤ To avoid starting from scratch, choose **File**, **New** and then click the **General Templates** link in the New Document task pane.

➤ When typing, press the **Enter** key only at the end of a paragraph, NOT at the end of every line.

➤ To create a new AutoText entry, drag over the desired text in your document, press **Alt+F3**, type a unique shorthand entry, and click **OK**.

➤ To highlight a chunk of text, drag the mouse pointer over it.

➤ To move a chunk of highlighted text, select it and then drag it to the desired location and release the mouse button.

➤ If you make a mistake, click the **Undo** button.

Chapter 5

Giving Your Text a Makeover

In This Chapter

➤ Making your text big and bold, like in magazines

➤ Aligning text left, right, and center

➤ Making bulleted and numbered lists

➤ Getting fancy with WordArt text boxes

➤ Automated formatting with styles

You need to breathe some life into your document, spice it up with some big bold headings, drop in a few bulleted lists, and maybe even add some color. (You do have a color printer, don't you?) In this chapter, you learn how to use Word's formatting tools to give your document that much-needed face-lift.

Fast and Easy Formatting with the Toolbar

The easiest way to format text is to use Word's Formatting toolbar. In case you haven't noticed this toolbar, it's the one with the B, I, and U buttons in the middle of it. Table 5.1 lists the Formatting toolbar buttons. Because the Formatting toolbar shares space with the Standard toolbar, only a few buttons are displayed. For additional buttons, click the **Toolbar Options** button (the double-headed arrow) at the right end of the toolbar or drag down the vertical line that's to the left of the toolbar to place the toolbar on a line of its own.

Table 5.1   Getting to Know Your Formatting Toolbar

Control	Description
Style	Enables you to select a style that contains several format settings. For example, in the Normal template, the Heading1 style uses Arial 14-point bold text. To learn more, skip ahead to "Baby, You've Got Style(s)," later in this chapter.
Font	Provides typefaces from which you can choose. The typeface is the design of the characters.
Font Size	Enables you to select the size of the characters.
B Bold	Makes text bold.
I Italic	Italicizes text.
U Underline	Underlines text.
Styles and Formatting	Turns the Styles and Formatting task pane on or off.
Align Left	Pushes the left side of the paragraph against the left margin.
Center	Centers the paragraph between the left and right margins.
Align Right	Pushes the right side of the paragraph against the right margin.
Justify	Spreads the text evenly between the left and right margins, as in newspaper columns.
Line Spacing	Changes the line spacing (for instance, to double-space your text).
Numbering	Creates a numbered list.
Bullets	Creates a bulleted list.
Decrease Indent	Decreases the distance that the text is indented from the left margin.
Increase Indent	Increases the distance that the text is indented from the left margin.
Borders	Draws a box around the paragraph.
Highlight	Highlights the text (you can select a different color from the drop-down list).
Font Color	Changes the color of the text.

You can use any of the buttons in the Formatting toolbar to format your text before or after you type it. To format on-the-fly, use the Formatting toolbar to set your preferences, and then start typing. If you have already typed the text, select it (as explained in Chapter 4, "Making and Editing Word Documents") and use the tools to apply formatting to the text.

Two More Formatting Tricks

The Formatting toolbar is pretty cool, but a couple of other formatting shortcuts are available that you can use to dazzle your friends and impress your boss. The first is to right-click highlighted text and select one of the formatting options (Font, Paragraph, or Bullets and Numbering) in the pop-up menu. This displays the dialog box for applying the desired format.

The second trick is much cooler. Use the Format Painter to copy the format of the text without copying the text itself. First, drag over the text whose format you want to use. Then, click the **Format Painter** button (you might have to click the **Toolbar Options** button to access the Format Painter). Now, for the grand finale, drag over the text to which you want to apply the format you just copied. Voilà!

Paint the Town

Double-click the **Format Painter** button to keep it on so that you can paint the copied format to several text selections. When you're finished, click the **Format Painter** button to turn it off.

Visiting the Font Smorgasbord

The Font and Type Size lists are great for some light text formatting, but you're not going to start your own magazine with those limited choices. You need more power! You need the Font dialog box—a box overflowing with fonts, sizes, and enhancements such as strikethrough, superscript, and double-underlining.

Using the Font dialog box is simple. You drag over the text you want to format, right-click the selected text, and select **Font** (or open the **Format** menu and select **Font**). The Font dialog

Change the Default Font

Do you want to use the same font for every document you create? Then change the default font. After making your selections in the Font dialog box, click the **Default** button in the lower-left corner of the dialog box, and then click **Yes** to confirm.

box, shown in Figure 5.1, spreads out like a table full of choice grub. Just point and click to pick the desired font, size, and attributes. In addition, the Font dialog box contains a Character Spacing tab that lists options for controlling the space between characters. Use those options to scrunch the characters together or spread them out.

Office

Remove All Formatting

If you're not sure what you did to your text, but you're sure you want it undone, you can clear all formatting from the text and return it to normal. Select the text and then go to the top of the Style list and click **Clear Formatting**.

➤ **General**—Provides an option for changing the text alignment. You can choose to align the paragraph left, right, or center, or justify it. You also can do this with the alignment buttons on the Formatting toolbar. The Outline level lets you set a heading level for the paragraph, so you can outline your document.

➤ **Indentation**—Enables you to indent the left or right side of the paragraph. This is useful for setting off long quotes and other chunks of text from surrounding text. The **Special** options are for creating first-line or hanging indents. A first-line indent is useful for indenting the first line of a standard paragraph. A hanging indent indents all lines of a paragraph *except* the first line; this is useful for creating bulleted and numbered lists.

➤ **Spacing**—The Before and After options enable you to set the amount of space between the current paragraph and the one preceding or following it. Setting the spacing this way is more accurate and efficient than trying to set the spacing by pressing the Enter key repeatedly. The Line Spacing option sets the space between lines of text within the paragraph. Just as on a typewriter, you can choose single-space, double-space, or other settings.

The Line and Page Breaks tab contains options for preventing awkward page breaks in multipage documents. The following list provides a brief description of each option:

➤ **Widow/Orphan Control**—Prevents the first line of a paragraph from being stranded at the bottom of a page and prevents the last line of a paragraph from being stranded at the top of the next page.

➤ **Keep Lines Together**—Bumps the entire paragraph to the next page if the paragraph does not fit on the current page.

➤ **Keep with Next**—Keeps this paragraph on the same page as the paragraph that follows it.

➤ **Page Break Before**—Inserts a page break before this paragraph, ensuring that the paragraph starts at the top of a page.

➤ **Suppress Line Numbers**—Hide line numbering for this paragraph if line numbering is turned on for the document. (Line numbering typically is used in legal and literary documents to make referring to specific passages easy.) You can turn on line numbering via the File, Page Setup command.

➤ **Don't Hyphenate**—Turns off the hyphenation feature for this paragraph if you have the hyphenation feature turned on for the entire document. (Use the Tools, Language, Hyphenation command to access the hyphenation options.)

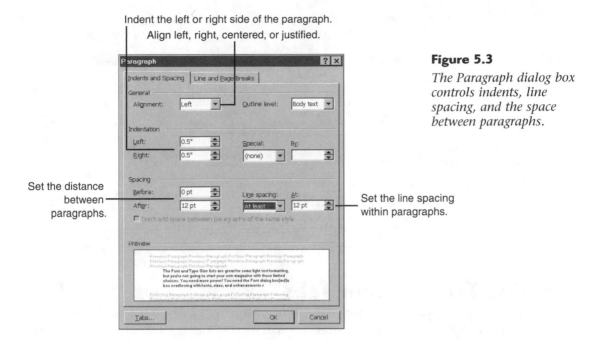

Indent the left or right side of the paragraph.
Align left, right, centered, or justified.

Set the distance between paragraphs.

Set the line spacing within paragraphs.

Figure 5.3

The Paragraph dialog box controls indents, line spacing, and the space between paragraphs.

Ruling Your Indented Servants: Indenting Paragraphs and Lists

Some people are good at judging measurements for the indents they want to create. Other people are men. We men need to see our indents in context to know whether they are correct. For us, Word offers the horizontal ruler (just above the document viewing area), as shown in Figure 5.4. If the ruler isn't on your screen, some joker must have turned it off. Open the **View** menu and select **Ruler**. The ruler contains four markers (three triangles plus a rectangle below the lower-left triangle), which you can drag to do the following:

➤ Drag the upper-left triangle to the right to indent the first line of the paragraph—so you won't have to press the spacebar five times at the beginning of each paragraph.

➤ Drag the lower-left triangle to indent the rest of the lines in the paragraph.

➤ Drag the rectangle that's below the lower-left triangle to move both left triangles at the same time (but retain their positions relative to one another). The lower-left triangle is glued to the rectangle, so the two always stay together. This indents all the lines of the paragraph.

➤ Drag the rightmost triangle to the left to indent all the lines of the paragraph in from the right margin.

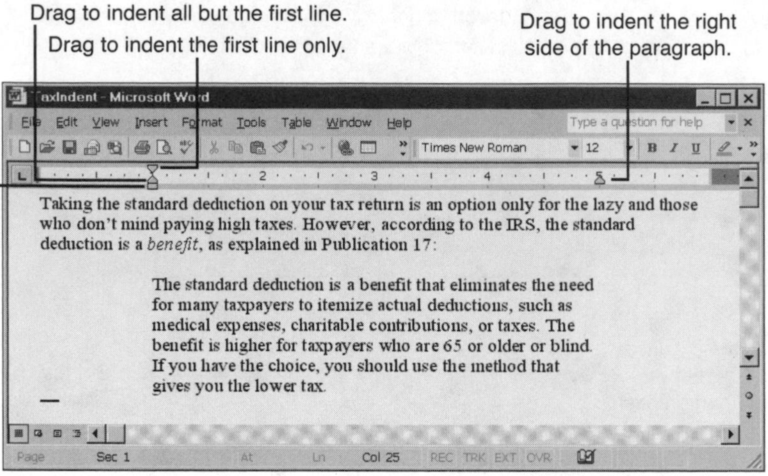

Drag to indent all but the first line.
Drag to indent the first line only.

Drag to indent the right side of the paragraph.

Figure 5.4

Use this picture as your guide to indents.

Drag to indent all lines in the selected paragraph(s).

Taking the standard deduction on your tax return is an option only for the lazy and those who don't mind paying high taxes. However, according to the IRS, the standard deduction is a *benefit*, as explained in Publication 17:

> The standard deduction is a benefit that eliminates the need for many taxpayers to itemize actual deductions, such as medical expenses, charitable contributions, or taxes. The benefit is higher for taxpayers who are 65 or older or blind. If you have the choice, you should use the method that gives you the lower tax.

Keeping Tabs on Your Tabs

By default, regular paragraphs have tab stops at every half inch. Whenever you press the Tab key, the insertion point moves one half inch to the right. It's tempting to just keep pressing the Tab key until you've nudged the insertion point to where you want it. Don't. This might work okay for simple indents, but this technique often results in making your text more difficult to realign later. Instead, set the tab stops yourself, and press the Tab key only once to get there. Trust me, you'll save yourself loads of work in the long run.

The easiest way to set tab stops is to use the horizontal ruler, as shown in Figure 5.5. At the far-left end of the ruler is a tab type symbol, which should be shaped like the letter L. Rest the mouse pointer on it to see which type of tab it is set to insert. Click it to select the type of tab you want to set—Left, Center, Right, or Decimal (for aligning a column of numbers on the decimal point). Click inside the lower half of the horizontal ruler where you want the tab stop inserted. An icon representing the tab stop appears on the ruler. To move a tab stop, drag it to a new position. To delete a tab stop, drag it off the ruler.

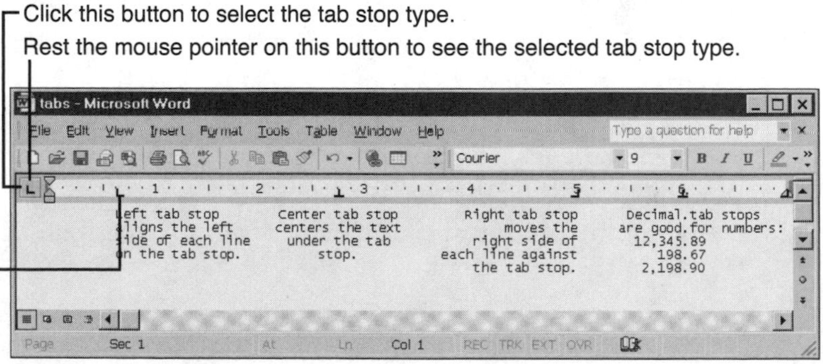

Click this button to select the tab stop type.
Rest the mouse pointer on this button to see the selected tab stop type.

Figure 5.5

The easiest way to set tab stops is to use the horizontal ruler.

Click inside the bottom of the ruler to set the tab stop.

| Left tab stop aligns the left side of each line on the tab stop. | Center tab stop centers the text under the tab stop. | Right tab stop moves the right side of each line against the tab stop. | Decimal tab stops are good for numbers: 12,345.89 198.67 2,198.90 |

More Tab Control

For more control over the look and behavior of your tab stops, open the **Format** menu and select **Tabs**. The Tabs dialog box enables you to set tab stops in inches, clear tab stops, and add *leaders* to tab stops. A leader is a string of characters that lead up to the text at the tab stop, like this:

Chapter 14 155

The Painted Word: Using Text as Art

Fancy fonts are great for headings and running text, but sometimes you need something a little different. Maybe you want to add a curving banner to the top of a page or set off a block of text in its own box. Word offers a couple of tools you can use to create these special effects: WordArt and text boxes.

Inserting WordArt Objects

With WordArt, you can create 3D text objects that curve, angle up or down, and even lean back. To insert a WordArt object on a page, move the insertion point to where you want the object inserted. Open the **Insert** menu, point to **Picture**, and select **WordArt**. The WordArt Gallery appears, displaying a bunch of styles from which to choose. Click the desired style and click **OK**. In the Edit WordArt Text dialog box, type your text and select the desired font, font size, and attributes (bold or italic). Click **OK**. Word creates the object, places it on the page along with the WordArt toolbar, and changes to Print Layout view (which is required for displaying graphics). At first, the WordArt object lays over any text on your page, but you can change its properties, as explained later, to make text wrap around the object.

The WordArt object is essentially a graphic object. When it first appears and whenever you click it, small squares called *handles* appear around it, and the WordArt toolbar appears, as shown in Figure 5.6. You can drag a handle to change the size of the object. If you move the mouse pointer over the object, the pointer appears as a four-headed arrow. You can drag the object to move it.

In addition to changing the object's size and position, you can use buttons on the WordArt toolbar to modify the object, as explained in Table 5.2.

Table 5.2   WordArt Toolbar Buttons

Button	Description
Insert WordArt	Inserts another WordArt object on the page.
Edit Text	Enables you to edit the text used in the WordArt object.
WordArt Gallery	Enables you to select a different style for this WordArt object from the WordArt Gallery.
Format WordArt	Displays a dialog box that enables you to change the WordArt object's size and position, control how surrounding text wraps around the object, change the object's color, and much more.
WordArt Shape	Enables you to pick a different shape for the object.
Text Wrapping	Controls the way surrounding text wraps around the WordArt object.
WordArt Same Letter Heights	Displays all the characters in the object (uppercase or lowercase) at the same height.
WordArt Vertical Text	Displays characters running from the top to the bottom, instead of left to right.
WordArt Alignment	Doesn't do anything if you have only one line of text. With two or more lines of text, this button enables you to align the text left, right, or center, or to justify it (so that it spreads out to touch both sides of the imaginary WordArt box).
WordArt Character Spacing	Enables you to change the space between characters in the WordArt object.

Setting Off Text in Text Boxes

Word is becoming more and more like a desktop publishing program with each new release. Word even offers text boxes, which you can use to set off a block of text from surrounding text. You've probably seen text boxes used in your favorite magazines to set off quotes or add a brief summary of an article. Because the text is in a box of its own, it captures the reader's attention.

Click the object to select it and display the WordArt toolbar.

Drag a handle to resize the object.

Drag the object to move it.   The WordArt toolbar

Figure 5.6
WordArt enables you to create graphical text objects.

To create a text box in Word, position the insertion point where you want the text box placed, open the **Insert** menu, and click **Text Box**. The mouse pointer turns into a crosshair pointer. Position the pointer where you want one corner of the text box to appear, and then drag the pointer to the opposite corner to define the box size and dimensions. Word inserts the box and displays the Text Box toolbar. Type your text in the box, and use the Formatting toolbar to style the text. As with WordArt, the text box is surrounded by handles you can drag to change the size or dimensions of the box.

On the left end of the Text Box toolbar are two Link buttons—**Create Text Box Link** and **Break Forward Link**. These buttons enable you to continue the contents of one text box inside another text box on the same page or on another page. (You can, for instance, start a story on the front page and continue it on page 5.) To create a link, create two text boxes and insert or type the desired text in the first text box. Then, click the **Create Text Box Link** button and click inside the second text box. If the text doesn't fit in that text box, you can create a third text box and link to it. The **Break Forward Link** button enables you to break the link between text boxes.

One last text box trick, and I'll let you move on. Activate the Drawing toolbar (right-click any toolbar and select **Drawing**). All the way to the right are two buttons called **Shadow** and **3D**. To add a drop shadow to the text box, click the **Shadow** button and select the desired shadow. To give your text box a 3D look, such as the one in Figure 5.7, click the **3D** button and select a 3D effect.

If you drop a text box on top of existing text, the text box hides the text under it. If you prefer, you can have the existing text wrap around the text box so that you can see all the text. To enter text wrap and other format settings for your text box, either open the **Format** menu and select **Text Box** or double-click the border that defines the text box.

A text box in 3D

Figure 5.7

Get out your 3D glasses, and turn on the Drawing toolbar.

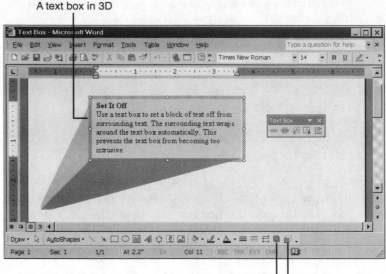

Shadow button ⌐ └3D button

Baby, You've Got Style(s)

You go to a lot of trouble to create a "wardrobe" for your documents. Maybe you designed the perfect title, created some great-looking bulleted lists, and spent way too much time playing with the various levels of headings. You don't want to do all that work over again, and you don't have to. Instead, you can save your format settings as *styles* and apply the styles to the text in any other documents you create.

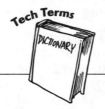

Tech Terms

What's a Style?

A style is a group of format settings. For example, if you create a heading using 18-point, Arial, bold, italic type that's centered, you must apply all formats separately the first time you format the heading. If you then create a style for that heading and name it, say, "Attitude," you can apply all those format settings to some other text by selecting the Attitude style from the style list.

Even better, you can modify a style and have your changes affect all the text you have formatted using that style. For instance, if you decide you want to bump down the type size for all the top-level headings from 18-point to 16-point, all you have to do is change the type size for the style you applied to those headings. All the headings you've formatted using that style are then automatically changed from 18-point to 16-point.

The two types of styles are paragraph and character. A *paragraph style* applies paragraph and character formatting to all the characters in the paragraph. Paragraph formatting includes alignment, indents, line spacing, space before and after the paragraph, and so on. Character formatting controls the font, size, and character attributes, such as bold and italic. A *character style* applies format settings only to selected text; it does not apply formatting to all the text in a paragraph. The style list (on the Formatting toolbar) marks paragraph styles with a ¶ and character styles with an a.

Applying Character and Paragraph Styles

Word's templates all come with a set of styles you can apply to your paragraphs and text. To apply a paragraph style, click anywhere in the paragraph to which you want to apply the style, open the **Style** drop-down list (in the Formatting toolbar or Formatting and Styles task pane), and click the desired style (you might need to click the **Toolbar Options** icon to display the Style drop-down list). To apply a character style, drag over the text to which you want to apply the style, open the **Style** drop-down list, as shown in Figure 5.8, and click the desired style.

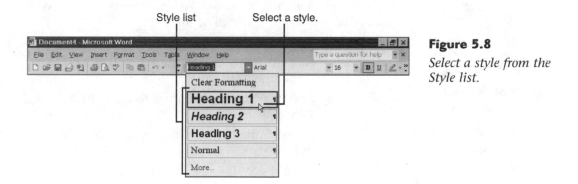

Figure 5.8

Select a style from the Style list.

If the drop-down list doesn't include the desired style, display the Styles and Formatting task pane (select **Format**, **Styles and Formatting**), and then open the **Show** list near the bottom of the taskbar and click **All Styles**. This displays a list of even more ready-made Word styles and styles that you have created (which you do in the next section).

Displaying the Style Bar

You can display the names of paragraph styles used in your document on the left side of the document window. Open the **Tools** menu, select **Options**, and click the **View** tab. Under the Outline and Normal options, use the **Style Area Width** spin box to set the style area to .5" or more.

Creating Your Own Styles

An easy way to create your own paragraph style is to use the **Style** box on the toolbar. (You can't use this box to create a character style, however.) First, set up the paragraph on which you want to base your style; include any special formatting you want to use. Be sure your insertion point is somewhere in that paragraph, and then click in the **Style** box in the Formatting toolbar. Enter a new style name, being careful not to duplicate an existing name. Click anywhere outside the box or press **Enter**. You can now apply your style by name to any new paragraphs you add to your document.

Apply Styles with a Keystroke

In previous versions of Word, you could assign a keystroke to a style right inside the New Style dialog box. You can't do that anymore. To assign a keystroke to a style, you must take the same steps as you would take to assign a keystroke to a macro or command. For details, see the section "Assigning Shortcut Keys for Quick Playback" in Chapter 27, "Macros for Mere Mortals."

To create a character style, you can't use the Style box on the Formatting toolbar. You must use the New Style dialog box, as explained in these steps:

1. Open the **Format** menu and select **Styles and Formatting** to display the Styles and Formatting task pane.
2. Click the **New Style** button to display the New Style dialog box.
3. In the **Name** text box, type a name for the style.
4. Open the **Style Type** list box and select **Character**.
5. Open the **Format** menu at the bottom of the dialog box and select **Font** to change the appearance of the text. This displays the Font dialog box.
6. Use the Font dialog box to select the desired character formatting and click **OK**. This returns you to the Style dialog box.
7. Click **Close** to save your new style.

Saving Your Styles in a Template

Behind every Word document is a template containing settings, styles, fonts, keystroke assignments, and other elements unique to the document. When you save your document, Word saves your new styles in the template for that document; you can use the styles you created only in that document. To use the styles in other documents, you have two choices: Save the document as a template or copy the styles from your current document to the document or template in which you want to use those styles.

To save a document as a template, open the **File** menu and click **Save As**. Open the **Save As Type** drop-down list and click **Document Template**. The Templates folder opens automatically. Name and save the document as you normally would. You now can create new documents based on this template. You also can attach this template to any document in which you want to use your styles. To attach a template to a document, open the **Tools** menu and click **Templates and Add-Ins**. Click the **Attach** button, select the desired template, and click **Open**. You also can use the File, New command to create a new document based on your template.

To copy a style from one document or template to another, first open the document that contains the styles you want to copy. Open the **Tools** menu and click **Templates and Add-Ins**, and then click the **Organizer** button. The available styles appear in the list on the left. The styles in the Normal template appear on the right. To copy a style to the Normal template, so it will be available to all documents, click the style in the list on the left; then click the **Copy** button. To copy a style to a different template or document, click the **Close File** button below the list on the right, and then click the **Open File** button and select the document or template to which you want to copy the styles. You can then select a style in either list and click the **Copy** button to add it to the other list.

Editing Styles On-the-Fly

In the lower-right corner of the Modify Style dialog box is the Automatically Update check box. If this option is checked, whenever you change the formatting for any text to which you applied a style, the style's definition is updated to reflect the change. All text formatted with this style is automatically reformatted accordingly.

Revamping Your Styles

Now for the fun part. As discussed earlier, you can reformat *all* text to which you applied a particular style simply by changing the format settings for that style. Here's what you do:

1. Open the **Format** menu and click **Styles and Formatting** to display the Styles and Formatting task pane.

2. In the **Pick Formatting to Apply** list, point to the style you want to change and click the arrow that appears to the right of the style. A list of options appears.

3. Click **Modify**. The Modify Style dialog box appears.

4. Click the **Format** button in the lower-left corner of the dialog box; then click the desired format settings you want to change.

5. Enter your changes, and then click **OK** to return to the Modify Style dialog box.

6. Repeat steps 4 and 5 to enter any additional changes; then click the **OK** button. Word updates all text formatted with that style to reflect the formatting changes.

The Least You Need to Know

About 50% of the time you spend creating a document is devoted to formatting it. If you have a severe case of writer's block, that percentage is even higher. So, before you move on, you should master these basic tasks:

➤ To make text bold, highlight the text and press **Ctrl+B** or click the **B** button in the Formatting toolbar.

➤ You can right-click selected text to display a context menu that lists your formatting options.

➤ To change the line spacing or indents for a paragraph, click in the paragraph, select **Format**, **Paragraph**, and then enter your preferences in the Paragraph dialog box.

➤ To quickly indent a paragraph, drag the indent markers on the ruler displayed just above the document viewing area.

➤ To check the format settings that control the appearance of selected text, open the **Format** menu and click **Reveal Formatting**.

➤ To insert a WordArt object, open the **Insert** menu, point to **Picture**, and click **WordArt**.

➤ To apply a style, select the text you want to format, display the **Styles and Formatting** task pane, and click the desired style.

Chapter 6

Aligning Your Text with Columns and Tables

In This Chapter

➤ Using newspaper–style columns to create your own newsletters

➤ Setting up a table to align text in rows and columns

➤ Drawing a table with your mouse—cool!

➤ Understanding section breaks

Text is fluid. As you type, text pours onto the page, filling every nook and cranny between the left and right margins. If you're typing paragraphs, this fluidity is fine, but when you need to arrange text in columns and rows, the text can be very uncooperative. No matter how hard you try to shove it around on the page with tabs and indents, there's only so much you can do.

Should you give up? No! Word has a whole box full of text-alignment tools for taking control of stubborn text and making it line up the way you want it to. With Word's columns and tables, you can make newspaper-style columns snake across the page from top to bottom, create perfectly aligned tables, and even decorate your tables with borders and shading. This chapter shows you how to use Word's advanced text-alignment tools to make your text behave.

Creating Your Own Newspaper Columns

Although text boxes, (discussed in the previous chapter) provide excellent control over columns of text, for basic newsletters you might want to use a more standard feature: *newspaper columns*. Newspaper columns divide the text into two or more columns that wrap the text from the bottom of one column to the top of the next column, just like in a newspaper or magazine.

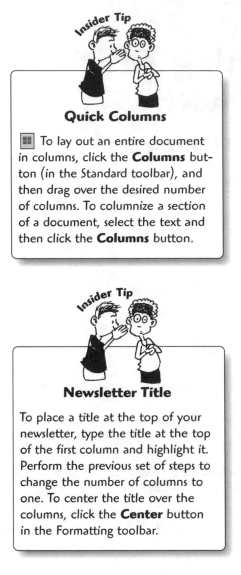

Quick Columns

To lay out an entire document in columns, click the **Columns** button (in the Standard toolbar), and then drag over the desired number of columns. To columnize a section of a document, select the text and then click the **Columns** button.

Newsletter Title

To place a title at the top of your newsletter, type the title at the top of the first column and highlight it. Perform the previous set of steps to change the number of columns to one. To center the title over the columns, click the **Center** button in the Formatting toolbar.

Before you create columns, figure out where you want the columns to start and end. Maybe you want the entire document divided into columns, or perhaps you want to apply columns to only a portion of the document. After you've decided, perform the following steps to create your columns:

1. Position the insertion point where you want the columns to start, or drag over the text you want to lay out in columns. (To format the entire document with columns, the insertion point can be anywhere within the document.)

2. Open the **Format** menu and select **Columns**. The Columns dialog box appears, prompting you to specify the desired number of columns.

3. Select one of the preset column styles at the top, and specify additional preferences as desired to modify the style. You can click the **Line Between** option to insert a vertical line between the columns. (For uniform columns, make sure **Equal Column Width** is checked.)

4. Open the **Apply To** drop-down list and click the option for applying columns to the whole document or to selected text or sections.

5. Click **OK**. Word automatically changes to Print Layout view to display the columns as they will appear in print. (You'll have an easier time moving around in columns by switching to Normal view.)

If you decide later to return the columns to normal text, position the insertion point where the columns start and repeat the steps for setting columns. This time, select the **One** column option from the Presets area. You can change the column layout anywhere inside the document; for instance, you might want to shift from two columns on one page to three columns on the next.

Whenever you create columns, the horizontal ruler displays markers for controlling the column boundaries, as shown in Figure 6.1. To quickly change the width of a column, drag its marker. (When the mouse pointer is over a column width marker, the pointer appears as a double-headed arrow.) To display the column width measurements in the ruler, hold down the **Alt** key while dragging.

You also can adjust the column widths by resetting the columns. To do so, move the insertion point to where the columns begin, open the **Format** menu, and select **Columns**. Enter the desired measurements for the width of each column. (Remember that you can make all the columns the same width by turning on **Equal Column Width**.)

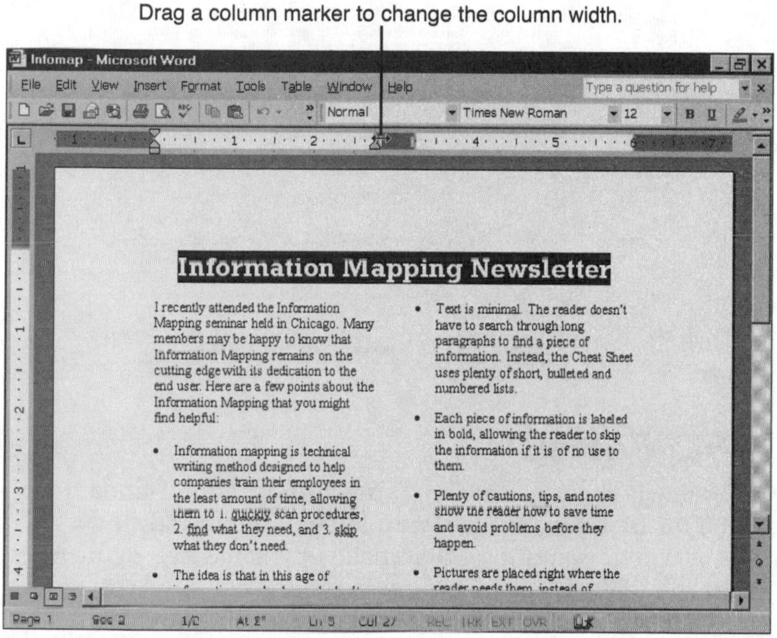

Drag a column marker to change the column width.

Figure 6.1

The easiest way to resize a column is to drag its marker.

Setting a Table for Precise Alignment

The most useful page layout tool in any word processing program is the Table feature. This tool enables you to align blocks of text side by side not only to create tables packed with small bits of information, but also to create professional-looking résumés, exams, study guides, and documentation. If you ever have trouble placing two items side by side in a document, the solution is usually a table. Figure 6.2 shows a table used to create a résumé.

The key to Word tables is that the information is organized in a systematic fashion. Like a well-designed city, a table is a grid consisting of *rows* and *columns* that intersect to form *cells*. The following sections teach you four techniques for creating your own tables. Later sections in this chapter show you how to insert text and pictures in the cells that make up the table, and how to change the look and layout of the cells.

Figure 6.2

A table disguised as a résumé.

	Susan K. Shiffer 1603 North Emerson Chicago, Illinois 60631 Home Phone: (312) 555-5555
Goals	To teach and share my love and knowledge of the Spanish language and culture in an environment that will further enrich and develop my personal and academic skills.
Education **May, 1993** **May, 1990**	*Purdue University, West Lafayette, Indiana* Master of Arts in Spanish Literature. Bachelor of Arts in Spanish/Education.
Sept., 1998- **June, 1999**	*University of Madrid, Spain.* Concentrated on all aspects of peninsular Spanish culture, including History, Economics, Architecture, Literature, and Art.
Sept., 1994- **Jan., 1995**	*University of the Americas, Cholula, Mexico* Emphasis on furthering language skills, plus first-hand cultural exchanges.
Honors **1990**	Delta Kappa Pi (Spanish Honorary Society) Distinguished Student Award, Purdue University. Dean's List and Honor Roll throughout my undergraduate career.
Special *Projects/* *Publications* **1994**	Presentation, "How to Organize a Successful Foreign Language Week," at the IFLTA Fall Conference.
Jan., 1983	Critical review of Gail L. Nemetz-Robinson's book, *Issues in Second Language and Cross-Cultural Education: The Forest Through the Trees.* Published in *The Canadian Modern Language Review*, Vol. 39, No.2, Jan., 1983.
1982	Graduate Assistant of Purdue's summer study program at the Universidad-Iberoamericana in Mexico City.
1981	Assistant Instructor for Purdue's "Super Saturday" educational program. Language instruction for exceptional children, ages 6-12.

Using the Insert Table Button

The easiest way to create a table is to use the **Insert Table** button in the Standard toolbar. When you click the **Insert Table** button, Word opens a menu showing a graphic representation of the columns and rows that make up a table (see Figure 6.3). Drag down and to the right to highlight the number of rows and columns you want your table to have (you'll learn how to insert and delete columns and rows later). Drag beyond the bottom or right side of the drop-down box to expand the table grid. When you release the mouse button, Word inserts the table.

The Insert Table button

Figure 6.3

Create a table of uniform row height and column width.

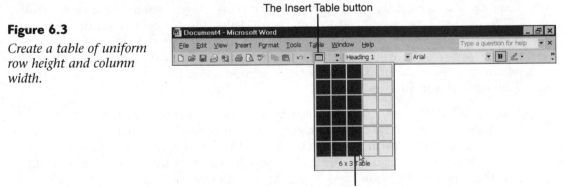

Drag over the desired number of columns and rows.

Setting Your Table with a Dialog Box

For more control over the structure and appearance of your table, use the Insert Table dialog box. Open the **Table** menu, point to **Insert**, and click **Table**. Then, enter your preferences in the Insert Table dialog box. To give your table a professional look, click the **AutoFormat** button and select a predesigned format from the **Formats** list.

Drawing a Table with Your Mouse

If you're looking for a more intuitive way to create a table, just draw it. Word offers a table drawing tool that enables you to create the overall table outline and then chop the table into little pieces by adding row and column lines.

The Tables and Borders Toolbar

Whenever you choose to draw a table, the Tables and Borders toolbar appears. You can start drawing a table with simple lines, or you can select options from the toolbar (such as line color and thickness) before you start drawing.

To draw a table, open the **Table** menu and select **Draw Table**. The mouse pointer turns into a pencil, the Tables and Borders toolbar appears, and Word switches to Print Layout view. Drag a rectangle of the desired length and width where you want the table to appear. When you release the mouse button, Word inserts a one-cell table. You can then drag vertical and horizontal lines across the table (within the original rectangle), using the pencil pointer to create columns and rows (see Figure 6.4). You also can draw a table by drawing individual cells side by side and on top of one another, as opposed to sectioning off a large cell.

Transforming Existing Text into a Table

Creating a table using tabs is like performing brain surgery with a meat cleaver; tabs just don't give you enough control over your columns and rows. If, however, you're reading this after having set up a table with tabs or inserting one from another program, don't despair. You can recover from your ill-conceived mistake by converting your tabular table into a genuine, bona fide Word table.

First, drag over all the text you want to include in the table. Then, open the **Table** menu, point to **Convert**, and click **Text to Table**. The Convert Text to Table dialog box appears, prompting you to specify the number of columns and rows and to enter other preferences. Make the desired selections and click **OK**. Word converts the text to a table, and you can start modifying it if necessary.

Figure 6.4

You can now draw tables.

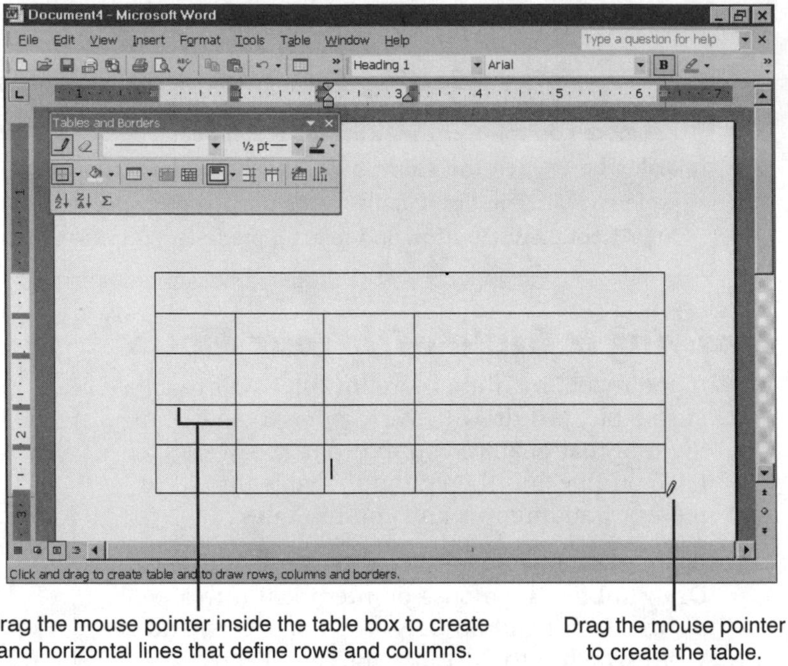

You can drag the mouse pointer inside the table box to create vertical and horizontal lines that define rows and columns.

Drag the mouse pointer to create the table.

Cruising Around Inside Your Table

Navigating a table with the mouse is fairly straightforward. You click inside a cell to move the insertion point to that cell. You also can use the keyboard to quickly move from cell to cell. Table 6.1 lists the keystrokes to use for moving around in a table.

Table 6.1   Moving Around in a Table

Press	To
Tab	Move to the next cell. With the insertion point at the end of the table, pressing Tab creates a new row and moves the insertion point into its first cell.
Shift+Tab	Move to the previous cell in the table.
Alt+Home	Move to the first cell in the row you're in.
Alt+PgUp	Move to the top cell in the column you're in.
Alt+End	Move to the last cell in the row you're in.
Alt+PgDn	Move to the bottom cell in the column you're in.

You select text inside a table the same way you select text in a paragraph—by dragging over it. To select an entire row, move the mouse pointer to the left of the row (outside the table) until the mouse pointer points to the right, and then click. To select a column, move the mouse pointer over the topmost line of the column until the pointer points down, and then click. To select multiple columns or rows, drag the mouse when the pointer is pointing down or to the right. To move selected columns or rows, you can drag and drop them to the desired location. You also can select a row, a column, or the entire table by choosing the desired option from the **Table**, **Select** sub-menu.

Aligning Graphics and Text

Although tables traditionally are used to align blocks of text, they're excellent for aligning pictures with text as well. Just place the insertion point in the cell where you want the picture to appear and select the **Insert**, **Picture** command.

Performing Reconstructive Surgery on Your Table

A table never turns out perfect the first time. Maybe you want more space between the topmost row and the rest of the table, or you need to shade some of the cells or add lines to divide the columns and rows. In the following sections, you learn all the tricks for restructuring and enhancing your table.

Adjusting the Row Height and Column Width

The easiest way to adjust the row height and column width is to drag the lines that divide the columns and rows. When you move the mouse pointer over a line, the pointer changes into a double-headed arrow; that's when you can start dragging. If you hold down the **Alt** key and drag, the horizontal or vertical ruler shows the exact row height or column width measurement. (You also can drag the column or row markers inside the rulers to change the row height and column width.)

Automated Adjustments

To have Word adjust the row height and column width for you, select the row(s) or column(s) you want to change; then open the **Table** menu, point to **AutoFit**, and select the desired option.

Inserting and Deleting Columns and Rows

When you start typing entries in a table, you might find that you have either too many rows or columns or too few. This problem is easy to correct:

➤ To insert one or more rows, click in the row where you want the new row added (or drag over the desired number of rows) and select **Table**, **Insert**, **Rows Above** or **Rows Below**.

➤ To insert one or more columns, first select an existing column (to insert two columns, select two columns). Then select **Table**, **Insert**, **Columns to the Left** or **Columns to the Right**.

➤ To delete rows or columns, drag over the rows or columns you want to delete and select **Table**, **Delete**, **Rows** or **Columns**. (If you press the Delete key instead, Word removes only the contents of the rows or columns.)

Splitting and Joining Cells

Although not quite as exciting as splitting atoms, splitting cells and joining them (fusion, I guess) can keep you entertained for hours—and give you a great deal of control over your tables. Figure 6.5 shows some instances in which you might want to join cells to create a single cell that spans several rows or columns.

A column heading can span two or more columns.

Figure 6.5

You can join cells to form a single cell, or split one cell into many.

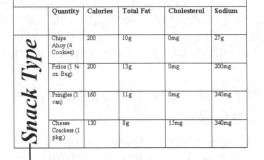

Snack Table					
	Quantity	Calories	Total Fat	Cholesterol	Sodium
Snack Type	Chips Ahoy (4 Cookies)	200	10g	0mg	27g
	Fritos (1 ¼ oz. Bag)	200	13g	0mg	200mg
	Pringles (1 can)	160	11g	0mg	340mg
	Cheese Crackers (1 pkg.)	130	8g	15mg	340mg

A row heading might span several rows.

Insider Tip

Split Tables

Word now allows you to split an entire table in two. With the insertion point in the row where you want the table split, open the **Table** menu and click **Split Table**. You can't, however, split a table vertically by columns.

To join cells, drag over the cells you want to transform into a single cell, open the **Table** menu, and select **Merge Cells**. Word transforms the multiple cells into a single-cell organism.

To split a cell into two or more cells, select the cell you want to split, open the **Table** menu, and select **Split Cells**. The Split Cells dialog box appears, asking you to specify the number of rows and columns you want to split the cell into. Enter your preferences and click **OK**. After the cells are split, you might have to drag the borders to adjust the width and height of the cells.

Giving Your Table a Face-Lift with Borders and Shading

Tables are bland at first; however, Word offers several seasonings, such as borders and shading, that can add spice to your tables. By far, the easiest way to embellish your table is to use the AutoFormat feature. Click anywhere inside the table, open the **Table** menu, and select **Table AutoFormat**. Select the desired design for your table and click **OK**.

If you don't like the prefab table designs Word has to offer, you can design the table yourself using the Borders and Shading dialog box. To change the borders or add shading to the entire table, make sure the insertion point is somewhere inside the table; you don't have to select the entire table. To add borders or shading to specific cells, select the cells. Then open the **Format** menu and select **Borders and Shading**.

As shown in Figure 6.6, the Borders and Shading dialog box has three tabs, two of which you can use to format your table: the Borders tab and the Shading tab. On the **Borders** tab, select any of the border arrangements on the left, or create a custom border by inserting lines of a specific thickness, design, and color.

First, select a line style, thickness, and color from the options in the center of the dialog box. Next, open the **Apply To** drop-down list, and select **Table** (to apply the lines to the entire table) or **Cell** (to apply lines only to selected cells). In the Preview area (just above the Apply to list), click the buttons or click locations in the preview to insert lines.

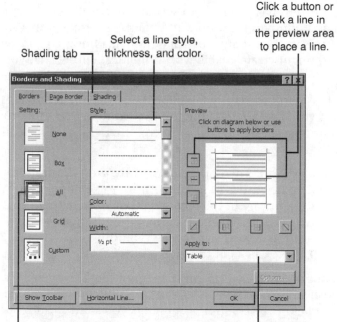

Figure 6.6

You can select a pre-designed border arrangement or create your own.

To shade cells with color or gray shading, click the **Shading** tab. In the Fill grid, click the color you want to use to shade the table or selected cells. Under Patterns, click a color and percentage to add a pattern of a different color to the shading. For example, you might select green as the fill and use a 50% yellow pattern to brighten the green. When you finish entering all your border and shading preferences, click **OK** to apply the changes to your table.

Use the Tables and Borders Toolbar

For quick formatting, use the Tables and Borders toolbar. To display the toolbar, right-click any toolbar and click **Tables and Borders**. In addition to buttons for formatting tables, this toolbar contains the Eraser button, which enables you to quickly erase the lines that define cell boundaries.

Sorting and Summing Table Entries

Tables commonly contain entries that you need to sort alphabetically or numerically. If you create a table of phone numbers for people and places you frequently call, for example, you might want to sort the list alphabetically to make finding people when you need to easier. You also might create a table with numerical entries that you need to total. Word offers a couple of tools that can help.

To sort entries in a table, first select the entire table (or the portion that contains the entries you want to sort). If you have a row at the top that contains descriptions of the contents in each column, make sure it is *not* selected; otherwise, it is sorted along with the other rows.

Open the **Table** menu and select **Sort**. Then open the **Sort By** drop-down list and select the column that contains the entries to sort by (for example, if you want to sort by last name and the last names are in the second column, select Column 2). Open the **Type** drop-down list and select the type of items you want to sort (**Number**, **Text**, or **Date**). Select the desired sort order: **Ascending** (1, 2, 3 or A, B, C) or **Descending** (Z, Y, X or 10, 9, 8). Click **OK** to sort the entries.

Although a Word table is not designed to perform the complicated mathematical operations an Excel spreadsheet can handle, tables can add a column of numbers. Click inside the cell directly below the column of numbers you want to add, open the **Table** menu, and click **Formula**. By default, the Formula dialog box is set up to total the values directly above the current cell. Click **OK** to total the numbers.

The Least You Need to Know

After you learn how to use tables and columns, you can pry the Tab key off your keyboard. Until then, just be sure you can do the following:

➤ To transform existing text into newspaper columns, highlight the text, click the **Columns** button, and click the desired number of columns.

➤ To adjust the width of newspaper columns, drag the column markers in the horizontal ruler.

➤ To insert a table, click the **Insert Table** button, drag over the desired number of rows and columns, and release the mouse button.

➤ Press the **Tab** key to move from one cell to the next in your table. Press **Shift+Tab** to move back one cell.

➤ To have Word format your table, click anywhere inside the table, open the **Table** menu, select **Table AutoFormat**, and enter your preferences.

➤ Although Word tables can perform some basic math, stick with Excel when you need math-intensive solutions.

Chapter 7

Spicing It Up with Graphics, Sound, and Video

In This Chapter

➤ Decorating your text-heavy pages with pictures

➤ Inserting audio and video clips

➤ Moving and sizing your pictures

➤ Drawing your own masterpieces

To catch the attention of today's media-savvy audience and effectively convey your ideas and insights, you now must know how to communicate visually as well as verbally. You must use graphics both to attract the reader and to convey information. And if you really want to captivate the audience of the future with your digital documents, you will have to dazzle them with multimedia elements, as well.

In this chapter, you learn how to use several tools in Word to add graphics, sound, and video to your documents.

Inserting Pictures, Sounds, and Video Clips from the Media Gallery

Maybe you can hold your own in a doodling contest or sketch Gumby and Pokey in your sleep, but chances are that you probably don't have the talent, ambition, or determination to become a professional artist. Fortunately, Word has gathered a collection of clip art, audio recordings, and video clips that you can use to transform your text-heavy pages into a dazzling multimedia document.

Although previous versions of Office included robust clip art galleries, Office XP has completely revamped the Clip Art Gallery and renamed it the *Media Gallery*. To insert

Web Work!

If you're connected to the Internet (currently online) and you have Internet Explorer installed, you can download additional clips from Microsoft's Web site. Click the **Clips Online** link near the bottom of the Insert Clip Art task pane.

an item from the gallery, first insert your Microsoft Office CD into the CD-ROM drive. The CD contains additional clips that were not installed when you installed Office. Open the **Insert** menu, point to **Picture**, and click **Clip Art**. The first time you choose to insert clip art, the Add Clips to Gallery dialog box appears, explaining that you can import images from your hard disk into the gallery now or later. Click **Later**, so you can forge ahead with clip art.

The Insert Clip Art task pane appears, which might leave you wondering, "Where's the clip art?!" Well, this pane might not look like much at first, but it does make the job of finding a specific image much easier. Click in the **Search Text** text box, type a brief description of the type of image for which you're looking (for instance, "football"), and click **Search**. As shown in Figure 7.1, the Insert Clip Art task pane displays thumbnail versions of all the images that match your search instructions. To modify the search or start a new search, click the **Modify** button below the thumbnails. Click the image to insert it.

Figure 7.1

The Insert Clip Art task pane helps you track down images in the vast clip art gallery.

Click the desired clip to add it to your document.

Images that match your search instructions

Click Modify to limit your search or to search again.

Click here to get additional clips from Microsoft's Web site.

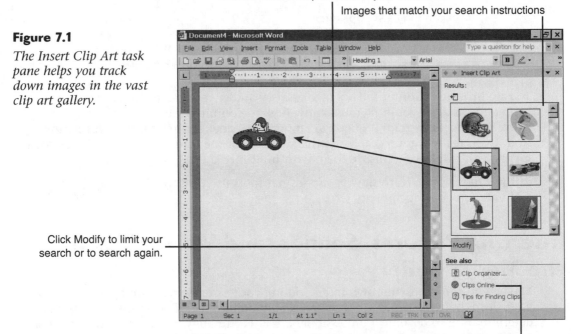

When you first enter your search instructions or click the Modify button to start a new search, you can make your search more selective. Open the **Search In** drop-down list and check the boxes next to only those folders in which you want to search. Open the **Results Should Be** drop-down list and place a check mark next to the types of media files you want: **Clip Art**, **Photographs**, **Movies**, or **Sounds**.

Can't I Just Browse the Gallery?

If you want to browse through the clip art collection and other media files, click the **Clip Organizer** link near the bottom of the Insert Clip Art task pane. This displays a Windows Explorer–like window that lists the folders in which the various media files are stored. Browse through the folders to view thumbnail versions of each clip art image.

Inserting Scanned Images On-the-Fly

If you have a scanner, you can insert a scanned image directly into your document. To insert a scanned image, select **Insert**, **Picture**, **From Scanner or Camera**, and then use your scanner to scan in the desired image. The first time you choose to scan an image, Word might prompt you to install the feature from your Office CD. Insert the CD and follow the instructions to install the feature. Then, follow the onscreen instructions to scan the image. The steps vary depending on your scanner and the scanning software you have installed.

Scan and File Paper Documents

If you have a scanner wired to your computer, you can use the Office document scanner to scan paper documents and file them as graphic images or convert them into editable text. Open the **Start** menu, point to **Programs, Microsoft Office Tools**, and click **Microsoft Office Document Imaging** (to scan documents for filing) or **Microsoft Office Document Scanning** (to scan in multi-page documents and convert them to editable text). Open the **File** menu and select **Scan New Document** to fire up the scanner.

Importing Graphics Files

To insert a graphic image stored on your disk, open the **Insert** menu, point to **Picture**, and click **From File**. The Insert Picture dialog box appears, prompting you to select the graphics file. By default, this dialog box is set up to display *all* the graphics file types that Word supports, which can include file types you have no intention of using. You can narrow the list by selecting a specific graphics file type from the **Files of Type** drop-down list.

Use this dialog box just as you would use the Open dialog box to open a document file. Select the drive, folder, and name of the graphics file you want to insert, and then click the **Insert** button.

Shoving Pictures Around on a Page

Pictures never land right where you want them on a page. You usually have to shove the picture around a little to give your page some balance. To move a picture, click the picture and then drag it to the desired location, as shown in Figure 7.2. When you release the mouse button, Word plops the picture in the current location. To fine-tune the position of an image, use the arrow keys to nudge it.

Rotate It

In Office 2000, you had to click the Free Rotate button in the Drawing toolbar before you could spin an image around its center point. In Office XP, free rotation is enabled for all graphics all the time. Just drag one the green circle that appears above the object. If the green circle does not appear, click the image, and then click the **Rotate Left** button in the Picture toolbar.

What happens to the surrounding text depends on the text wrapping setting for this picture. By default, the picture is set to have text appear above it and below it, but not on either side. To change the way text wraps around a picture, click the image, click the **Text Wrapping** button in the Picture toolbar, and then click the desired text wrap style. For more wrapping options, right-click the picture and select **Format Picture** or **Format Object**. Click the **Layout** tab and select the desired wrapping style. For additional wrapping options, click the **Advanced** button to display the Advanced Layout dialog box.

Drag the picture to the desired
location in the document.

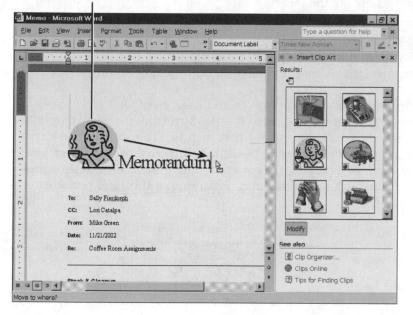

Figure 7.2
*You move pictures by
dragging them.*

The Advanced Layout dialog box also contains a
Picture Position tab, which enables you to fine-
tune the position of a picture on the page and
control whether the picture moves with its surrounding text (so you can keep the picture on
the same page as the text that refers to it). In
the Advanced Layout dialog box, click the
Picture Position tab, enter your preferences,
and click **OK**.

Resizing and Reshaping Your Pictures

Pictures rarely fit in where they're first placed.
Either they're so large that they take over the
entire page, or they're too dinky to make any
impression at all. Changing the size of a picture
is a fairly standard operation. When you click the picture, squares or circles (called
handles) surround it, as shown in Figure 7.3. You can drag the handles to change the
picture's size and dimensions:

Insider Tip

**Copying and Cutting
Pictures**

The Cut, Copy, and Paste commands work for pictures as well as
text. You also can copy a picture by
holding down the **Ctrl** key and
dragging it, or you can right-click a
picture and select the desired command from the pop-up menu.

➤ Drag a top or bottom handle to make the picture taller or shorter.

➤ Drag a side handle to make the picture skinny or fat.

➤ Drag a corner handle to change both the height and width proportionally.

➤ Hold down the **Ctrl** key while dragging to increase or decrease the size from the center out. If you hold down the Ctrl key while dragging a handle on the right side out, for example, the picture gets fatter on both the left and right sides.

For more control over the size and dimensions of an image, right-click the image, click **Format Picture** (or **Format Object**), and click the **Size** tab. This page of options enables you to enter specific measurements for your picture. (The Size tab also has an option called Lock Aspect Ratio, which is on by default. This ensures that when you change the height or width of a picture, the corresponding dimension is resized proportionally. That way, you don't turn a tall, thin person into a short, fat person.)

Figure 7.3

You can use the handles around an object to resize it.

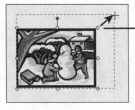

Drag a handle to resize or reshape a picture.

Touching Up a Picture with the Picture Toolbar

The Picture toolbar is like a graphics program built right into your desktop. With about 10 buttons, this toolbar enables you to adjust the picture's brightness and contrast, crop the image (to use only a portion of it), transform a color picture into grayscale or black-and-white, add a border around the picture, and even change the way text wraps around it. Table 7.1 lists the buttons in the Picture toolbar and describes the function of each button.

Table 7.1   Moving Around in a Table

Button	Name	Function
	Insert Picture	Enables you to insert a graphics file from disk.
	Color	Displays a menu that enables you to transform a color image into grayscale, black-and-white, or a watermark (a ghost image that can lie on top of text without hiding it).
	More Contrast	Is similar to a TV control that increases the contrast of the image.

Table 7.1 CONTINUED

Button	Name	Function
	Less Contrast	Decreases the contrast in an image.
	More Brightness	Makes the image brighter.
	Less Brightness	Makes the image darker.
	Crop	Turns the mouse pointer into a cropping tool. Move the pointer over one of the handles and drag it to chop off a portion of the picture. You can use the cropping tool to uncrop a cropped picture, as well.
	Rotate Left	Rotates the image 90° counterclockwise around its centerpoint.
	Line Style	Enables you to add a border around the picture.
	Compress Pictures	Automatically reduces the file size of pictures in your document, so they take up less disk space and download and print more quickly.
	Text Wrapping	Does the same thing as the options on the Layout tab described earlier, but this control is a lot easier to use.
	Format Picture	Displays the Format Picture dialog box, which offers plenty of options for changing the appearance and layout of the image.
	Set Transparent Color	Makes the selected color in a picture transparent so that the background of the page (paper) or screen shows through. Click this button, and then click the color you want to make transparent. (This button is unavailable for most clip art images.)
	Reset Picture	Changes the options back to their original settings in case you mess up while entering changes.

Compress Your Monster Graphics

Large, full-color graphics are notorious for consuming gobs of disk space and taking loads of time to e-mail or copy over a network or the Internet. To reduce the size of images in your document, click the **Compress Pictures** button and enter your preferences. Compression provides two options for reducing image sizes: It can decrease the resolution (image quality) and delete cropped areas of an image.

Looking Classy with Watermarks

When you're trying to make a good impression with your written correspondence, nothing is more effective than a sheet of fancy stationery, especially if it carries a watermark. Now, with Office XP, you no longer need to run out to your local neighborhood office store and pay big bucks for fancy stationery. You can insert a watermark in Word. Here's what you do:

1. Open the document in which you want to add a watermark.

2. Open the **Format** menu, point to **Background**, and click **Printed Watermark**.

3. Perform one of the following steps:

> Click **Picture Watermark**, click **Select Picture**, and click the image you want to use as a watermark.

> Click **Text Watermark**, select the text you want to use (from the **Text** drop-down list), and enter any additional preferences to control the appearance of the text.

4. Click **OK**. Word inserts the specified watermark on every page of the document.

Sketching Custom Illustrations

Word offers a Drawing toolbar, shown in Figure 7.4, that has several tools you can use to create your own drawings, logos, flow charts, illustrations, and other simple graphics. You also can use these tools to modify and enhance existing drawings. To turn on the Drawing toolbar, click the **Drawing** button (in the Standard toolbar) or right-click any toolbar and select **Drawing**. The following sections show you how to use the drawing tools to create your own custom illustrations.

Click the button for the
desired line or shape.

Figure 7.4

The Drawing toolbar contains buttons for drawing lines and basic shapes.

Stretch Your Canvas

Whenever you start a drawing—by clicking a shape in the Drawing toolbar—the new *drawing canvas* appears. Draw all objects inside the canvas to keep them together and treat them as a single graphic image. You can even include text boxes! The drawing canvas prevents your images from being split by awkward page breaks, making managing your custom illustrations within a document much easier.

Creating Drawings with Simple Lines and Shapes

Technical illustrators typically have a collection of rulers and templates they use to draw lines, ovals, rectangles, curves, triangles, and other shapes. They assemble these very basic geometric shapes to create complex illustrations. This is the same technique you use to create drawings in Word.

The Drawing toolbar enables you to place five geometrical objects on a page: a line, an arrow, an oval, a rectangle, and an AutoShape (a predrawn object, such as a diamond, heart, or starburst). In addition, you can use the Shadow and 3D tools to transform two-dimensional objects, such as squares, into three-dimensional objects, such as cubes.

You follow the same procedure for drawing any of these objects. Click the button for the object you want to draw (or select a shape from the **AutoShapes** menu), and then drag the mouse on the page to create the object, as shown in Figure 7.5. For more control over the drawing tool, use the following techniques:

➤ Hold down the **Ctrl** key while dragging to draw the object out from an imaginary center point. Without the Ctrl key, you drag the object out from its corner or starting point.

➤ Hold down the **Shift** key while dragging to create a uniform shape (a perfect square or circle).

➤ Hold down **Ctrl+Shift** while dragging to draw the object out from its center point and create a uniform shape.

Draw Your Own Organizational Charts

Click the new **Insert Diagram or Organizational Chart** button to display six diagrams commonly used in business, including an organizational chart, a pyramid, and a target diagram. Select the desired diagram type, click **OK**, and follow the onscreen directives to customize your diagram.

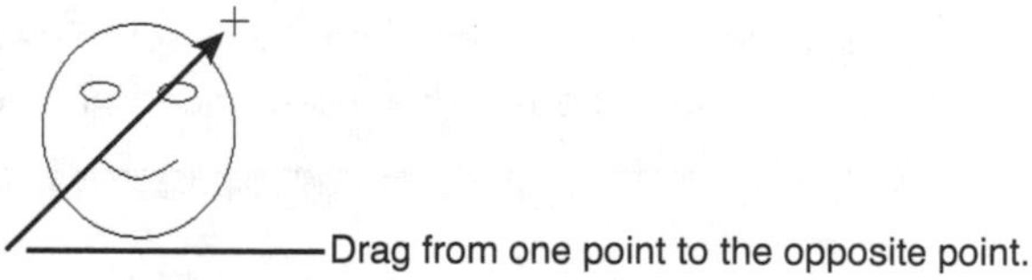

Figure 7.5

Click a drawing tool, and then drag the object into existence.

Drag from one point to the opposite point.

After you have an object on the page, you can use some of the other buttons in the Drawing toolbar to change qualities of the object, such as its fill color and the color and width of the line that defines it. First, select the shape whose qualities you want to change. Then use the buttons listed in Table 7.2 to change the object's qualities.

Table 7.2   Changing the Appearance of Drawn Objects

Button	Name	Function
Draw ▾	Draw	Provides options for turning on a grid (for more precise positioning), changing the order of layered objects, grouping objects, flipping objects, and wrapping text.
⬚	Select Objects	Turns the mouse pointer into a selection tool, so you can use it to select objects rather than draw them.
⬚	Fill Color	Colors inside the lines (as you would in a coloring book). Click the button to fill the object with the color shown. To change the fill color, click the arrow next to this button and select the color from the menu.

Table 7.2 CONTINUED

Button	Name	Function
	Line Color	Changes the color of the line that defines the shape. Click the button to use the color shown. To change the color, click the arrow next to this button and select the color from the menu.
	Font Color	Is for text boxes only. Drag over the text inside the box, open **Font Color**, and select the desired color.
	Line Style	Displays a menu from which you can choose the line thickness and style you want to use for the line that defines the shape.
	Dash Style	Enables you to use dashed lines instead of solid lines.
	Arrow Style	Works only for arrows you have drawn. Select the arrow, and then use this menu to select the type of arrow you want to use or to change the direction in which it points.
	Shadow Style	Works only for ovals, rectangles, AutoShapes, and other two-dimensional objects (including text boxes). This menu contains various drop-shadow styles you can apply to objects.
	3-D Style	Works for ovals, rectangles, AutoShapes, and text boxes. It turns rectangles into blocks and ovals into cylinders. What it does to AutoShapes, you have to see for yourself.

Working with Layers of Objects

Working with two or more drawing objects on a page is like playing with a Colorforms toy; you know, those storyboards with the vinyl characters you stick on and peel off to create various scenes? The trouble with these objects is that when you place one on top of another, the top object blocks the bottom one and prevents you from selecting it. You must flip through the deck to find the object you want. Word

Graphics and Text

You can add some interesting special effects to a document by combining text with AutoShapes. For sales brochures or announcements, for example, you might consider placing small bits of text inside a starburst. Just lay a text box on top of the starburst.

offers a couple of drawing tools that can help you flip through the stack and create groups of objects, which makes maneuvering them easier.

The first thing you must do is reorder the objects. You can send an object that's up front back one layer or all the way to the bottom of the stack, or you can bring an object from the back to the front. First, click the object you want to move (if possible). Some objects are buried so deep you can't get to them. In such a case, you must move objects from the front to the back to get them out of the way until you find the one you want.

After selecting the object you want to move, right-click it, point to **Order**, and select the desired movement: **Bring to Front**, **Send to Back**, **Bring Forward**, **Send Backward**, **Bring in Front of Text**, or **Send Behind Text**.

Working with Two or More Objects as a Group

After you've created a drawing or a portion of a drawing consisting of several shapes, moving this loose collection of shapes or resizing it becomes difficult. If you drag one object, you ruin its relative position with the other objects. Similarly, if you need to shrink or enlarge the drawing, you shouldn't have to resize each object separately. And you don't have to. Word enables you to group two or more objects so you can move and resize them as if they were a single object.

 To create a group, click the **Select Objects** button in the Drawing toolbar and drag a selection box around all the objects you want to include in the group (or just Shift+click each object). Handles appear around all the selected objects. (When dragging a selection box, make sure the box completely surrounds all desired objects; if a portion of an object is outside the box, it might not get selected.)

Next, right-click one of the selected objects, point to **Grouping**, and click **Group** (or open the **Draw** menu in the Drawing toolbar and select **Group**). The handles around the individual objects disappear, and a single set of handles appears around the group, as shown in Figure 7.6. You can now drag a handle to resize all the objects in the group, or you can drag any object in the group to move the group.

To turn off grouping so you can work with an individual object, open the **Draw** menu again and click **Ungroup**. After you're finished working with the individual object, you can regroup the objects by opening the **Draw** menu and selecting **Regroup**.

Drag this handle to rotate the image.

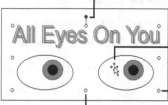

Drag any object in the group to move all the objects.

Drag a handle to resize all objects.

A single set of handles appears around the group.

Figure 7.6
You can group two or more objects and treat them as a single object.

Editing Existing Pictures

Suppose one of your friends or colleagues sent you a graphic or you copied one off the Internet. You like the overall design, but it needs a few minor adjustments. You definitely don't want to redraw it from scratch. The solution? Insert the graphic into a Word document (as explained earlier in this chapter) and double-click it. This opens the picture in a drawing window.

When Word displays the picture in the drawing window, gray lines surround the picture. These define the object's boundaries; whatever is inside the gray lines will be inserted as a picture into your document. Anything outside the lines will be chopped off. To change the position of these lines, drag the markers in the vertical and horizontal toolbars.

Try This!

If you insert a picture from your hard disk using Insert, Object, you might be able to select the image, ungroup its component parts, and edit the image. Unfortunately, this doesn't work with the Office clip art.

After you've set up the markers, use the buttons in the Drawing toolbar to add shapes to the existing drawing. Keep in mind that you can use the Picture toolbar to modify the existing picture. When you're finished, click the **Close Picture** button.

The Least You Need to Know

Microsoft has revamped the way Word and other Office products deal with graphics. To take full advantage of these enhancements, you first need to master some basic tasks:

➤ To insert a clip art image from the Office Media Gallery, open the **Insert** menu, point to **Picture**, and click **Clip Art**.

➤ To insert a picture that is stored as a file on your hard disk, open the **Insert** menu, point to **Picture**, and click **From File**.

➤ To move a picture, drag it.

➤ To change the size of a picture, drag one of its handles.

➤ To insert a scanned image, load the image into your scanner and select **Insert**, **Picture**, **From Scanner or Camera**.

➤ To touch up a picture or digitized photo, use the tools on the Picture toolbar.

➤ You can create your own custom illustrations by using the line and shape tools on the Drawing toolbar.

Chapter 8

Proofreading Your Document: Word Can Help

In This Chapter

➤ Proofreading for lazy people

➤ Checking spelling and grammar as you type

➤ Using AutoCorrect to automatically correct common typos

➤ Using a thesaurus to find just the right word

In this era of electronic communications in which people are sharing documents, rifling off e-mail messages, and having virtual meetings with chat programs, written communications skills are becoming much more important. No matter how well you speak, if your writing is unclear and packed with typos and grammatical errors, your colleagues and customers are going to think you're a dolt.

Word offers a couple of tools that can help you clean up your writing. The spelling checker can catch most of your spelling errors and typos; the grammar checker can help you avoid passive voice and other grammatical no-no's; and the thesaurus can help you think up just the right word. In this chapter, you learn how to use these tools and a few others to clean up your prose.

Looking for Mis Spellings

Word provides more than one way for you to check your spelling. Word can check your spelling on-the-fly (as you type) or after you're finished typing. You also can customize the spelling checker to have it skip over special character strings, such as acronyms (NASA, for instance) and Internet addresses (such as www.whitehouse.gov). The following sections show you what to do.

Spell-Checking on the Go

By default, Word is set up to check for possible spelling errors as you type. If you type a word that does not have a matching entry in Word's spelling dictionary, Word displays a squiggly red line below the word. You have several options at this point:

What About the Other Office Applications?

The spelling checker is shared among all Office applications, including Excel and PowerPoint. So if you need to check your spreadsheets and presentations for spelling errors and typos, refer to this chapter for instructions.

➤ Ignore the line.

➤ Backspace over the misspelled word and type the correct spelling.

➤ Right-click the word in question to display a pop-up menu that very likely contains the correct spelling, as shown in Figure 8.1. Then, if you see the correct spelling, click it.

➤ Right-click the word and select **Ignore All** to have Word remove its annoying red squiggly line and tell it not to question the spelling of this word in this document again.

➤ Right-click the word and select **Add to Dictionary** to add the word to the Office spelling dictionary. After the word is in the dictionary, the spelling checker does not question its spelling in any document ever again.

➤ Right-click the word, point to **AutoCorrect**, and select the correct spelling of the word. (See "Making Word Automatically Correct Your Typos," later in this chapter, for details.) The next time you mistype the word the same way, AutoCorrect automatically inserts the correct spelling in its place.

Personally, I find the squiggly red lines offensive. They give me flashbacks to grade school, where good writing meant every word was spelled correctly and you followed the grammar rules. To turn off automatic spell checking, open the **Tools** menu, select **Options**, and click the **Spelling & Grammar** tab. Click **Check Spelling As You Type** to remove the check from the box, and then click **OK**. If you turn off this option, be sure to check the document's spelling before you print it, as explained in the following section.

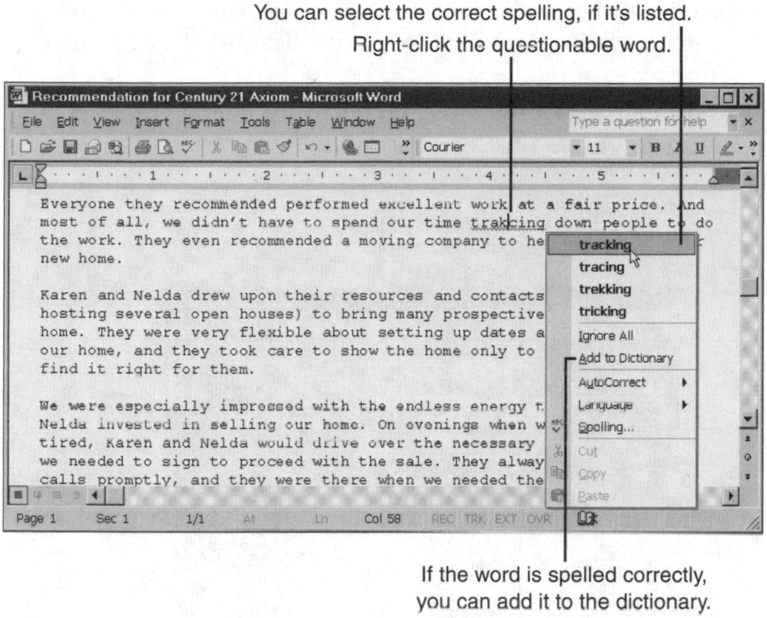

You can select the correct spelling, if it's listed.
Right-click the questionable word.

Figure 8.1
Right-click the word to display a list of suggested corrections.

If the word is spelled correctly,
you can add it to the dictionary.

Spell-Checking When You're Almost Done

If you took my advice and turned off the check-as-you-type option, you can use Word to perform one of these last-minute spell checks for you. To do so, open the **Tools** menu and select **Spelling and Grammar** or click the **Spelling and Grammar** button in the Standard toolbar. Word starts checking your document and stops on the first questionable word. The Spelling and Grammar dialog box displays the word in red and usually displays a list of suggested corrections, as shown in Figure 8.2. You have several options:

➤ Double-click the word in the **Not in Dictionary** text box, type the correction, and click **Change** or **Change All**. Change changes only this one occurrence of the word; Change All changes all occurrences of this word in this document.

➤ Click **Ignore Once** if the word is spelled correctly and you want to skip it just this once. Word stops on the next occurrence of the word.

➤ Click **Ignore All** if the word is spelled correctly but is not in the dictionary and you want Word to skip any other occurrences of this word in this document.

➤ Click **Add to Dictionary** to add the word to the dictionary so that the spelling checker never questions it again in any of your Office documents (the dictionary is shared by all Office applications).

➤ If the word is spelled incorrectly and the Suggestions list displays the correct spelling, click the correct spelling and click **Change** to replace only this occurrence of the word.

➤ To replace this misspelled word and all other occurrences of the word in this document, click the correct spelling in the **Suggestions** list and click **Change All**.

➤ To have AutoCorrect automatically insert the correct spelling when you make this same typo in the future, click **AutoCorrect**.

The spelling checker highlights
the questionable word.

Figure 8.2

If the spelling checker finds a misspelling and displays the correct spelling, your options are simple.

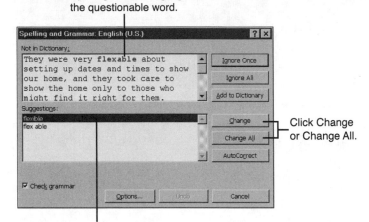

Click Change
or Change All.

Click the correct spelling, if it's listed.

When Word completes the spelling check, it displays a dialog box telling you so. Click **OK**.

Check a Word

To check the spelling of a single word or paragraph, double-click the word or triple-click the paragraph to select it before you start the spelling checker. When Word is finished checking the selection, it displays a dialog box asking whether you want to check the rest of the document.

Customizing the Spelling Checker

The spelling checker is your flunky. You tell it what to do and how to do it, and the spelling checker carries out your instructions. To display the spelling checker options, either click the **Options** button during a spelling check, or open the **Tools** menu, click **Options**, and click the **Spelling & Grammar** tab, as shown in Figure 8.3.

Most of the options on this tab are self-explanatory, but a couple might give you trouble, such as **Hide Spelling Errors in This Document**. This option tells Word to hide the squiggly red lines under questionable words as you type. **Always Suggest Corrections** tells Word to display a list of possible corrections for any questionable word. You should probably keep this option on. If any other options confuse you, right-click the option and select **What's This?**.

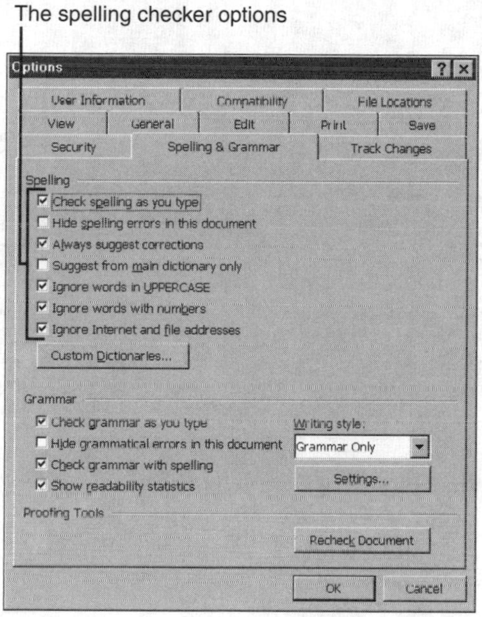

The spelling checker options

Figure 8.3

You can tell the spelling checker how to do its job.

Making Word Automatically Correct Your Typos

One of my favorite features in Word is AutoCorrect. I type *teh*, and Word inserts *the*. I start a sentence with a lowercase character, and AutoCorrect capitalizes it. Now *that's* a feature!

To create an AutoCorrect entry on-the-fly, simply select the **AutoCorrect** option when the spelling checker stops on a questionable word. When you create an AutoCorrect entry, you pair a commonly misspelled (or mistyped) word with its correct spelling. Whenever you type the misspelling and follow it with a space or punctuation mark, Word automatically inserts the correction.

You can edit the list of paired words to create additional AutoCorrect entries or to delete entries. Open the **Tools** menu and select **AutoCorrect Options**. The AutoCorrect dialog box appears, displaying a list of options for controlling the behavior of AutoCorrect and a list of AutoCorrect pairs. Set your preferences using the check box options at the top of the dialog box.

103

To create a new AutoCorrect pair, click in the **Replace** text box and type the text you want Word to automatically replace, as shown in Figure 8.4. Tab to the **With** text box, and type the text with which you want Word to replace it. You can type more than one word in either or both text boxes, and you can choose to have the replacement text formatted. When you're finished, click the **Add** button. To remove a pair from the list, click the pair and then click the **Delete** button.

Figure 8.4

Create AutoCorrect entries for all your most common typos.

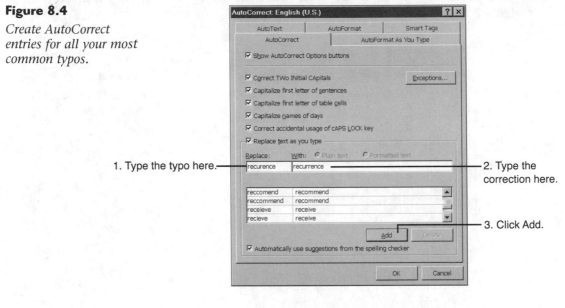

1. Type the typo here.

2. Type the correction here.

3. Click Add.

Insider Tip

Create Your Own Shorthand

You can create your own shorthand by using AutoText entries (explained in Chapter 4, "Making and Editing Word Documents"), but then you have to type and press the F3 key to insert a word or phrase. Instead of creating AutoText entries, create an AutoCorrect entry, so you won't have to press F3.

Writing Good with the Grammar Checker

Grammar checkers are easy to fool. If you write short subject-verb sentences without contractions, the grammar checker ranks your writing skills right up there with

Dr. Seuss. The grammar checker doesn't care whether your writing is entertaining, insightful, or even well organized. As long as you don't break any rules, you're a genius. In addition, grammar checkers aren't always correct and often suggest changes that are downright absurd.

With that in mind, I'm going to keep this section brief. The grammar checker options are similar to those of the spelling checker (and they're on the same tab). To change them, open the **Tools** menu, select **Options**, and click the **Spelling & Grammar** tab. Enter your preferences for the following:

➤ **Check Grammar As You Type**—Draws a green squiggly line under questionable phrases and sentences.

➤ **Hide Grammatical Errors in This Document**—Hides the green squiggly lines as you type.

➤ **Check Grammar with Spelling**—Tells Word to check both grammar and spelling at the same time whenever you spell check a document.

➤ **Show Readability Statistics**—Displays a message at the end of the grammar check showing the reading level required to understand your writing. For instance, if you're writing a children's book and the readability statistics show that you're writing for college kids, you might need to scale back on the compound complex sentences and multisyllabic words.

➤ **Writing Style**—Lets you specify whether you want the grammar checker to check grammar and style or just grammar.

➤ **Settings**—Enables you to turn individual grammar rules on or off.

➤ **Recheck Document**—Rechecks the document using the preferences you just entered.

Word's Helpful, Useful, Beneficial Thesaurus

Suppose you're writing a letter of resignation to your supervisor, and you can't think of a less offensive word than "stupid." The dictionary's no help, and you can't really ask around the office. What do you do? Follow these steps to look up alternative words in the thesaurus:

1. Click the word to place the insertion point somewhere inside it.

2. Open the **Tools** menu, point to **Language**, and click **Thesaurus** (or just press **Shift+F7**). Word displays the Thesaurus dialog box, as shown in Figure 8.5, providing a list of alternative words or phrases.

Whoa!

No Thesaurus?!

If "Thesaurus" does not appear on your Tools, Language menu, it might not be installed. Run the Office installation again. You'll find the thesaurus under Office Shared Features/Proofing Tools/English (or whatever language Office is installed to use).

Right-Click for Synonyms

For quick access to a list of synonyms, right-click the word you're thinking of replacing and point to **Synonyms**. If you see the word you want, click it.

3. If the Meanings list has more than one word, click the word that most closely matches your intended meaning. If you look up "stupid," for example, the Meanings list displays "unintelligent," "dim," "brainless," and so on. The Replace with Synonym list displays suggested replacement words.

4. If the Replace with Synonym list contains a word that's pretty close to the one you want but just not quite it, click the word and click the **Look Up** button, or double-click the word. (If the list of synonyms that you get next is worse than the previous list, click the **Previous** button.)

5. When you find the word you want or a word that's close enough to satisfy you, click it and click the **Replace** button. (The Replace with Synonym list also might include antonyms, cleverly marked with "(antonym)" following the word.)

Figure 8.5

The thesaurus can help you find the perfect word.

1. Click a meaning that's close.

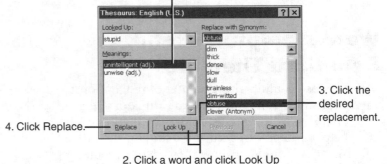

3. Click the desired replacement.

4. Click Replace.

2. Click a word and click Look Up to display its synonyms.

Where's a Real Dictionary When You Need One?

The dictionary that Office uses to check spelling is not a bona fide dictionary—it has no definitions. However, if you installed Office over a previous version of Office that had Microsoft Bookshelf installed, you can access Bookshelf's dictionary from Word to look up definitions. Simply right-click the word and click **Define**. (You can purchase Microsoft Bookshelf separately and install it on your system to give Office its added functionality.)

What About Foreign Languages? (Translating in Office)

Office XP just hired a translator, and you can put it to work translating foreign terms and brief phrases in your Word documents. However, before you can use the translator, you must install the foreign language dictionaries you plan to use. Run the Office installation again. You'll find translation dictionaries under Office Shared Features/Proofing Tools/<Language>, (where <Language> is the language you want to translate).

I Lost Bookshelf in the Upgrade!

If your previous version of Office included Bookshelf and you lost the ability to look up definitions in Word when you upgraded, try reinstalling Bookshelf from your old Office CDs.

Complete Document Translations Via the Web

The Office translator is not designed to translate entire documents or even whole sentences. To translate lengthy selections, select a translation, service from the **Translate Via the Web** list (near the bottom of the Translate task pane), and then click **Go**.

After you have installed the required, dictionary, perform the following steps to translate a word or phrase:

1. Highlight the word or phrase you want to translate.

2. Open the **Tools** menu, point to **Language**, and click **Translate** (or right-click the selection and click **Translate**). The Translate task pane appears, as shown in Figure 8.6.

3. Make sure the correct foreign language dictionary is selected in the **Dictionary** list.

4. Click the **Go** button. The translator displays one or more translations in the Results box.

5. Highlight the desired translation in the **Results** box.

6. Click the **Replace** button (below the Results box) to replace the selected text in your document with the highlighted translation from the Results box.

Figure 8.6

Use the Translate task pane to translate foreign words or phrases.

1. Highlight the word or phrase you want to translate.

2. Select the desired foreign language dictionary.

3. Click Go.

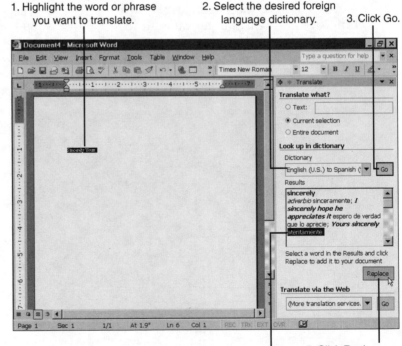

4. Highlight the desired translation.

5. Click Replace.

The Least You Need to Know

In this chapter, you learned how to use several of Word's writing tools to perfect and polish your documents. Before you become overconfident with your spelling and grammar skills, however, make sure you know the following:

➤ A squiggly red line below a word indicates that it's probably misspelled or mistyped.

➤ Right-click a misspelled word to view a list of suggested corrections, and then click the desired correction.

➤ To spell check your document, click the **Spelling and Grammar** button in the Standard toolbar.

➤ To have Word automatically correct a word you commonly misspell or mistype, open the **Tools** menu, click **AutoCorrect Options**, and use the resulting dialog box to add a misspelling and correction pair for the word.

➤ To customize the way the spelling and grammar tools work, open the **Tools** menu, click **Options**, click the **Spelling & Grammar** tab, and enter your preferences.

➤ To view a list of synonyms for a word, right-click the word in your document and point to **Synonyms**.

➤ To translate a word or phrase, highlight it, right-click the selection, and click **Translate**. Highlight the desired translation in the **Results** box and click **Replace**.

Chapter 9

Everything You've Always Wanted to Know About Printing Documents

---

In This Chapter

➤ Making a two-page essay run three pages with a few clever margin adjustments

➤ Forcing Word to number your pages for you

➤ Printing a footer on the bottom of every page

➤ Interior decorating with page borders

➤ Sending your document to the printer

Up to this point, you have been micromanaging your document—formatting blocks of text, adding tables and columns, and inserting pictures and other clips. Before you print your document, however, you need to perform a few macro management tasks, such as setting the page margins, correcting any funky page breaks, adding page numbers, and perhaps even decorating your page with an attractive border.

This chapter shows you how to perform these preprinting tasks and how to send your completed document off to the printer.

Setting Up Your Pages for Printing

After typing a document, it's tempting to just click the **Print** button in the Standard toolbar to crank out a paper copy of the document. Avoid the temptation. You usually end up wasting paper and being sorely disappointed with the results. Before you print, you should first check the Page Setup options.

Publishing Electronically

Although the paperless age hasn't quite arrived, you can publish your document electronically on the World Wide Web. If that's your intent, skip to Chapter 26, "Creating and Publishing Your Own Web Pages."

To display the Page Setup options, open the **File** menu and select **Page Setup**. The Page Setup dialog box appears, presenting four tabs for changing various page and print settings. In the following sections, you learn how to use this dialog box to set margins and control the way Word prints a document.

Setting the Page Margins

The very first time the Page Setup dialog box appears, the Margins tab is up front. If it's hiding, click it to bring it to the front. This tab enables you to change the top, bottom, left, and right margins. Click the up or down arrow to the right of each margin setting to change the setting in increments of .1 inch, or click in a margin setting text box and type a more precise measurement.

The Margins tab, shown in Figure 9.1, offers several additional options for special printing needs:

➤ **Gutter**—Enables you to add margin space to the inside margin of the pages, in case you plan to insert the pages into a book or binder.

➤ **Gutter Position**—Gives you the option of placing the gutter margin at the top or left side of the pages, depending on how you plan to bind the document.

➤ **Orientation**—Gives you the option of printing your pages right-side up *(portrait orientation)* or sideways *(landscape orientation)* on the page.

➤ **Multiple Pages**—This drop-down list provides several options for helping you cram more text on fewer pages and conserve paper. Mirror Margins is helpful if you plan to print on both sides of a sheet. 2 Pages Per Sheet shrinks the pages so Word can print two pages on a single sheet of paper. Book Fold prints the text in two columns—sort of like newspaper columns—so you can fold the pages in half and staple in the middle to create a booklet.

➤ **Apply To**—Enables you to apply the margin settings to the entire document, from this point forward in the document, or to only selected text. This is useful for long documents that might require different page layouts for some sections.

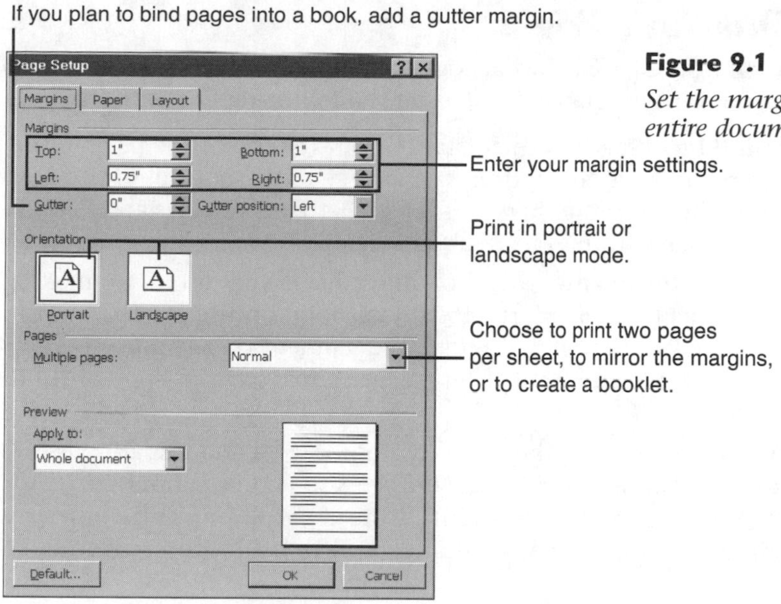
If you plan to bind pages into a book, add a gutter margin.
Page Setup
Margins
Paper
Layout
Top: 1"
Bottom: 1"
Left: 0.75"
Right: 0.75"
Gutter: 0"
Gutter position: Left
Orientation
Portrait
Landscape
Pages
Multiple pages: Normal
Preview
Apply to: Whole document
Default...
OK
Cancel
Enter your margin settings.
Print in portrait or landscape mode.
Choose to print two pages per sheet, to mirror the margins, or to create a booklet.

Figure 9.1

Set the margins for the entire document.

Whoa!

Encroaching on the Non-Printing Area

Most printers are incapable of printing all the way to the edges of a sheet. If you make the margins too small, your text might fall into this non-printing area and get chopped off. Fortunately, Word displays an error message if you set the margins too small and can automatically adjust the margins to fix the problem.

Picking a Paper Size and Source

If you always print on standard 8 1/2×11-inch paper, you don't really need to worry about the paper size or where the paper is coming from. Your printer is set up to use the default paper tray, which is typically loaded with 8 1/2×11-inch paper, and all your programs know that. If, however, you need to print envelopes, banners, or any other paper that's not 8 1/2×11-inch, check the Paper tab before you start printing just to ensure that Word is set up to use the correct paper size and tray.

Laying Out Your Pages

The last tab in the Page Setup dialog box is the Layout tab. Ignore most of the options on the Layout tab and focus on the following four options:

➤ **From Edge**—Specifies the distance from the top of the page to the top of the header and from the bottom of the page to the bottom of the footer. (For details about headers and footers, see "Head-Banging Headers and Foot-Stomping Footers" later in this chapter.)

➤ **Vertical Alignment**—This drop-down list is very useful for making one-page documents (such as short letters) look good on the page. Open the drop-down list and select **Center** to center the document on the page. This option is especially useful for printing cover pages. To make the document fill the page, select **Justified**.

➤ **Line Numbers**—This button is useful for legal and literary pieces. These types of documents often contain line numbers so people can refer to the line numbers when discussing the documents, instead of quoting entire lines and sounding really boring. To insert line numbers, click the button and enter your preferences.

➤ **Borders**—Opens the Borders and Shading dialog box, which allows you to add a border around your entire page or at the top, bottom, left, or right margin. For a more graphic border, open the **Art** list and click the desired design.

Adding Page Numbers

You really have no excuse for not numbering the pages in a multipage document, because Word can do it for you. You can insert a page number code in a header or footer (see "Head-Banging Headers and Foot-Stomping Footers" later in this chapter), or you can use the Insert, Page Numbers command. Follow these steps to use the latter method:

1. Open the **Insert** menu and select **Page Numbers**. The Page Numbers dialog box appears.

2. Open the **Position** drop-down list and specify whether you want the page numbers printed at the top or bottom of the page.

3. Open the **Alignment** drop-down list and select where you want the page number placed in relation to the left and right margins. (The Inside and Outside options are for positioning page numbers on pages that will be bound in a book.)

4. If the first page is a cover page or you just don't want a page number on the first page, make sure there is no check mark in the **Show Number on First Page** box.

5. Click the **Format** button, enter any additional preferences, and click **OK**. The Page Number Format dialog box, shown in Figure 9.2, enables you to change the numbering scheme, include chapter numbers, or start with a page number other than 1.

6. Click **OK** to save your changes. The page number is inserted inside a header or footer.

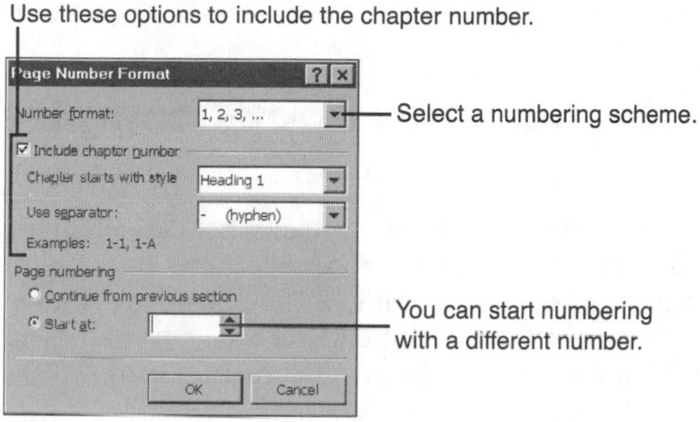

Use these options to include the chapter number.

Page Number Format	
Number format:	1, 2, 3, ...
☑ Include chapter number	
Chapter starts with style	Heading 1
Use separator:	- (hyphen)
Examples: 1-1, 1-A	
Page numbering	
○ Continue from previous section	
⦿ Start at:	
OK	Cancel

— Select a numbering scheme.

You can start numbering with a different number.

Figure 9.2

The Page Number Format dialog box offers additional controls.

Insider Tip

Viewing Page Numbers

Page numbers do not appear in Normal view. To view page numbers, switch to Print Layout view or Print Preview. You also can view, edit, and format page numbers in the header or footer: Open the **View** menu and select **Header and Footer**. If you're in Print Layout view, simply double-click the header or footer.

Chopping Your Text into Pages

Typing in Word is like working in a sausage factory. As you type, Word stuffs your text and divides it into neat little pages. Word divides the text into pages using *soft page breaks*, which can move automatically as you add or delete text. The trouble is that you might not like where Word divides your text. Word might divide an important list over two pages or perform other similar atrocities. You need a way to control these breaks.

In Print Layout view, you easily can identify a page break by the top or bottom edges of the onscreen pages. In Normal view, a soft page break appears as a dotted horizontal line. If you don't like where Word inserted the page break, insert your own break (a *hard page break*, which stays put). Move the insertion point to the beginning of the paragraph before which you want the break inserted and press **Ctrl+Enter**.

If you insert a break and later decide that it's not working out, you can delete the break or move it. First, change to Normal view (**View**, **Normal**). To select a break, click it. To delete a selected break, press the **Del** key. To move a break, drag it.

Head-Banging Headers and Foot-Stomping Footers

Headers and footers are great tools for stitching together a document and helping your audience find specific pages and information. Headers and footers can include all sorts of useful information, such as the title of the document or a section inside the document, the date on which the document was created, chapter numbers, page numbers, and the total number of pages in the document. Figure 9.3 shows a sample header displayed in Print Layout view.

Figure 9.3

Header in Print Layout view.

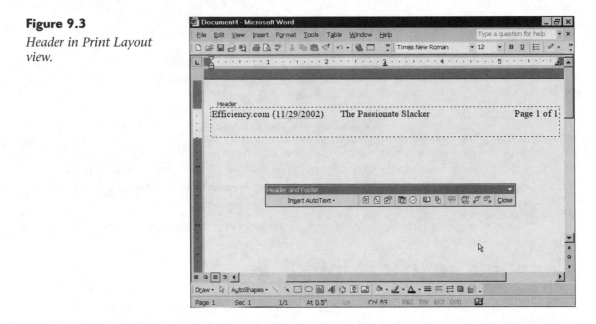

To insert a header or footer, open the **View** menu and select **Header and Footer**. This displays the Header and Footer toolbar and the header of the first page (which should be empty, unless you have gremlins or you inserted page numbers earlier). You can scroll down to see the footer. Before you start typing, familiarize yourself with the Header and Footer toolbar buttons:

Insert Page Number. Automatically inserts the correct page number on each page. To insert the word "Page," you must type it. Then, click the **Insert Page Number** button to insert a page number code that automatically inserts the correct page number on each page.

 Insert Number of Pages. Inserts the total number of pages in the document. You can use this feature to create headers or footers that say "Page 2 of 27," for example. This feature is very useful for faxed documents.

Keeping Lines of Text Together

To prevent soft page breaks from breaking up a list or other text you want to keep together, select the text and then select **Format, Paragraph**. Click the **Line and Page Breaks** tab, click **Keep Lines Together**, and click **OK**.

 Format Page Number. Displays the Page Number Format dialog box, which enables you to include the chapter number and enter other preferences.

Insert Date. Inserts a field code that plugs in the date from your computer's internal clock.

Automatic Date/Time Changes

When you use the Insert Date or Insert Time button to insert the date or time, Word inserts a field code that pulls the date or time from your computer's clock. The date and time change automatically to reflect the current date and time on your computer. To keep the date from changing, click it and press **Ctrl+Shift+F9**.

Insert Time. Inserts a field code that inserts the current time from your computer's clock.

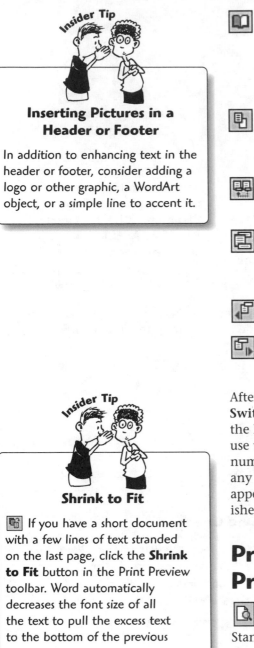

Insider Tip

Inserting Pictures in a Header or Footer

In addition to enhancing text in the header or footer, consider adding a logo or other graphic, a WordArt object, or a simple line to accent it.

Page Setup. Enables you to create a different header or footer for odd pages and even pages. Use the Show Previous and Show Next buttons to move between the boxes for entering the odd and even page headers or footers.

Show/Hide Document Text. Turns the document text display on or off. When Hiding, all you see onscreen is the header or footer text box.

Same as Previous. Enables you to use the same header or footer for this section that you used for the previous section.

Switch Between Header and Footer. Tells Word to display the footer box if you are currently using the header box and vice versa.

Show Previous. Moves to the previous header or footer so you can edit it.

Show Next. Moves to the next header or footer.

After you are familiar with the buttons, click the **Switch Between Header and Footer** button to display the Header box or the Footer box. Type your text and use the Insert buttons as desired to insert the page number, date, time, or total page count. You can use any of the text formatting options to enhance the appearance of your header or footer. When you're finished playing around, click the **Close** button.

Insider Tip

Shrink to Fit

If you have a short document with a few lines of text stranded on the last page, click the **Shrink to Fit** button in the Print Preview toolbar. Word automatically decreases the font size of all the text to pull the excess text to the bottom of the previous page.

Previewing Pages Before Printing Them

Before you print the document, click the **Print Preview** button Print Preview buttonin the Standard toolbar. This gives you a bird's-eye view of the page, enables you to quickly flip pages, and provides rulers you can use to drag the margin settings around. Figure 9.4 shows a document in Print Preview.

Display or hide rulers
for changing margins.

Click to start printing.

The Shrink to
Fit button

Click here to close
Print Preview.

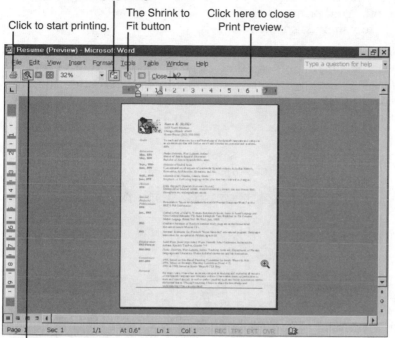

Figure 9.4

Print Preview enables you to make minor adjustments before you commit the document to paper.

Turn on the Magnifier and
then click the page to zoom
in or right-click to zoom out.

Ready, Set, Go to the Printer

When you have your printer working successfully with any of your Windows applications, printing is pretty simple. Make sure your printer has plenty of paper and ink or toner, turn on the printer, open your document, and click the **Print** button.

To take more control of the printing—to print extra copies, print sideways on the page (landscape mode), collate copies, select a print quality, or enter other settings—you must display the Print dialog box. To do this, open the **File** menu and select **Print** instead of clicking the Print button. You can then use the Print dialog box to enter your preferences, as shown in Figure 9.5.

Although most of the printing options are straightforward, two might throw you: Page Range and Collate. In most cases, you want to print all the pages in your document. To do this, use the default Page Range setting of All. To print only specified pages, select **Pages** and type the numbers of the pages you want to print. You might type 1,3,9, for example, to print only pages 1, 3, and 9, or 2-4 to print only pages 2, 3, and 4. If you choose to print more than one copy of the document, the Collate option completely prints one copy of the document before printing the next copy. With this option off, Word prints all copies of the first page, all copies of the second page, and so on, so you must collate manually.

One more option that's pretty cryptic is the new **Manual Duplex** option, which enables you to print your document on two sides of a sheet. First, Word prints the odd pages (1, 3, 5, and so on) and then displays a prompt for you to reinsert those pages in the paper feed tray, so it can print the even pages (2, 4, 6, and so on) on the backside of the first pages.

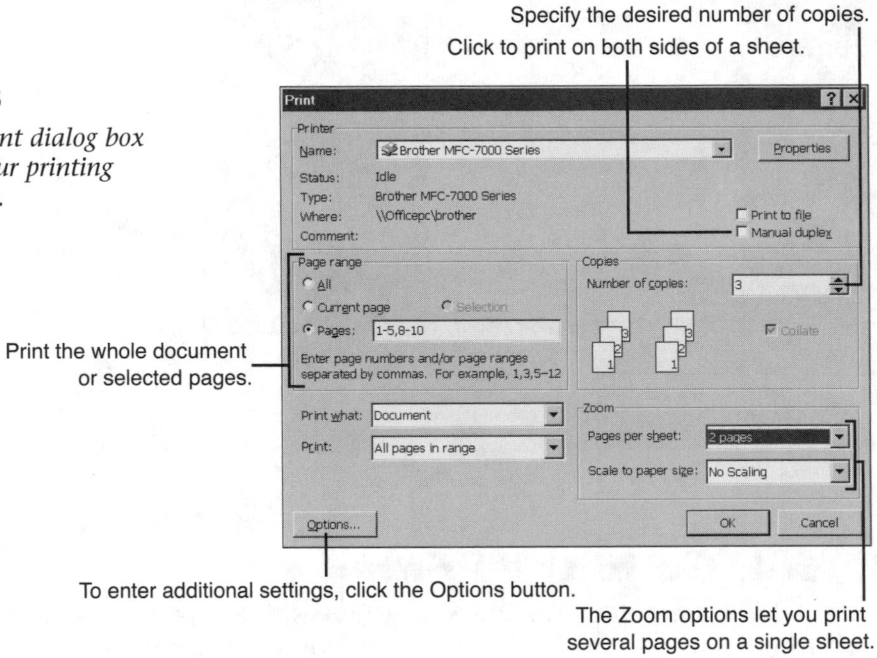

Figure 9.5

Use the Print dialog box to enter your printing preferences.

Specify the desired number of copies.
Click to print on both sides of a sheet.

Print the whole document or selected pages.

To enter additional settings, click the Options button.

The Zoom options let you print several pages on a single sheet.

The Least You Need to Know

After you have set up your printer properly in Windows, you don't need to know much about printing documents from any of your Windows applications. You click the Print button and wait for your printer to spit out a clean, fresh copy. For additional control over printing Word documents, make sure you can perform the following tasks:

➤ To control the overall page layout for a document, including the page margins, open the **File** menu, click **Page Setup**, and enter your preferences.

➤ To number the pages of your document, open the **Insert** menu, click **Page Numbers**, specify where you want the numbers printed, and click **OK**.

➤ To force a page break, place the insertion point at the beginning of the line that you want to appear on the *next* page and press **Ctrl+Enter**.

➤ To view the header and footer area, open the **View** menu and click **Header and Footer**.

➤ To print an attractive page border, open the **File** menu, click **Page Setup**, click the **Layout** tab, click the **Borders** button, and enter your preferences.

➤ Click the **Print Preview** button and flip through the pages to inspect your document before printing it.

➤ To print a document quickly, click the **Print** button (in the Standard toolbar).

Chapter 10

HERE YA' GO.

Printing Envelopes, Mailing Labels, and Form Letters

In This Chapter

➤ Addressing an envelope with your printer

➤ Laying out and printing address labels

➤ Creating your very own personalized form letters

➤ Doing mass mailings with mail merge

Face it, you're a mail junkie. Your motivation to wake up in the morning comes only from the possibility that you might receive a piece of mail addressed to you or to some guy named "Current Resident." You stare out the window to catch the familiar gait of your mail carrier. You're on a first-name basis with the UPS driver. You just can't get enough. And you know that the only way to get mail is to send mail.

This chapter shows you how to use a couple of features that can help you address your paper mail correspondence. You learn how to easily print addresses on envelopes or mailing labels and merge a form letter with a list of names and addresses to create a stack of personalized letters for mass mailings.

Addressing an Envelope or Mailing Label

Most of the letters I receive from friends and family members have obviously been typed and printed using a computer; but for some strange reason, they arrive in hand-written envelopes. I guess it just takes too much time and effort to position the two addresses on the front of that skinny little envelope. Fortunately, Word can print addresses for you on envelopes or mailing labels.

Quick and Easy Letters

The easiest way to write and format a letter is to use the Letter Wizard. Select **File**, **New**, click the **General Templates** link, click the **Letters & Faxes** tab, and double-click **Letter Wizard**. Or, create a new document and then select **Tools**, **Letters and Mailings**, **Letter Wizard**. The Letter Wizard dialog box displays a fill-in-the-blank form you can use to specify your preferences and enter information such as the inside address, the salutation, and the closing.

Addressing an Envelope

To print an address on an envelope, open the **Tools** menu, point to **Letters and Mailings**, click **Envelopes and Labels**, and make sure that the Envelopes tab is up front. Type the recipient's name and address in the **Delivery Address** text box, as shown in Figure 10.1. (If you already wrote your letter, Word lifts the recipient's address from the letter and inserts it in the Delivery Address text box.) Tab to the **Return Address** text box and type your address. You can format selected text in the Delivery or Return Address text boxes by highlighting the text and pressing the key combination for the desired formatting—for example, Ctrl+B for bold. You also can right-click the text to choose additional formatting options.

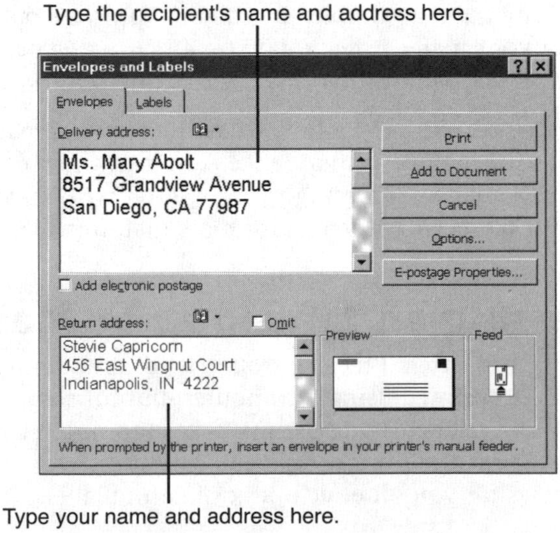

Figure 10.1

Enter the delivery and return addresses.

Type the recipient's name and address here.

Envelopes and Labels

Envelopes | Labels

Delivery address:

Ms. Mary Abolt
8517 Grandview Avenue
San Diego, CA 77987

Print
Add to Document
Cancel
Options...
E-postage Properties...

☐ Add electronic postage

Return address: ☐ Omit

Stevie Capricorn
456 East Wingnut Court
Indianapolis, IN 4222

Preview   Feed

When prompted by the printer, insert an envelope in your printer's manual feeder.

Type your name and address here.

If you hate peeling and pasting postage stamps, Word's new e-postage feature can print the postage right on your envelopes or labels. Click the **E-postage Properties** button and follow the onscreen instructions to install the e-postage software and buy your postage online (you'll need your credit card number, of course). To print postage on the envelope or label, click the **Add Electronic Postage** check box.

Before you print, click the **Options** button. This displays the Envelope Options dialog box, which allows you to specify the envelope size and the fonts for the delivery and return addresses. The Printing Options tab enables you to specify how the envelopes feed into your printer. Enter your preferences and click the **OK** button.

Dry Run

Before printing on a relatively expensive envelope or a sheet of mailing labels, print the envelope or mailing labels on a normal sheet of paper to check the position of the print. You can then make adjustments without wasting costly supplies.

If you need to manually load the envelope into your printer, load away. All printers are different; check your printer's documentation to determine the proper loading technique. When the envelope is in position, click the **Print** button to print it.

Addressing a Mailing Label

To print a single label or a whole page of labels with the same address or other information, open the **Tools** menu, point to **Letters and Mailings**, select **Envelopes and Labels**, and make sure the **Labels** tab is up front. In the **Address** text box, type the name and address you want printed on the mailing label. (You can print your return address by clicking the **Use Return Address** check box, instead.) Under Print, specify whether you want to print a single label (and specify the location of the label on the label sheet) or a full page of labels.

Click the **Options** button, use the Label Options dialog box to specify the type of label on which you are printing, and click **OK**. Load the sheet of labels into your printer and click the **Print** button.

Merging Your Address List with a Form Letter

You've been getting them for years from Publisher's Clearing House, *Reader's Digest*, MasterCard, Visa, window installers, and even America Online, selling you products you don't need and dreams of being someone you're not.

Now it's your turn. The following sections show you how to do your own mass mailings right from your desktop.

Make a Personal Address Book

Just above the text boxes in which you type the delivery and return addresses (for either an envelope or a mailing label) is the **Insert Address** button. Click this button to create an address book containing the names and addresses of people to whom you commonly send letters. You can then quickly insert a person's address by clicking the arrow next to the button and selecting the person's name. You also can use the address book in mail merges, as explained in the next section.

First You Need Some Data

To perform a mail merge, you need a letter and a list of the names, addresses, and other information you want to insert in the letter. Let's start with the list of names and addresses (hence referred to as the *data source*). You can use any of the following several data sources for the mail merge:

➤ An Outlook address book. (See Chapter 23, "Keeping Track of Dates, Mates, and Things to Do.")

➤ An Access database.

➤ An Excel spreadsheet with column headings.

➤ A Word table. The first row must contain headings describing the contents of the cells in that column. Each row contains information about an individual (see Figure 10.2).

Then You Need a Form Letter

How you compose your form letter is your business. You can type it from scratch, use a template, or seek help from the Letter Wizard. Omit any information that Word obtains from the data source during the merge, such as the addressee's name and address. After you complete the letter, you insert field label codes into the letter (one for the person's name, one for the address, and so on). During the merge operation, these codes pull information from the data source and insert it into a copy of the letter to create a customized letter for each person in your data source.

A field name can be as many
as 40 characters, no spaces,
and must begin with a letter.   Each cell contains a piece of information.

Title	First Name	Last Name	Address	City	State	ZIP Code	
Ms.	Mary	Abolt	8517 Grandview Avenue	San Diego	CA	77987	
Ms.	Carey	Bistro	987 N. Cumbersome Lane	Detroit	MI	88687	
Ms.	Adrienne	Bullow	5643 N. Gaylord Ave.	Philadelphia	PA	27639	
Mr.	Chuck	Burger	6754 W. Lakeview Drive	Boston	MA	56784	
Mr.	Nicholas	Capetti	1345 W. Bilford Ave.	New Orleans	LA	12936	
Ms.	Gary	Davell	76490 E. Billview	New York	NY	76453	
Mr.	Kathy	Estrich	8763 W. Cloverdale Ave.	Paradise	TX	54812	
Ms.	Joseph	Fugal	2764 W. 56th Place	Chicago	IL	60678	
Mr.	Marie	Gabel	8764 N. Demetrius Blvd.	Miami	FL	88330	
Mr.	Lisa	Kasdan	8976 Westhaven Drive	Orlando	FL	88329	
Ms.	William	Kennedy	5567 Bluehill Circle	Indianapolis	IN	46224	
Ms.	Marion	Kraft	1313 Mockingbird Lane	Los Angeles	CA	77856	
Ms.	John	Kramden	5401 N. Bandy	Pittsburgh	PA	27546	
Mr.	Mitch	Kroll	674 E. Cooperton Drive	Seattle	WA	14238	
Mr.	Gregg	Lawrence	5689 N. Bringshire Blvd.	Boston	MA	56784	
Mr.	Allison	Milton	32718 S. Visionary Drive	Phoenix	AZ	97612	
Ms.	Barry	Strong	908 N. 9th Street	Chicago	IL	60643	

Each row, called a record, contains
information for one person.

Figure 10.2

*You can use a Word table
or an Excel spreadsheet as
your data source.*

Now You Can Merge

After you have your form letter and data source, let the fun begin! This is a long process; but if you follow me step by step, you can pull off this merge thing without a hitch:

1. Create or open your form letter.

2. Crank down the **Tools** menu, point to **Letters and Mailings**, and select **Mail Merge Wizard**. The Mail Merge task pane appears, as shown in Figure 10.3, providing instructions on how to proceed.

3. Under Select Document Type, click **Letters** to tell Word to use your letter as the main document in the merge.

4. Click **Next: Starting Document**. The Mail Merge Wizard prompts you to specify the document you want to use.

5. Make sure **Use the Current Document** is selected and then click **Next: Select Recipients**. The Mail Merge Wizard prompts you to specify your data source.

6. Select one of the following options and perform the necessary steps to select the source of data you want to use for the merge:

Use an Existing List—Lets you use a data source you have already created. Select this option and then click **Browse** to display a dialog box that enables you to pick the data source file.

Select from Outlook Contacts—Lets you use your Outlook contact list as the data source. Select this option and then click **Choose Contacts Folder** to select the contacts file you want to use as the data source.

Type a New List—Leads you through the process of creating an address book containing the data you want to merge with your form letter. Select this option and then click **Create** to display a fill-in-the-blank dialog box for adding names and addresses to your address book.

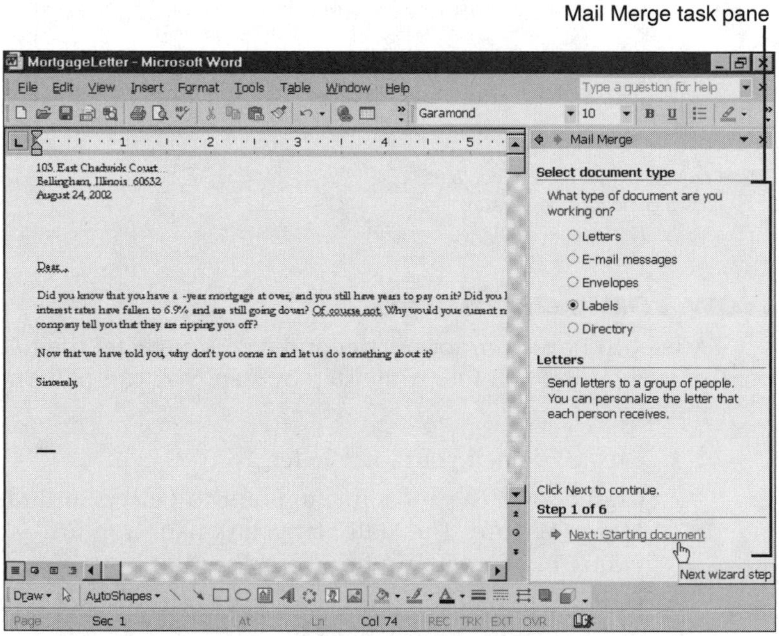

Mail Merge task pane

Figure 10.3

The Mail Merge task pane leads you through the six-step process.

7. Click **Next: Write Your Letter**. The Mail Merge Wizard instructs you to compose your letter if you have not already done so and provides a list of options for inserting codes into your letter.

8. Position the insertion point where you want to insert a piece of data from the database. For example, you might move the insertion point just below the date to insert the person's name and address.

9. Click the link for inserting the desired information. For example, click **Address Block** to insert the recipient's name and address. Click **Greeting Line** to insert

a greeting, such as "Dear Mr. Spock,". To insert individual merge codes that correspond with fields in your database, click the **More Items** link and select the desired code.

10. Enter your preferences in the resulting dialog box, as shown in Figure 10.4, and click **OK**. For example, if you chose to insert a greeting line, you can choose to insert the person's first name, title, and last name, or just the last name in the greeting. The Mail Merge Wizard inserts a merge code into the document, such as {{{{AddressBlock}}}}, which extracts the corresponding data from the data source.

11. Repeat steps 8–10 to insert additional merge field codes.

The Address Fields Are All Wrong!

The Mail Merge Wizard in Office XP tries its best to match its fields to the fields in your data source, but it's not perfect. Click the **Match Fields** button in the lower-left corner of the Insert Address Block or Insert Greeting Line dialog box to adjust the match-ups.

2. Select the information you want to include.

3. Specify the format.

1. Click the Address Block link to insert the recipient's name and address.

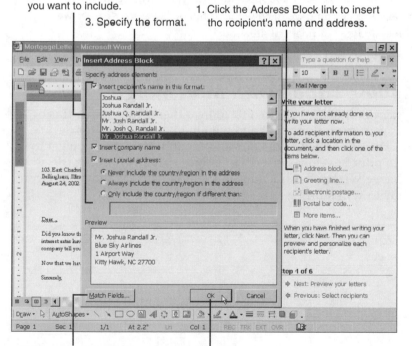

4. Click Match Fields to be sure Word is looking for the information in the correct data source fields.

5. Click OK.

Figure 10.4

Insert codes to pull entries from the data source into your letter.

12. Click **Next: Preview Your Letters**. The Mail Merge Wizard merges your form letter with your data source, creates a collection of personalized letters, and displays the first letter.

13. Click the >> button to preview the next letter or the << button to preview the previous letter. (You can edit individual letters, if desired.)

14. When you're satisfied with your letters, click **Next: Complete the Merge**.

15. To print your letters, click the **Print** link.

Other Data You Can Merge

If your data source contains specific information about each person, you can insert that information into the body of your letter. A financial advisor, for instance, might keep a list of clients along with the dates of their last appointments. The advisor could then insert something such as, "The last time we discussed your finances was on <date>. We should meet soon to reevaluate your financial situation."

Churning Out Mailing Labels with Mail Merge

Now that you have a stack of letters, you need to address them. You can do this by using a mailing label as your main document and merging it with the database. Perform the same steps you performed in the previous section, but when you get to step 3, select **Labels**. (To print envelopes, select **Envelopes**.) There's nothing tricky here; follow the Mail Merge Wizard's instructions in the task pane, as shown in Figure 10.5, and you'll be ready to start stuffing envelopes in no time.

Follow the wizard's instructions.

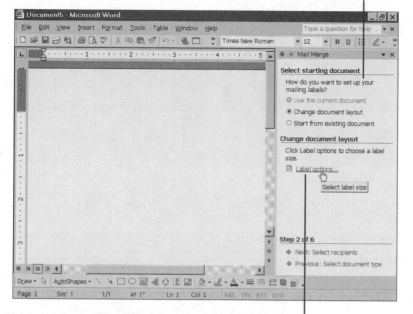

Figure 10.5

You can use Mail Merge to create pages of address labels.

Click Label Options to specify the type and size of labels to print.

The Least You Need to Know

With the letter templates, the Letter Wizard, and the Envelopes and Labels text box, you're primed to turn your office into a junk mail factory. Just make sure you've mastered these basic tasks:

➤ To print a delivery and return address on an envelope, open the **Tools** menu, point to **Letters and Mailings**, click **Envelopes and Labels**, enter the delivery and return addresses, and click **Print**.

➤ To print a full sheet of custom return address labels, open the **Tools** menu, point to **Letters and Mailings**, click **Envelopes and Labels**, click the **Labels** tab, enter the return address and any preferences, and click **Print**.

➤ To merge data from an address book with a form letter and create a stack of letters for a mass mailing, use the Mail Merge Wizard.

➤ You can use Mail Merge to extract data from a Word table, an Outlook address book, an Excel worksheet, or an Access database.

➤ To start the Mail Merge Wizard, open the **Tools** menu, point to **Letters and Mailings**, and click **Mail Merge Wizard**.

Part 3

Crunching Numbers with Excel Worksheets

You know your multiplication tables, and you've mastered long division. Now, you want to spend a little less time with your calculator and a little more time with your golf clubs.

Well, dust off your clubs. Excel is ready and willing to do your math homework for you. You type some text and values, insert a few formulas, and Excel takes care of the rest—adding, subtracting, multiplying, dividing, and even graphing the results!

Whether you're refinancing your home, analyzing sales figures, or creating a business plan, this part shows you how to automate your calculations with Excel.

Chapter 11

Worksheet Orientation Day

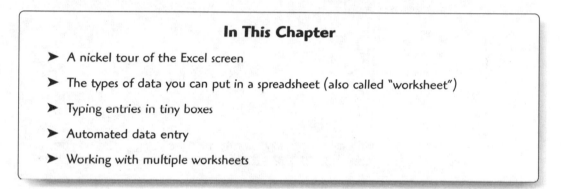

In This Chapter

➤ A nickel tour of the Excel screen

➤ The types of data you can put in a spreadsheet (also called "worksheet")

➤ Typing entries in tiny boxes

➤ Automated data entry

➤ Working with multiple worksheets

Contrary to popular belief, you don't have to be a mathematical wizard or a CPA to crunch a few numbers. All you need is a good spreadsheet program such as Excel (and a little instruction), and soon, you too will be juggling numbers, entering complex formulas and calculations, balancing budgets, and doing other high-profile tasks to impress your friends and colleagues. You'll probably even impress yourself!

Before you start juggling numbers, however, you have to enter them. In this chapter, you learn how to move around in Excel and enter the raw data Excel needs to perform its magic. Along the way, I even show you some quick ways to pour data into your spreadsheets and rearrange the data.

Taking Excel on the Open Road

How do you start Excel? First, you must know where to find the Excelerator. Get it? Excel-erator! Okay, enough of that. Although I told you how to start the Office programs back in the first part of this book, I'll tell you again. To run Excel, select **Start**,

Programs, **Microsoft Excel**, or use one of the alternative methods discussed in Chapter 1, "Up and Running with Office XP."

After Excel starts, you're left staring at a big blank workbook (as shown in Figure 11.1) containing three worksheets.

Figure 11.1

The Excel window might display some unfamiliar items.

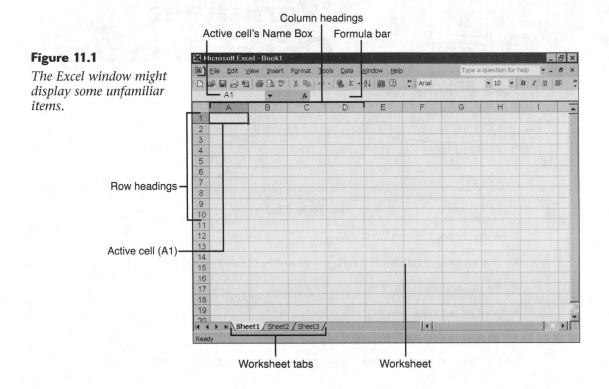

Active cell's Name Box   Column headings   Formula bar

Row headings

Active cell (A1)

Worksheet tabs   Worksheet

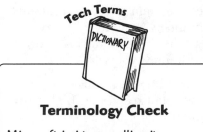

Terminology Check

Microsoft insists on calling its spreadsheets *worksheets*. When you first run Excel, it displays a *workbook* consisting of three worksheets.

The area surrounding the workbook shows you all the typical application controls, including toolbars, menu bars, and scrollbars. You also see the following less-familiar items:

➤ **Worksheet tabs**—Enable you to flip sheets in your workbook. Click a tab to select it. Right-click a tab for additional options. See "Working with Worksheets," later in this chapter, for instructions.

➤ **Formula bar**—Enables you to enter data into *cells* (the little boxes in the worksheet) and edit entries. You'll learn all about this bar when you start typing entries.

➤ **Column headings**—The gray boxes at the top of the columns. Each column is labeled with a letter of the alphabet (A–Z and then AA–AZ, BA–BZ, and so on to column IV—256 columns in all). To select a column, click its column heading.

➤ **Row headings**—The gray boxes at the left of the rows that indicate each row's number (1–65536). To select a row, click its row heading.

➤ **Active cell**—The cell with the thick border around it. When you start Excel, the active cell is A1, the cell in the upper-left corner of the worksheet. When you click a cell, it becomes the active cell.

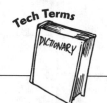

What's with the Letters and Numbers?

In a worksheet, rows and columns intersect to form the boxes we fondly refer to as *cells*. Each cell has an *address* made up of its column letter and row number. For example, the address of the cell in the upper-left corner of the worksheet is A1. Addresses are used in formulas to refer to values in particular cells. For instance, the formula =A1+A2+A3 would determine the total of the values in cells A1–A3. When you click a cell, Excel lights up its row number and column letter and displays its address in the Name Box to the left of the formula bar.

All Data Entries Are Not Created Equal

As with most high-end applications, Excel can accept just about any type of data that can be digitized. You can insert pictures, sounds, video clips, Web page addresses, e-mail addresses—you name it. But that type of data is merely a decoration for a worksheet. What a worksheet really needs are numbers, formulas, and some labels to indicate what the numbers and formulas stand for:

➤ **Labels**—The text entries you usually type at the top of a column or the left end of a row to indicate what is in that column or row (see Figure 11.2).

➤ **Numbers (values)**—The raw data that Excel needs. You enter this data in rows or columns to keep it all neat and tidy.

➤ **Formulas**—Entries that tell Excel to perform calculations. If you type the formula =A6+C3 into cell D5, for example, Excel adds the value in cell C3 to the value in A6 and inserts the answer in cell D5. When you type a formula and press Enter, the result appears in the cell. You learn all about formulas in Chapter 12, "Doing Math with Formulas."

➤ **Functions**—Predesigned formulas that perform relatively complex calculations, such as determining compounding interest on an investment, using a single operator. This also is covered in Chapter 12.

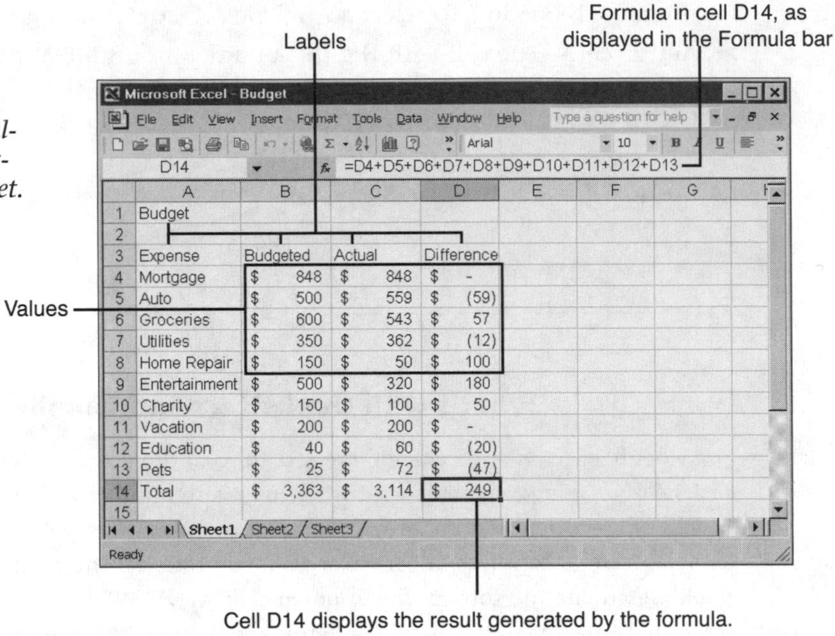

Figure 11.2

You can enter labels, values, formulas, and functions into your worksheet.

Labels

Formula in cell D14, as displayed in the Formula bar

Values

Cell D14 displays the result generated by the formula.

Entering Data

To enter data, first select a cell; click the cell or use the arrow keys or Tab key to move to it. A bold box (the *selection box*) appears around the selected cell. When you start typing data into a selected cell, the data immediately appears in that cell and in the formula bar above the workbook window. Two buttons also appear in the formula bar—a red × and a green check mark. Click the green check mark (or press **Enter**) to accept your entry and insert it into the cell. Click the red × (or press **Esc**) to cancel the entry. (If you press Enter, the selection box automatically moves down so that you can type an entry in the next cell.)

To edit an entry as you type it, use the **Backspace** and **Delete** keys as you normally would to delete characters, and then type your correction. If you accept your entry and then decide to change it, you have three options: Double-click the cell that contains the entry and edit it right inside the cell; select the cell and edit its entry in the formula bar; or select the cell, press **F2**, and edit the entry right inside the cell.

If you type a relatively long entry in a cell, the entry remains in its own cell, but it might appear to spill over into the cells on the right, as shown in Figure 11.3. If the cell on the right is occupied by another entry, your long entry might appear to be chopped off (if it is a label); or it might appear as a series of pound signs (########) if it is a value. No, Excel isn't trying to drive you crazy; the pound signs alert you to the fact that the entire numerical value cannot be displayed—instead of displaying only a portion of the value (which could be misleading), Excel displays the pound signs.

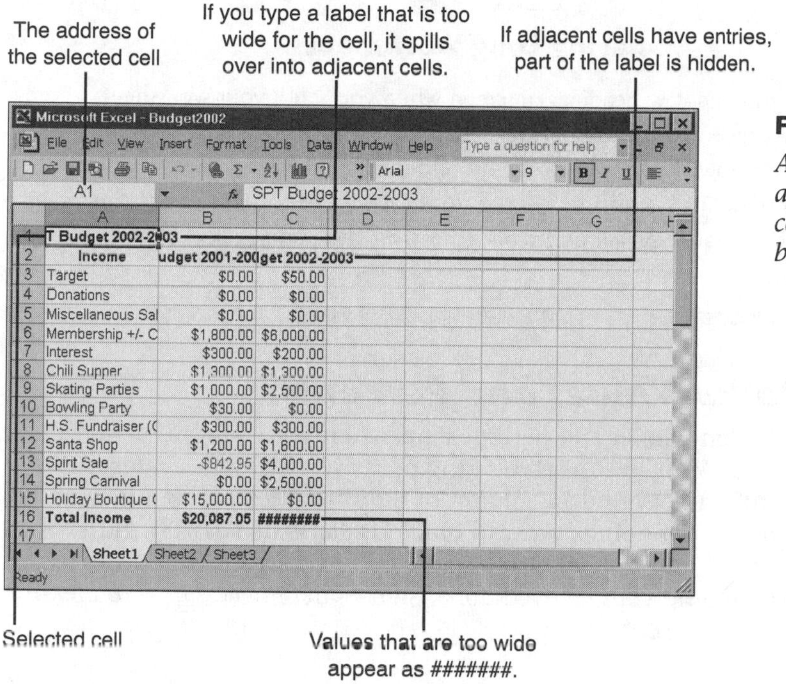

The address of the selected cell

If you type a label that is too wide for the cell, it spills over into adjacent cells.

If adjacent cells have entries, part of the label is hidden.

Figure 11.3

As you type, your entry appears in the selected cell and in the formula bar.

Selected cell

Values that are too wide appear as #######.

In any case, don't panic. Although you can't see your entry, it's still there and is displayed in the formula bar. You just need to widen your column. Click anywhere in the column, open the **Format** menu, select **Column**, and select **AutoFit Selection**. This command automatically widens the column so that your text fits. As an alternative, you can place your mouse pointer between the column headings until it becomes a double-headed arrow and then double-click. (For additional control over column width and row height, see "Tweaking Row Heights and Column Widths," in Chapter 13, "Giving Your Worksheet a Professional Look.")

Another way to fit a long text entry into a cell is to have Excel *wrap* the text from line to line and expand the cell vertically. To turn on text wrap, first highlight the cell(s) in which you want the text to wrap. Open the **Format** menu and select **Cells**. Click the **Alignment** tab and select **Wrap Text** to check its box. Click **OK**.

Managing Long Worksheets

To keep your column and row headings onscreen when you scroll your worksheet, freeze a block of cells to prevent them from moving. Click a cell to the right of the column(s) or directly below the row(s) you want to freeze. Open the **Window** menu and select **Freeze Panes**. A dark line appears below the frozen row(s) or to the right of the frozen column(s), indicating that they will not scroll. To defrost the panes, select **Window**, **Unfreeze Panes**.

What About Dollar Values and Percents?

Although you can include dollar and percent signs when you enter numeric values, you might not want to. Why? Because you can apply formatting that adds this for you. For example, instead of typing a column of hundred-dollar amounts including the dollar signs and decimal points, you can type numbers such as 700 and 19.99, and then change the column to Currency format. Excel changes your entries to $700.00 and $19.99, adding your beloved dollar signs where necessary. (You learn how to do this in Chapter 13.)

How Come Excel Can't Calculate This Number?!

After you tell Excel to treat a number as text, you cannot use that number in a calculation. Double-click the cell and delete the quotation mark to have Excel treat the number as a value rather than as text.

Numbers As Text

What if you want your numbers to be treated like text? You know, say you want to use numbers for a ZIP code instead of a value. To do this, precede your entry with a single quotation mark ('), as in '90210. The single quotation mark is an alignment prefix that tells Excel to treat the following characters as text and left-align them in the cell.

Numbers As Dates and Times

To use any date or time values in your spreadsheet, type them in the format in which you want them to appear (see Table 11.1). When you enter a date using one of the formats shown in the table, Excel converts the date into a number that represents how many days it falls after January 1, 1900. Excel does this so that it can perform calculations using the dates, but you never see that mysterious number. Excel always displays a normal date onscreen. And don't worry about the Y2K bug mucking up your dates. Excel is set up to handle dates up to the year 9999.

Table 11.1 Valid Formats for Dates and Times

Format	Example
MM/DD	9/9
MM/DD/YY	9/9/03 or 09/09/03
MMM-YY	Aug-03 or August-03
DD-MMM-YY	16-Sep-03
DD-MMM	29-Mar
Month, D, YYYY	March 29, 2003
HH:MM	16:50
HH:MM:SS	9:22:55
HH:MM AM/PM	6:45 PM
HH:MM:SS AM/PM	10:15:25 AM
MM/DD/YY HH:MM	11/24/03 12:15

Secrets of the Data Entry Masters

Microsoft realized a long time ago that people don't like to type. In Word, Microsoft built in the AutoCorrect and AutoText features so that people wouldn't have to waste time correcting common typos and typing every character of commonly used words and phrases. In Excel, Microsoft offers these same features and more. The following sections explain how you can use these timesaving features to turbocharge your data entry.

Fill 'Er Up

Let's say you need to insert the same label, date, or value in 20 cells. The mere thought of retyping a date 20 times makes your fingers twitch. You could use the Copy and Paste commands to do it, but that's only slightly less tedious. The solution? Use the Fill feature.

Whoa!

We're in the Army Now

Unless you type AM or PM, Excel assumes that you are using a 24-hour military clock; therefore, Excel interprets 8:20 as AM (not PM) unless you type 8:20 PM. In military time, you would have to type 20:20 for 8:20 PM.

It Talks!

Excel now offers a text-to-speech feature that automatically reads your entries back to you (assuming your computer has a sound card and speakers). This provides you with an audio verification of your entries as you type them. To turn on this feature, right-click any toolbar or the menu bar and click **Text to Speech**. Click the **Speak on Enter** button (the rightmost button on the Text to Speech toolbar). Whenever you type an entry and press Enter, Excel reads the entry back to you. To have Excel read back a block of cell entries, highlight the block, and then click the **Speak Cells** button (the leftmost button).

To fill neighboring cells with the same entry, drag over the cell that contains the entry and the cells into which you want to copy the entry (up, down, left, right—it doesn't matter). Open the **Edit** menu, point to **Fill**, and click the direction in which you want to fill: **Down**, **Right**, **Up**, or **Left**. Excel pours the entry into the selected cells.

A Faster Fill Up

That submenu thing was fun, but there's an easier way. First click the cell that contains the entry you want to insert into neighboring cells. In the lower-right corner of the cell is a tiny square called the *fill handle*, as shown in Figure 11.4. Move the mouse pointer over the fill handle and it turns into a crosshair pointer. Drag the fill handle over the cells that you want to fill, and then release the mouse button.

Figure 11.4

You can drag the fill handle for quick fills.

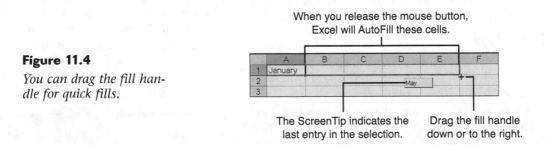

In some cases, this inserts the same entry into all the cells. In other cases, it inserts entries that complete a series. For example, if you use the fill handle to fill January into four neighboring cells, Excel inserts February, March, April, and May. Why?

Excel has some built-in *fill series*, which it uses to make AutoFill a more intelligent tool. To fill cells with the identical entry, right-drag the fill handle, release the mouse button, and click **Copy Cells**.

Fill with Formatting

You can copy the formatting from one cell into neighboring cells without changing the contents of those cells. Click the cell whose formatting you want to copy. Then, drag the cell's fill handle to highlight the cells to which you want to copy the formatting. Release the mouse button and click **Fill Formatting Only**.

Creating Your Own AutoFill Series

To create your own AutoFill series, first type the series in a column or row (or open a workbook that already has the series in it). Drag over the entries in the series. Open the **Tools** menu, select **Options**, and click the **Custom Lists** tab. Click **Import**. You can add items manually to the AutoFill list by typing them in the **List Entries** text box. Click **OK** when you're done.

Fill In the Blanks with AutoComplete

Many spreadsheet users spend a lot of time entering repetitive data or the same labels over and over again in their columns. Excel can help you speed up such entries with AutoComplete. It works like this: Excel keeps track of your entries for each column. Instead of retyping an entry, you right-click an empty cell in the column and select **Pick from List**. A list of entries you already typed in that column appears below the selected cell, as shown in Figure 11.5. You can then select from the list, which is a lot faster than typing the word again.

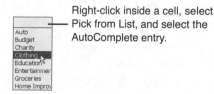

Right-click inside a cell, select Pick from List, and select the AutoComplete entry.

Figure 11.5

You can quickly insert entries you have already typed.

143

You might notice the AutoComplete feature kicking in while you enter text. If you repeat the first few letters of a previous entry, AutoComplete guesses that you're typing repeat information and finishes your word for you. If the word Excel inserts is not the correct word, keep typing and ignore AutoComplete.

AutoComplete also might try to enter values for you, which can become annoying if all the values you're typing are different. To turn off AutoComplete for values, open the **Tools** menu, select **Options**, click the **Edit** tab, and click **Enable AutoComplete for Cell Values** to remove the check from the box.

Grabbing Data from the Web

With Office XP, Excel has become much more Web savvy, enabling you to copy and paste data from Web pages into your worksheets and have that data automatically updated when it changes on the Web. You can, for instance, create a worksheet that tracks your investments. By copying and pasting stock prices from the Web into your worksheet and telling Excel to set up a Web query, you can have Excel create a live link between your worksheet and the Web page. Here's what you do:

1. Start your Web browser and open the page that has the data you want.
2. Highlight the data and press **Ctrl+C** to copy it.
3. Click in the worksheet cell in which you want to paste the data.
4. Press **Ctrl+V**. The Paste icon appears outside the lower-right corner of the cell.
5. Click the **Paste** icon and click **Create Refreshable Web Query**. The New Web Query dialog box appears, displaying the Web page from which you copied the data.
6. Click the yellow-boxed arrow icon next to the table of data you want to import.
7. Click the **Import** button.

To insert the latest data from the Web page into your worksheet, open Excel's **Data** menu and click **Refresh Data**.

Life in the Cell Block: Selecting Cells

So far, we've talked about typing entries into cells. After you have some entries, however, you might need to select the entries to copy, move, delete, format, or perform other operations on a group of cells. To select cells, use the following techniques:

➤ To select a group of cells, drag over them.
➤ To select a column, click the letter at the top of the column. Drag over column letters to select more than one column.
➤ To select a row, click the number to the left of the row. Drag over row numbers to select more than one row.

➤ To select an entire worksheet, click the **Select All** button. (It's that blank button above the row numbers and to the left of the column letters.)

➤ To select multiple neighboring cells, columns, or rows, select the first cell, column, or row. Then press and hold down the **Shift** key and select the last cell, column, or row.

➤ To select multiple non-neighboring cells, columns, or rows, select the first cell or group of cells, columns, and rows. Then press and hold down the **Ctrl** key and click other cells, columns, or rows.

Work Smart with Smart Tags

Whenever you insert a person's name or address, a date, a stock symbol, or any other special data that Excel recognizes, a light red underline appears below the entry. Move the mouse pointer over the entry to display a smart tag icon and then click the icon to view your options. If smart tags do not appear, open the **Tools** menu, click **AutoCorrect Options**, click the **Smart Tags** tab, and enter your preferences.

Roaming the Range

After you become accustomed to selecting cells, you might notice that you often need to select the same group of cells to format, copy, print, or refer to in other cells. Instead of dragging over this group of cells every time you want to perform some operation with it, consider creating a *range*. A range is a rectangular group of cells. You can name the range to make it even easier to select and refer to. (In Chapter 12, I show you how to use ranges in formulas.)

Excel refers to ranges by specific anchor points: the upper-left corner and the lower-right corner. For instance, if you drag over the cells from C3 to E5, you create a range that Excel fondly refers to as C3:E5. (Doesn't this sort of remind you of that game Battleship? You know, A5:D10—Hey! You sunk my battleship!) A range uses a colon to separate the anchor points.

After you have selected a range, you should name it to make it easier to recognize and locate. To name the range, click the **Name** box (at the left end of the formula bar), type the desired name, and press **Enter**. When naming a range, follow these naming conventions:

➤ Start the range name with an underscore or a letter. You can type numbers in a range name, but not at the beginning.

➤ Do not use spaces. You can use an underscore character, a period, or some other weird character to separate words.

➤ You can type as many as 255 characters (but if you type any more than 15, you should be committed).

➤ The name can't be the same as a cell address. (As if you'd want a range name to be as cryptic as those cell addresses.) For example, a range of entries from the fourth quarter of this year can't be named Q4 because Q4 is already the address of a cell in the worksheet. Try FourthQuarter or Qtr4, or something similar.

To select a named range quickly, open the **Name** box and click the range's name. You also can open the **Edit** menu and select **Go To** (or press **Ctrl+G**). Excel displays a list of named ranges. Click the desired range and click **OK**.

Working with Worksheets

In most cases, a single worksheet is all you need. However, sometimes you might need additional worksheets. To keep track of income and expenses for a small business, for instance, you might want to list income categories on one worksheet and expense categories on another. You can then use a third worksheet to summarize income minus expenses (see Figure 11.6).

To change from one worksheet to another, simply click the tab for the desired worksheet. You can take control of your tabs by doing the following:

➤ **Insert a worksheet**—Click the tab before which you want the new worksheet added; then open the **Insert** menu and click **Worksheet**.

➤ **Delete a worksheet**—Right-click the worksheet's tab and click **Delete**. A warning appears, asking you to confirm the deletion. Click **OK**.

➤ **Rename a worksheet**—Right-click the worksheet's tab and select **Rename**, or double-click the tab. The sheet's current name is highlighted. Type a name for the sheet (up to 31 characters) and press **Enter**. (Keep names short so that the tab doesn't take up the entire tab area.)

➤ **Recolor a worksheet tab**—Excel 2002 has a new option for color-coding your tabs. Right-click a tab, click **Tab Color**, and click the color you want to use.

➤ **Move or copy worksheets**—To move a worksheet, drag its tab to the left or right. To copy a worksheet, hold down the **Ctrl** key while dragging. To move or copy a worksheet to another workbook, open both workbooks and then right-click the tab and click **Move or Copy**. Enter your preferences to specify the destination of the worksheet and click **OK**.

➤ **Scroll**—If you have more tabs than fit inside the tab area, use the tab scrolling buttons to the left of the tabs to bring hidden tabs into view. The two buttons in the middle scroll one tab at a time back or forward. The button on the left displays the first tab, and the button on the right displays the last tab in the workbook.

➤ **Select multiple worksheets**—Ctrl+click the tab of each worksheet you want to select. Alternatively, click the first tab you want to select, and then Shift+click the last tab in the range.

Click a tab to display
the worksheet.

	Inc&Exp							
	A	B	C	D	E	F	G	
1	Online Services				Total			
2	4/10	IQuest	$23.71		$345.08			
3	4/17	America Online	$ 9.95					
4	5/16	IQuest	$15.00					
5	5/16	America Online	$19.03					
6	6/15	IQuest	$15.00					
7	7/19	IQuest	$15.00					
8	8/23	IQuest	$15.00					
9	6/15	America Online	$15.71					
10	6/29	CompuServe	$ 9.95					
11	7/17	America Online	$ 9.95					
12	7/20	CompuServe	$18.97					
13	8/7	CompuServe	$12.75					

Shipping \ **Online Services** / Office Supplies / Bank Fees

Tab scroll buttons   Worksheet tabs

Figure 11.6

Excel enables you to create an entire workbook full of worksheets.

All This and a Database, Too?

Microsoft Office includes a high-powered database program, Access (which you learn all about in Part 5, "Mastering the Information Age with Access"). Excel, however, provides some great database tools you might find a little easier to use. If you need a simple database for your address book or to keep track of your video or CD collection, Excel is all the database you need. You won't have to deal with the complexities of Access.

To create a database in Excel, you type *field names* in the topmost row, as shown in Figure 11.7. You might create a simple address book by typing field names, such as Title, FirstName, LastName, Address, and so on, in row A. Make the field names bold, or use some other formatting to set them off from the *field entries* (the actual names and addresses of the people in your database). In the remaining rows, type your field entries. Each set of field entries (each row) constitutes a *record* in your database.

Insider Tip

Start with More Worksheets

You can change the default number of worksheets Excel creates for a new workbook. Open the **Tools** menu, select **Options**, and click the **General** tab. Use the **Sheets in New Workbook** spin box to enter the desired number of worksheets. Click **OK**.

When you have entered all the records, you can then use commands on the Data menu to sort, filter, and perform other database management operations. If you need a more full-featured database to manage your records, however, you should consider using Access instead. For example, if you're running your own business and need to keep track of customers, billing, inventory, and employees, you should spend the time learning Access because it saves you time in the long run.

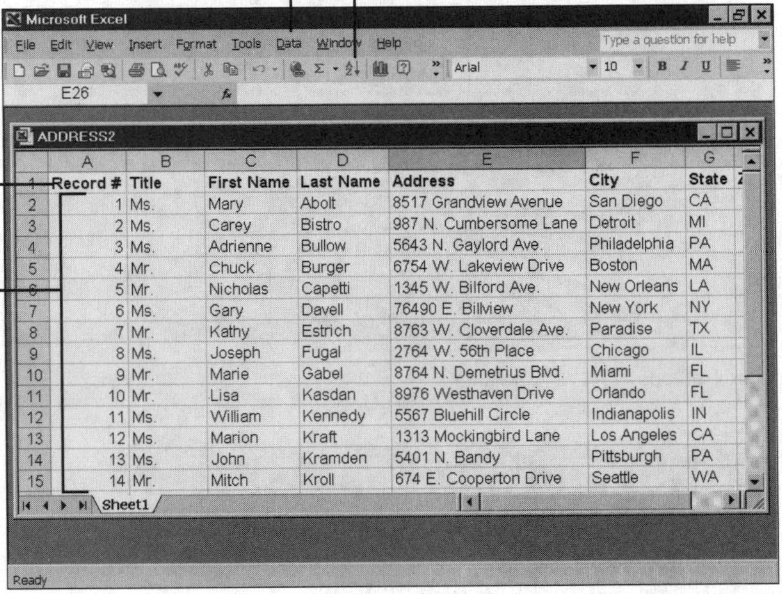

The Data menu contains commands
for sorting and filtering your records.

You can quickly sort records
in an Excel database.

Figure 11.7

You can create a simple database in Excel.

Type field names in
the topmost row.

Type records in the
remaining rows.

The Least You Need to Know

Before you can put a worksheet to work for you, the worksheet must contain some data. Before moving on to the next chapter, make sure you have mastered these basic data entry concepts and tasks:

➤ A cell is a box formed by the intersection of a row and a column.

➤ A cell's address consists of the cell's column letter and row number.

➤ To type an entry in a cell, click the cell or tab to it and start typing.

➤ If an entry is too wide for a cell, adjust the column width by double-clicking the border to the right of the column's heading.

➤ To copy a cell's contents into neighboring cells, drag the cell's fill handle.

➤ To highlight a group of neighboring cells, drag the mouse pointer over them.

➤ To rename a worksheet, right-click its tab, click **Rename**, and type the new name.

➤ You can create a simple database in Excel by typing field names in the top row and entering your records in the rows that follow.

➤ When you see #### in a cell, this means your numeric data is too large for that cell size. Click anywhere in the column, open the **Format** menu, select **Column**, and select **AutoFit Selection**.

Chapter 12

Doing Math with Formulas

Although an Excel worksheet is ideal for arranging entries in columns and rows, that's not its main purpose. You can do that with Word's Table feature. What makes a work-sheet so powerful is that it can perform calculations using various values from the worksheet and values you supply. In addition, you can set up unlimited scenarios for your worksheet that supply different numbers in the calculations, enabling you to play "What if...?" with various sets of numbers!

In this chapter, you learn how to unleash the power of Excel's formulas, functions, and other calculation tools.

Understanding Formulas and Concocting Your Own

The term *formula* might conjure up the image of Albert Einstein scrawling abstract mathematical operations on a chalkboard. Excel formulas are much more practical than that. These formulas perform mathematical operations (addition, subtraction, multiplication, and division) on the entries in your worksheet to determine totals, grand totals, percentages, and other practical results. To help you understand how formulas work in a spreadsheet, here are some helpful facts about formulas:

➤ You type a formula into the cell in which you want the answer to appear.

➤ All formulas start with an equal sign (=). If you start with a letter, Excel thinks you're typing a label. If you start with a number, Excel thinks you're typing a static (unchanging) value.

➤ Formulas use cell addresses to pull values from other cells into the formula. For example, the formula =A1+D3 adds the values in cells A1 and D3.

➤ Formulas use the following symbols:

+	addition
–	subtraction
×	multiplication
/	division
^	raise to the ___ power of
%	percentage

➤ You can include your own numbers in formulas. To determine your annual income, for instance, you would multiply your monthly income by 12. If your monthly income were in cell C5, the formula would be =C5×12.

A simple formula might look something like =A1+B1+C1+D1, which determines the grand total of the values in cells A1–D1. Formulas can be much more complex, however, using values from two or more worksheets and even values from different workbooks!

Getting Your Operators in Order

You're probably dying to start entering formulas to see what happens. Whoa, little filly. First you need a refresher course on a little rule in math that determines the *order of operations*. In any formula, Excel performs the series of operations from left to right in the following order, which gives some operators *precedence* over others:

1st	All operations in parentheses
2nd	Exponential equations or operations
3rd	Multiplication and division
4th	Addition and subtraction

This is important to keep in mind when you are creating equations because the order of operations determines the result.

If you want to determine the average of the values in cells A1, B1, and C1, and you enter =A1+B1+C1/3, you probably get the wrong answer. Excel divides the value in C1 by 3 and then adds that result to A1+B1. It calculates this way because division takes precedence over addition. So, how do you correctly determine this average? You must group your values in parentheses. In this little example, you want to total A1–C1 first. To do that, enclose the cell addresses in parentheses: =(A1+B1+C1)/3. This tells Excel to total the values before dividing them.

Pointing and Clicking Your Way to Formulas

You can enter formulas in either of two ways: by *typing* the formula or by *selecting* cell references.

To type a formula, click the cell in which you want the result to appear, type the formula (starting with an equal sign), and press **Enter**. Excel calculates the result and enters it into your selected cell (assuming you have entered some values to calculate).

Error!

If an error message appears in the cell in which you typed your formula, make sure you did not enter a formula that told Excel to do one of the following: divide by 0 or a blank cell, use a value from a blank cell, delete a cell being used in a formula, or use a range name when a single cell address was expected.

To enter a formula by selecting cell references, take the following steps, and don't press Enter until you've entered the entire formula (it's tempting, but don't do it):

1. Select the cell in which you want the formula's result to appear.
2. Type the equal sign (=).
3. Click the cell whose address you want to appear first in the formula. The cell address appears in the Formula bar.
4. Type a mathematical operator (+, –, and so forth) after the value to indicate the next operation you want to perform.
5. Continue clicking cells and typing operators until you finish entering the formula, as shown in Figure 12.1. (Remember to group operations using parentheses, if necessary, to control the order of the operations.)
6. When you finish, press **Enter** to accept the formula.

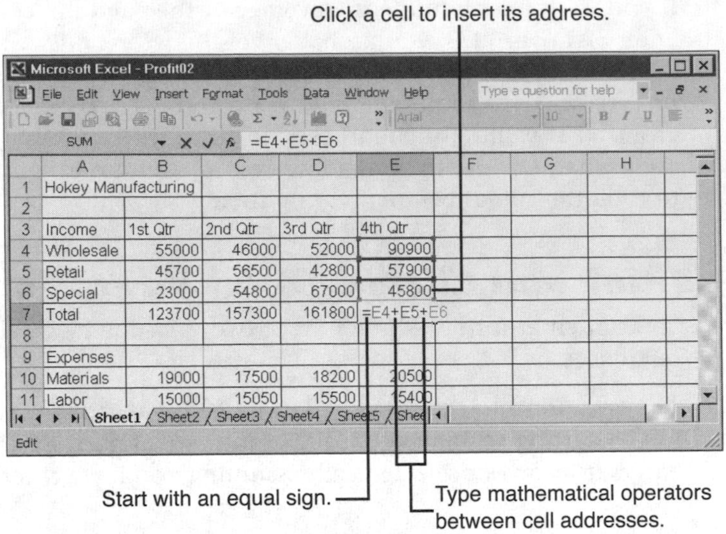

Click a cell to insert its address.

Figure 12.1

The easiest way to compose formulas is to point and click.

Start with an equal sign. ⎯

Type mathematical operators between cell addresses.

If you make a mistake while entering a formula, simply backspace over it and enter your correction as you would with any other cell entry. If you already accepted the entry (by pressing **Enter** or clicking the check mark button), double-click the cell (or click it and then click in the Formula bar where you want to make changes).

As you enter formulas, you might notice that Excel automatically performs the calculation. If you change a value in a cell that the formula uses, Excel instantly recalculates the entire worksheet! If you have a long worksheet with a lot of formulas and a slow computer, this can slow down Excel significantly, so you might want to change the recalculation settings. To turn off the Auto Calculation option, open the **Tools** menu, select **Options**, and click the **Calculation** tab. Select **Manual** and click **OK**. From now on, when you want to recalculate the worksheet, press **F9**.

Going Turbo with Functions

Functions are ready-made formulas you can use to perform a series of operations using two or more values or a range of values. For example, to determine the sum of a series of values in cells A5–G5, you can enter the function =SUM(A5:G5) instead of entering +A5+B5+C5+D5+E5+F5+G5, which is way too much typing. Functions can save a lot of time. Other functions can perform more complex operations, such as determining the monthly payment on a loan when you supply the values for the principal, interest rate, and number of payment periods.

Every function must have the following three elements:

> ➤ **The equal sign (=)**—Indicates that what follows is a formula, not a label.

> ➤ **The function name**—An example is SUM. This indicates the type of operation you want Excel to perform.

154

> ➤ **The argument**—An example is A3:F11. This indicates the cell addresses of the values on which the function acts. The argument is often a range of cells, but it can be much more complex.

One other thing to remember is that a function can be part of another formula. For example, =SUM(A3:A9)+B43 uses the SUM function along with the addition operator to add the value in cell B43 to the total of the values in cells A3–A9.

The Awesome AutoSum Tool

One of the tasks you perform most often is summing up values you've entered in your worksheet cells. Because summing is so common, Excel provides a tool devoted to summing—AutoSum.

Σ To quickly determine the total of a row or column of values, first click an empty cell to the right of the row or just below the column of values. Then, click the **AutoSum** button in the Standard toolbar, as shown in Figure 12.2. AutoSum assumes you want to add the values in the cells to the left of or above the currently selected cell, so it displays a marching ants box (called a *marquee*) around those cells. If AutoSum selects an incorrect range of cells, you can edit the selection by dragging over the cells whose values you want to add. After the AutoSum formula is correct, press **Enter** or click another cell.

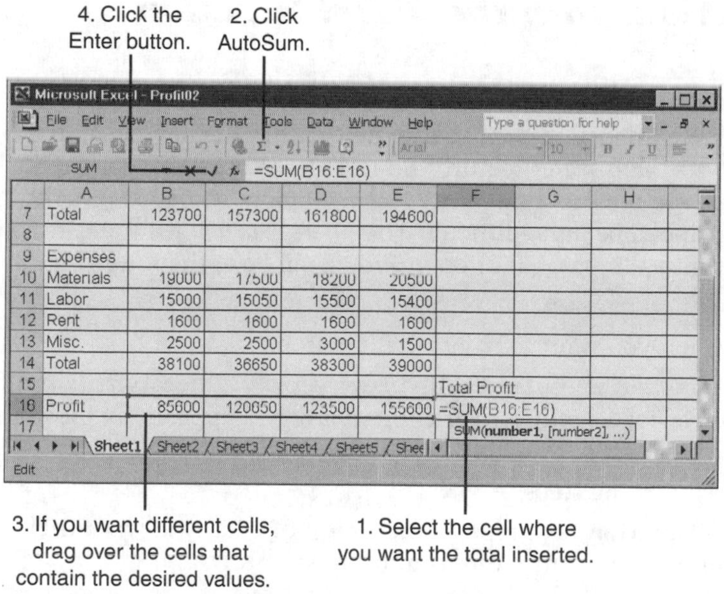

4. Click the Enter button.   2. Click AutoSum.

Figure 12.2

With a click of a button, AutoSum determines the total.

3. If you want different cells, drag over the cells that contain the desired values.

1. Select the cell where you want the total inserted.

If your worksheet contains two or more cells that contain subtotals, you also can use AutoSum to determine the grand total. Click the cell in which you want to insert the grand total and then click the **AutoSum** button. Click the first subtotal and then Ctrl+click any additional subtotals you want to include in the grand total. Press **Enter**.

AutoCalculate

Drag over a range of values and look in the status bar. You see Sum=, followed by the total of the values in the selected cells. This feature, called *AutoCalculate*, can help you determine totals without inserting the total in a cell. Right-click the status bar to display a pop-up menu that enables you to show the average of the selected cells or the count (the number of values in the cells).

Demystifying Functions with the Insert Function Feature

The SUM and AVERAGE functions are fairly easy to enter. Some of the other functions, however—such as the financial function that determines the payment on a loan—might contain several values and require you to enter those values in the proper *syntax* (order). To type the function, you must remember its name and know the required syntax, which can be quite difficult. The *Insert Function* feature can make the process much less painful. To paste a function into a cell, take the following steps:

1. Select the cell in which you want to insert the function.

2. Open the **Insert** menu and select **Function**; better yet, click the **Insert Function** button in the Formula bar. The Insert Function dialog box appears, as shown in Figure 12.3, displaying a list of available functions.

3. Perform one of the following steps:

   In the **Search for a Function** box, type a description of what you want the function to do, and then click the **Go** button or press **Enter**.

   Open the **Or Select a Category** list and select the type of function you want to insert. If you're not sure, select **All** to display the names of all the functions. They are listed alphabetically.

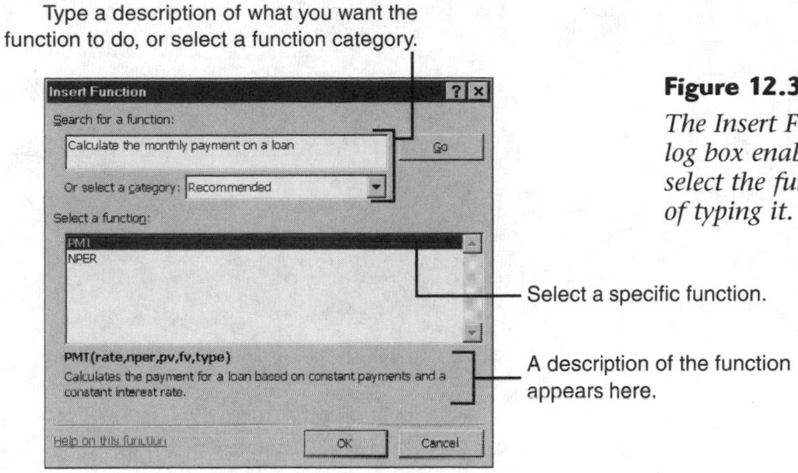

Type a description of what you want the
function to do, or select a function category.

Insert Function ? ✕

Search for a function:

| Calculate the monthly payment on a loan | | Go |

Or select a category: Recommended ▼

Select a function:

| PMT |
| NPER |

PMT(rate,nper,pv,fv,type)
Calculates the payment for a loan based on constant payments and a
constant interest rate.

Help on this function   OK   Cancel

Figure 12.3

*The Insert Function dia-
log box enables you to
select the function instead
of typing it.*

Select a specific function.

A description of the function
appears here.

4. Select the function you want to insert from the **Select a Function** list and click
   OK. The Function Arguments dialog box appears, as shown in Figure 12.4,
   prompting you to type the argument. You can type values or cell addresses in
   the various text boxes. Alternatively, you can click the button to the right of the
   text box and then click the cell that contains the specified value.

Where Did the Function Arguments Dialog Box Go?!

If you click a button for one of the items in the Function Arguments dialog box, Excel
tucks the dialog box out of the way, displaying the address of the currently selected cell
and a button for bringing the dialog box back into view. After you select the desired cell,
click the button to the right of the cell address to redisplay the dialog box.

5. Enter the values or cell ranges for the argument. You can type a value or an
   argument, or click the cells that contain the required values. (Some arguments,
   such as those that start with "If," are optional. Excel must "decide" which
   action to perform based on entries in your worksheet.)

6. Click **OK** or press **Enter**. Excel inserts the function and argument in the selected
   cell and displays the result.

Click one of these buttons to hide the dialog box, and
then click the cell that contains the specified value.

Figure 12.4

*Enter the values and cell
references that make up
the argument.*

Function Arguments		? ✕

PMT

Rate	C7	= 0.007083333
Nper	C8	= 360
Pv	C5	= 100000
Fv	C11	= 0
Type		= number

= -768.9134836

Calculates the payment for a loan based on constant payments and a constant interest rate.

Rate is the interest rate per period for the loan. For example, use 6%/4 for
quarterly payments at 6% APR.

Formula result =   ($768.91)

Help on this function   OK   Cancel

When you need to edit a function, select the cell that contains the function you want
to edit. (Make sure you're not in Edit mode—that is, the insertion point should not
appear in the cell.) Open the **Insert** menu and select **Function**, or click the **Insert
Function** button. This displays the Function Arguments dialog box, which helps you
edit your argument.

Seeing a Real Live Investment Function in Action

To get some hands-on experience with functions, check out the FV *(future value)* function. This function enables you to play around with some numbers to determine how
much money you'll have socked away when you're ready to retire. Let's say you plan
to retire in 20 years, and you invest $200 per month at 8% interest. You would enter
the following function:

=FV(8%/12,240,-200,0,1)

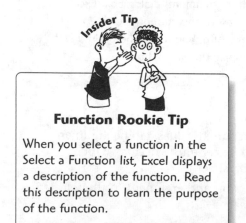

Function Rookie Tip

When you select a function in the
Select a Function list, Excel displays
a description of the function. Read
this description to learn the purpose
of the function.

Let's break this down:

= is an essential element in the function statement, as
explained earlier.

FV is the function name, which stands for "future
value."

8%/12 is the annual percentage paid to you divided by
12 months.

240 is the number of payments (12 months times 20
years).

-200 is the amount that you invest each month. Note
that this number is negative, because you are *paying
out* money to the investment account.

0 is the amount invested right now. If you already have some money socked away at this same percentage rate, replace 0 with that amount entered as a negative value.

1 specifies that the monthly investment is made at the beginning of the month. If you invest at the end of the month, use 0 instead or leave a blank.

As you might have already guessed, you can use cell references in place of the values. Figure 12.5 shows a sample worksheet used to determine the future value of an investment. Note that each value listed previously is in a separate cell.

C9		*fx* =FV(C4/12,C5,C6,C7,C8)						
	A	B	C	D	E	F	G	H
1								
2		Investment Worksheet						
3								
4		Annual Interest Rate	0.0800					
5		Payment Periods	240					
6		Payment Amount	($200.00)					
7		Current Investment	0.00					
8		1st of the Month	1					
9		After 20 Years	$118,589.44					
10								

Figure 12.5

Use cell references instead of values.

Track Down Errors

Excel's worksheet auditors can help you track down errors in formulas and functions. Click the cell that contains the function or formula that is not working properly (or the cell that is referenced by a problem formula or function). Then, open the **Tools** menu, point to **Formula Auditing**, and select the desired auditing tool: **Trace Precedents**, **Trace Dependents**, or **Trace Error**. The auditing tool displays arrows that point to the referenced cells or highlights errors. To remove the arrows, select **Tools, Formula Auditing, Remove All Arrows**.

Cloning Formulas for Quick and Easy Entry

When you copy a formula from one cell in the worksheet and paste it into another cell, Excel adjusts the cell references in the formula to reflect their new positions in the worksheet. In Figure 12.6, cell B9 contains the formula =B4+B5+B6+B7, which determines the total sales revenue for Fred. If you copy that formula to cell C9 (to determine the total sales revenue for Wilma), Excel automatically changes the formula to =C4+C5+C6+C7.

Formula copied into cell C9 determines Wilma's sales revenue.

Figure 12.6

Excel adjusts cell references when you copy formulas.

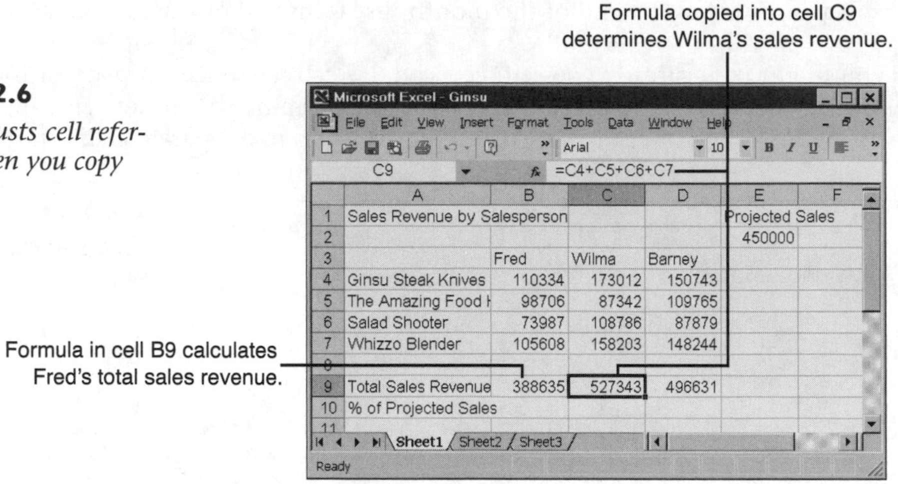

Formula in cell B9 calculates Fred's total sales revenue.

The preceding example shows a formula in which the cell references are *relative:* Excel changes the cell addresses relative to the position of the formula. In this example, the formula was moved one cell to the right, so all the addresses in the formula are also adjusted one cell to the right.

Sometimes, however, you might not want Excel to adjust the cell references. To keep a cell reference from changing when you copy or move the formula, you must mark the cell reference in the formula as an *absolute reference*. To mark a reference as an absolute, press the **F4** key immediately after typing the reference or move the insertion point inside the cell reference and press **F4**. This places a dollar sign before the column letter and the row number (as in E2). You can type the dollar signs yourself, but it's usually easier to let Excel do it.

You also can mark the column letter *or* the row number (but not both) as absolute. This enables the column letter or row number to change when you copy or move the formula. Keep pressing **F4** until you have the desired combination of dollar signs.

Playing "What If...?" with Scenarios

After you have some values and formulas in place, let the fun begin! Excel offers a tool that enables you to plug various sets of values into your formulas to determine the effects of different values on the outcome.

Say you're purchasing a home and need some idea of how much your monthly mortgage payment is going to be for various loan amounts. You have successfully created a worksheet that determines the monthly payment for a $120,000 house at 8.5%; but you want to know what the payment would be for a $110,000, a $130,000, and a $140,000 home. You also want to see the effects of other loan rates. You could create a bunch of separate worksheets, but a better solution is to create several scenarios for the same worksheet. A *scenario* is simply a set of values you plug into variables in the worksheet.

The Making of a Scenario

Making a scenario is fairly simple. You name the scenario, tell Excel which cells have the values you want to play with, and then type the values you want Excel to use for the scenario. The following step-by-step instructions walk you through the process of creating a scenario:

1. Display the worksheet for which you want to create a scenario.

2. Open the **Tools** menu and click **Scenarios**. The Scenario Manager appears, indicating that this worksheet has no current scenarios.

3. Click the **Add** button. The Add Scenario dialog box appears, as shown in Figure 12.7.

4. Type a name for the scenario that describes the specific changes you're going to make. For example, if you were creating this scenario to determine payments for a $130,000 house at 9.25%, you might type **130K @ 9.25%**.

5. Click the **Changing Cells** text box and click the cell that contains the value you want to change in your scenario. To change values in other cells, hold down the **Ctrl** key and click them. (This inserts the addresses of the changing cells, separating them with commas.)

6. Click **OK**. The Scenario Values dialog box displays the current values in the cells you want to change.

7. Type the values you want to use for this scenario and click **OK**. The Scenario Manager displays the name of the new scenario.

8. To view a scenario, click its name and click the **Show** button. Excel replaces the values in the changing cells with the values you entered for the scenario.

Managing Your Scenarios

Whenever you want to play with the various scenarios you've created, open the **Tools** menu and select **Scenarios**. This displays the Scenario Manager, which you met in the previous section. The Scenario Manager offers the following buttons for managing and displaying your scenarios:

➤ **Show**—Displays the results of the selected scenario right inside the worksheet.

➤ **Add**—Enables you to add another scenario.

➤ **Delete**—Removes the selected scenario.

➤ **Edit**—Enables you toselect different cells used for the scenario and insert different values for the variables.

➤ **Merge**—Takes scenarios from various worksheets and places them on a single worksheet.

➤ **Summary**—Displays the results of the various worksheets on a single worksheet. As you can see in Figure 12.8, this is great for comparing the various scenarios you've created.

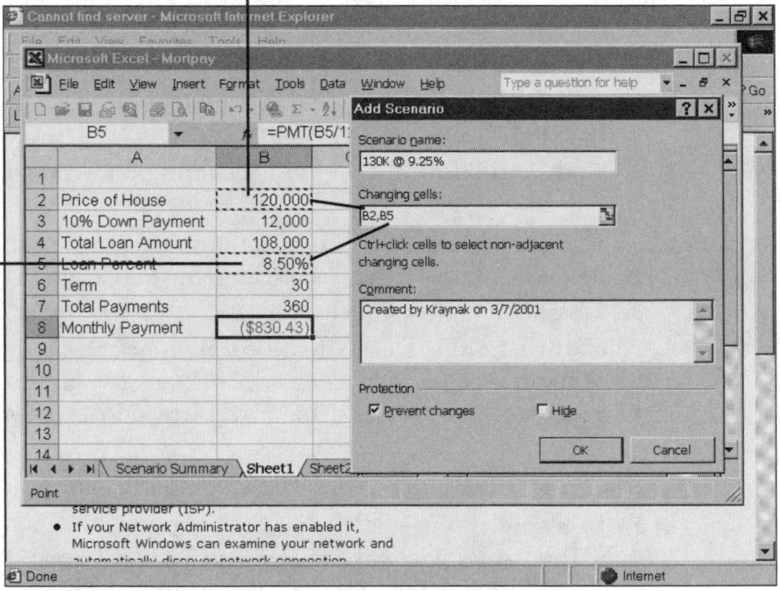

Figure 12.7

To make a scenario, enter different values for the variables.

This entry replaces the price of the house in cell B2.

This entry replaces the loan rate in cell B5.

Figure 12.8

Scenario Manager can create a summary of the results from various scenarios.

Scenario Summary				
	Current Values:	120K @ 8.25%	110K @ 9.25%	130K @ 9.625%
Changing Cells:				
B2	110,000	120,000	110,000	130,000
B5	9.25%	8.50%	9.25%	9.63%
Result Cells:				
B8	($814.45)	($830.43)	($814.45)	($994.40)
Notes: Current Values column represents values of changing cells at time Scenario Summary Report was created. Changing cells for each scenario are highlighted in gray.				

The Scenario Summary creates a new worksheet. When you're finished with it, simply click the tab for the worksheet on which you were working before creating your scenarios. To get rid of the sheet altogether, right-click the **Scenario Summary** tab and select **Delete**.

The Least You Need to Know

Your success with formulas depends on your ability to think of the right formula for a particular application and enter the formula correctly. Before moving on to the next chapter, make sure you've mastered these formula concepts and tasks:

➤ A formula consists of cell addresses and mathematical operators arranged in accordance with the proper order of operations.

➤ The easiest way to enter a formula is to type an equal sign, and then alternately click values and type mathematical operators to complete the formula.

➤ Unless you group certain operations using parentheses, Excel performs all multiplication and division operations before performing addition and subtraction.

➤ To quickly total a row or column of values, click in the cell to the right of the row or below the column of values; then click the **AutoSum** button and press **Enter**.

➤ The easiest way to enter a function is to click the **Insert Function** button and then follow the onscreen instructions.

➤ By default, Excel uses relative cell references in formulas, so that when you copy a formula from one cell to another, Excel can automatically adjust the cell references to retrieve the correct data.

➤ To add a scenario for a worksheet, open the **Tools** menu, click **Scenarios**, click the **Add** button, and follow the onscreen instructions.

Chapter 13

Giving Your Worksheet a Professional Look

In This Chapter

➤ Inserting blank rows, columns, and cells

➤ Adding dollar signs, decimals, percent signs, and other valuable ornaments

➤ Spiffing up a worksheet with clip art

➤ Adding borders, shading, and other fancy stuff

➤ Mastering a few formatting tricks and shortcuts

If you win the lottery or make some savvy investments in the stock market, numbers might grab your attention. In most cases, however, numbers look about as exciting as a stack of dirty laundry.

To make your numbers a little more appealing and make the rows and columns easier to follow, you need to format your worksheet. You can format by inserting blank rows and columns to give your values a little elbow room, laying down a few lines around your cells, or even shading individual cells, rows, or columns to make them stand out.

In this chapter, you learn several ways to adorn your worksheets and make your numbers a little more exciting.

Tweaking Row Heights and Column Widths

Worksheet cells are pretty dinky. You can't cram more than about nine characters into a cell without the entry spilling over into the next cell or being lopped off. To accommodate long entries or tall fonts, Excel enables you to adjust the column width and row height.

The easiest way to adjust the column width and row height is to drag the edge of the column or row heading, as shown in Figure 13.1. First select the cell(s) or column(s) you want to resize. Move the mouse pointer over the right edge of the column heading or the bottom edge of the row heading so the mouse pointer appears as a two-headed arrow. Then drag the edge to adjust the column width or row height.

Quick Alterations with AutoFit

To resize a column or row quickly, double-click the right edge of the column heading (the box with the letter in it at the top of the column) or the bottom edge of the row heading (the box with the number in it to the left of the row). You'll also find this feature on the Format, Rows and Format, Columns submenu.

A ScreenTip shows the new
column width as you drag.

Figure 13.1

The mouse provides an intuitive way to change the row height and column width.

Drag the bottom edge of a row heading to adjust the row height.

	A	B	C	D	E	F
	A1	Width: 21.89 (204 pixels)	nue by Sales Person			
1	Sales Revenue by Sales Person			Projected Sales		
2				560000		
3		Bill	Jack	Jane		
4	Widgets	150729	151252	152124		
5	Whackits	70327	65752	66254		
6	Whosits	82182	71046	85562		
7	Whatsits	260348	255458	275142		
8						
9	Total Sales Revenu	563586	543508	579082		
10	% of Projected	1.00640357	0.97055	1.034075		
11						

Drag the right edge of the column
heading to adjust the column width.

For more precise control over the column width and row height, select **Format**, **Row**, **Height** or **Format**, **Column**, **Width**, and enter the desired settings.

Fission and Fusion: Merging and Splitting Cells

As you enter data, you might need to merge two or more cells to create a single mega-cell that spans two or more rows or columns. In this single merged cell, you can then type a single entry that acts as a row or column heading. For example, you might want to merge the cells at the top of the worksheet to enter a worksheet title that spans the entire worksheet.

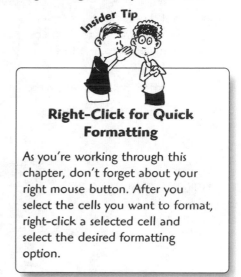

Right-Click for Quick Formatting

As you're working through this chapter, don't forget about your right mouse button. After you select the cells you want to format, right-click a selected cell and select the desired formatting option.

The easiest way to merge cells is to use the Merge and Center button in the Formatting toolbar. Drag over the cells you want to merge (the cells must be *contiguous*, neighboring), and then click the **Merge and Center** button (in the Formatting toolbar). (If the Merge and Center button is not visible, click the **Toolbar Options** button, at the right end of the Formatting toolbar, and then click the **Merge and Center** button.) Excel transforms the selected cells into a single cell and centers any text inside the cell. You can click any of the alignment buttons to change the text alignment.

You also can merge cells by changing the cell formatting. Take the following steps:

1. Drag over the cells you want to merge.
2. Open the **Format** menu and select **Cells**.
3. Click the **Alignment** tab and check the **Merge Cells** option.
4. Click **OK**.

To return the cells to their original (nonmerged) condition, repeat these steps to turn off the Merge Cells option.

Add a Few Rows, Toss in Some Columns

As you are building your worksheet, you might need to add a few columns or rows to insert data that you hadn't thought of when you were laying out your worksheet. On the other hand, maybe you need to delete a row or column if your design was a little too ambitious. Whatever the case, adding and deleting cells, rows, and columns is fairly simple.

Look to the Insert Menu

If your right mouse button is broken, you can always use the options on the Insert menu to insert cells, rows, or columns.

To insert cells, columns, or rows, first select the number of rows, columns, or cells you want to insert (drag over the row or column headings to select entire rows or columns).

After selecting columns, rows, or cells, right-click anywhere inside the selection and click **Insert**. If you selected columns or rows, Excel inserts them immediately. If you selected a block of cells, the Insert dialog box appears, as shown in Figure 13.2, asking which way you want the data in the currently selected cells to be shifted. Select **Shift Cells Right** or **Shift Cells Down** and click **OK**.

Specify the direction in which you want data from the currently selected cells to be shifted.

Figure 13.2

When you insert a block of cells, Excel shifts data down or to the right to make room.

	A	B	C	D	E	F	G
1	**House Sale**						
2				Insert			
3	**New House Cost**			Insert			
4				○ Shift cells right			
5	House	$120,000.00		● Shift cells down	95,000.00		
6	Interest	$ 325.00			42,744.30		
7	Title Insurance	$ 486.00		○ Entire row	4,000.00		
8	Deed Affidavit	$ 35.00		○ Entire column	5,700.00		
9	6 mos. Property Tax	$ 257.00			1,000.00		
10	Express Payoff	$ 25.00		OK Cancel	4,000.00		
11	Termite Report	$ 50.00		Stove and Refrigerator	$ 2,000.00		
12	FHA Required?	$ 350.00		**Total Profit**	$ 35,555.70		
13	**Total Cost**	**$121,528.00**					
14							

House Sale #2

Nuking Rows, Columns, and Cells

It's usually easier to destroy than to create. But that's not the case with worksheets because, when you delete in a worksheet, all sorts of things can happen. You might destroy only the data in the cells, or you might wipe out the cells or columns entirely, forcing adjacent cells to shift. Therefore, when you set out on any mission of mass destruction, keep the following points in mind:

➤ If you select columns, rows, or cells, and press the **Delete** key, Excel leaves the cells intact, deleting only the contents of the selected cells. This is the same as entering the Edit, Clear, Contents command.

➤ The **Edit**, **Clear** command opens a submenu that enables you to clear All (contents, formatting, and comments), Contents (just the cell entries, not the formatting), Formats (the cell formatting, not the contents), or Comments (only the cell comments).

➤ To remove cells, columns, or rows completely, select them, open the **Edit** menu, and select **Delete**. (Alternatively, right-click the selection and select **Delete**.)

➤ When you remove a row, rows below it are pulled up to fill the space. When you delete a column, columns to the right are pulled to the left to fill the void.

➤ If you choose to remove a block of cells (otherwise known as a *range*), Excel displays a dialog box asking you how to shift the surrounding cells.

If you delete cells by mistake, click the **Undo** button right away to get them back. If you make several mistakes, consider closing your workbook *without* saving your changes. You can then reopen the workbook and start over.

Fit Your Worksheet to the Browser Window

If you are formatting your worksheet to place it on the Web or on your company's intranet, try to keep the worksheet narrow. If the worksheet is wider than the Web browser window, the people viewing your worksheet have to use the horizontal scroll button to bring columns into view. This can make the worksheet a royal pain to navigate.

Making It Look Great in 10 Minutes or Less

Although the content of your worksheet is more important than its appearance, a little creative formatting can make your worksheet more attractive and functional. For example, you can add shading to rows and columns to make the spreadsheet easier to follow, add lines to set off totals and grand totals, and even have Excel display negative numbers in color to raise a flag when your business is in the red.

The following sections show you how to use the various formatting tools available in Excel to give your worksheets a more professional look.

Drive-Through Formatting with AutoFormat

Excel offers a formatting feature called *AutoFormat* that makes formatting your worksheet as easy as picking up a bag of burgers at the local drive-through. With AutoFormat, you apply a predesigned format to selected cells. The format controls everything from fonts and alignment to shading and borders.

To use AutoFormat, select the cells you want to format, open the **Format** menu, and select **AutoFormat**. In the AutoFormat dialog box, click the desired format. To turn off any format settings, such as shading or borders, click the **Options** button and select your preferences, as shown in Figure 13.3. Then click **OK**.

Click Options to display additional settings.

Figure 13.3

You can pick a pre-designed table format for your worksheet.

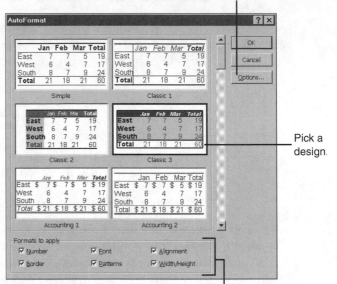

Pick a design.

When you click Options, these options appear.

Insider Tip

Highlight Key Values with Conditional Formatting

You can apply *conditional formatting* to a cell to make Excel display a value in a unique way if the value falls within a certain range. For example, you can apply a conditional format telling Excel that if this value falls below 0, it should shade the cell red and place a big, thick border around it to alert you. To apply conditional formatting, select the cell that contains the formula or value you want to format, open the **Format** menu, select **Conditional Formatting**, and enter your preferences.

Don't Forget Your Formatting Toolbar

Overlooking the Formatting toolbar in any of the Microsoft Office applications is like forgetting your laptop when you're going on a business trip. Without it, you have to resort to a system of awkward pull-down menus, dialog boxes, and pop-up menus to get anything done. The Formatting toolbar, shown in Figure 13.4, offers the fastest way for you to change fonts, increase or decrease the type size, align text in cells, change the text color, add borders, and more.

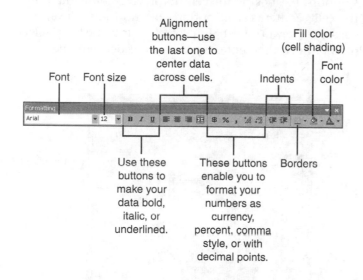

Figure 13.4

Excel's Formatting toolbar.

More Control with the Format Cells Dialog Box

For additional formatting options, use the Format Cells dialog box. Open the **Format** menu and select **Cells** to open the dialog box. You can easily change many of the formatting features for your data by clicking the appropriate tabs in this dialog box:

➤ **Number**—Provides various formats to control the appearance of values, including currency, percentages, dates, and times. Select the desired category and then click the specific format you want to use, as shown in Figure 13.5.

➤ **Alignment**—Enables you to control the way labels and values are positioned inside cells. You can even rotate text to display it on an angle inside a cell; under Orientation, drag the line next to Text to the desired angle.

➤ **Font**—Enables you to select a typeface and size for your text and to add enhancements, such as bold, italic, and color.

➤ **Border**—Provides options for adding lines between and around cells. (The light gray *gridlines* that Excel uses to mark cell boundaries do not print.) Before you select a border, select a line style from the **Style** list and a color from the **Color** drop-down list. The **Presets** buttons enable you to add an outline (a line around the outside of the entire selection) and inside lines (between all the cells in the

171

selected area). Click a button to turn the lines on or off. The **Border** buttons (below the Presets) enable you to add or remove individual lines.

➤ **Patterns**—Enables you to shade the selected cells. Under Color, click the main color you want to use for the cell shading. To overlay a pattern of a different color, open the **Pattern** drop-down list and click a pattern (from the top of the list). Then, open the **Pattern** drop-down list again and click a color (from the bottom of the list). Click **OK**. -

➤ **Protection**—Provides options for locking the cell (to prevent someone from editing it) or hiding the cell's contents. This option does nothing, however, unless you choose to protect the worksheet. To protect your worksheet, select **Tools**, **Protection**, **Protect Sheet**; then enter a password (if desired) and click **OK**.

Figure 13.5

Use number formatting for currency, dates, and percentages.

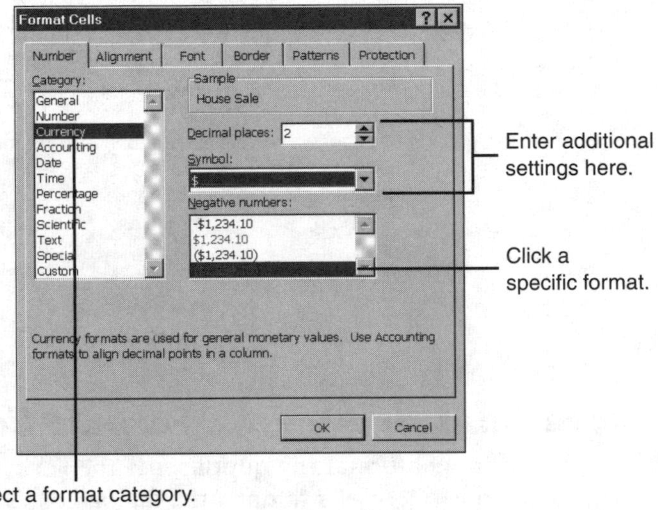

Excel 2002 now offers a Draw Border feature, which makes the process of adding borders much more intuitive. Right-click any toolbar or the Excel menu bar and click **Borders** to display the Borders toolbar. To draw a border around a block of cells, drag over the cells. To have lines appear around *and within* the block (to form a grid), open the **Draw Border** list (the leftmost button in the Borders toolbar) and click **Draw Border Grid**. Then, drag over the cells around which you want borders placed.

Changing the Default Font

To use any font as the normal font for all your worksheets, you can change the default font. Open the **Tools** menu, select **Options**, and click the **General** tab. Open the **Standard Font** drop-down list and click the desired font. Open the **Size** drop-down list and click the font size you want. Then click **OK**. The change doesn't take effect until you restart Excel.

Applying Formats with a Few Brush Strokes

You can quickly copy the formatting from one cell or a block of cells to other cells by using the Format Painter. Select the cell that contains the formatting you want to copy and click the **Format Painter** button (in the Standard toolbar). Drag your pointer (which now has a paintbrush icon next to it) over the cells to which you want to copy the formatting. Format Painter applies the formatting! To paint the format in multiple locations, double-click the **Format Painter** button to lock it in the on position. Then paint away. When you're done, click the **Format Painter** button again to turn it off.

Hanging a Few Graphical Ornaments

In Chapter 14, "Graphing Data for Fun and Profit," you learn how to add graphs to your worksheets to give your data meaning and to make your worksheets more graphical; however, Excel offers a few additional tools for adding graphics to your worksheets.

The **Insert, Picture** submenu contains several options for inserting clip art images, graphics stored on your disk, WordArt, AutoShapes, and even scanned images (assuming you have a TWAIN-compatible scanner or digital camera).

These graphics tools are similar (some are even identical) to the tools that Word offers. To learn how to use these tools (clip art, WordArt,

Give Your Web Worksheet an Attractive Background

If you're planning to place your Excel worksheet on the Web, give it a background design. Open the **Format** menu, point to **Sheet**, and select **Background**. In the Sheet Background dialog box, select one of the background designs.

AutoShapes, drawing, and so on), see Chapter 7, "Spicing It Up with Graphics, Sound, and Video."

The Least You Need to Know

With all the formatting tricks you learned in this chapter, your worksheets should inspire some "wows" from friends and colleagues alike. As you're sprucing up your other worksheets, make sure you've mastered these formatting basics:

➤ To change the height of a row or width of a column, drag the borders in the column and row headings.

➤ To insert rows or columns, highlight the number of rows or columns you want to insert, right-click the selection, and click **Insert**.

➤ To delete the contents of selected cells, columns, or rows, press the **Delete** key. To completely remove selected cells, columns, or rows, open the **Edit** menu and click **Delete**.

➤ To have Excel format your worksheet for you, open the **Format** menu and click **AutoFormat**.

➤ Use the buttons in the Formatting toolbar to apply most of the cell formatting you need.

➤ For more control over the formatting of selected cells, open the **Format** menu and click **Cells** or press **Ctrl+1**.

➤ To apply formatting that changes depending on the value of the selected cell, open the **Format** menu, click **Conditional Formatting**, and enter your preferences.

Chapter 14

Graphing Data for Fun and Profit

During the 1992 presidential race, Ross Perot made charts famous. With his prime-time voodoo pointer and his stack of charts, he managed to upset an election and change the political strategies of both parties. At the same time, he proved that a well-designed graph could convey data much more clearly and effectively than could any page full of stodgy numbers.

In this chapter, you learn how to use Excel's charting tools to make your data more graphical and give your numbers context.

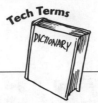

Graphs or Charts?

Completely ignoring the fact that most of us grew up calling graphs *graphs*, Excel and most other spreadsheet programs insist on calling them *charts*. They're still graphs, but to make Excel happy and to prevent confusion, let's agree to call graphs "charts" from now on.

Charting Your Data

To make charting a painless exercise, Excel offers a tool called the Chart Wizard. You select the data you want charted, and then start the Chart Wizard, which leads you step by step through the process of creating a chart. All you have to do is enter your preferences. To use the Chart Wizard, take the following steps:

1. Select the data you want to chart. If you typed names or other labels (Qtr 1, Qtr 2, and so on) and you want them included in the chart (as labels), include them in the selection.

2. Click the **Chart Wizard** button in the Standard toolbar. The Chart Wizard Step 1 of 4 dialog box appears, asking you to select the desired chart type. (Ignore the Custom Types tab for now.)

3. Make sure the **Standard Types** tab is up front, and then click the desired chart type in the **Chart Type** list, as shown in Figure 14.1. The Chart Sub-type list displays various renditions of the selected type.

4. In the **Chart Sub-type** list, click the chart design you want to use. (To see how this chart type appears when it charts your data, point to **Press and Hold to View Sample** and hold down the mouse button.)

5. Click the **Next** button. The Chart Wizard Step 2 of 4 dialog box appears, asking you to specify the worksheet data you want to chart. (I know, I already told you to select the data; but the Chart Wizard is just making sure you selected the correct data. Note that the worksheet name, followed by an exclamation point, appears at the beginning of the range.)

6. If the data you want to graph is already selected, go to step 7. If the Chart Wizard is highlighting the wrong data, drag over the correct data in your worksheet, as shown in Figure 14.2. (You can move the Chart Wizard dialog box out of the way by clicking the **Collapse Dialog Box** button just to the right of the Data Range text box.)

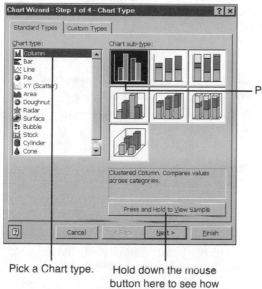

Figure 14.1

The Chart Wizard leads you through the process of charting your data.

Pick a Chart sub-type.

Pick a Chart type.

Hold down the mouse button here to see how your data looks with the selected type.

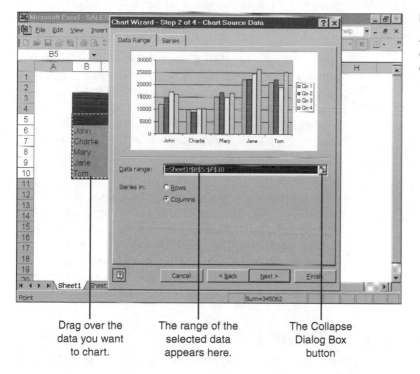

Figure 14.2

If you selected the wrong data, you get a second chance to change it.

Drag over the data you want to chart.

The range of the selected data appears here.

The Collapse Dialog Box button

7. Under Series In, click **Rows** or **Columns** to specify how you want the data graphed. Your selection tells Excel which labels to use for the category axis and which ones to use for the legend. This is a tough choice that is best done by trial and error.

8. Click the **Next** button. The Chart Wizard Step 3 of 4 dialog box appears, prompting you to enter additional preferences for your chart.

9. Enter your preferences on the various tabs to give your chart a title, name the X and Y axes, turn on additional gridlines, move the legend, enter data labels, and more. Most of these options are described in "Adding Text, Arrows, and Other Objects," later in this chapter.

10. Click the **Next** button. The Chart Wizard Step 4 of 4 dialog box appears, asking whether you want to insert the chart on the current worksheet or on a new worksheet.

11. If you want the chart to appear alongside your data, select **As Object In** and select the worksheet on which you want the chart to appear. To have the chart appear on a worksheet of its own, select **As New Sheet** and type a name for the sheet.

12. Click **Finish**. Excel makes the chart and slaps it on a worksheet.

If your chart has only two or three data types to graph, it probably looks okay. If you choose to graph several columns or rows, chances are that all your data labels are scrunched up, your legend is chopped in half, and several other eyesores litter your chart. Fortunately, you can fix most of these problems by resizing the chart.

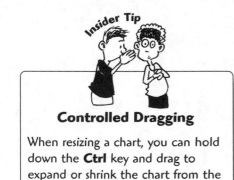

Controlled Dragging

When resizing a chart, you can hold down the **Ctrl** key and drag to expand or shrink the chart from the center. Hold down the **Shift** key and drag to ensure that the chart retains its relative dimensions.

If you inserted the chart as an object, you can move and resize the chart. First click the chart's background to select it. (If you haven't clicked outside the chart since creating it, it is already selected and the Chart toolbar is displayed.) Make sure you click the chart's background and not some object on the chart itself. If you click an object, such as the data area, that object is selected. This can be a bit tricky at first.

Excel displays tiny squares around the chart, called *handles*. To resize the chart, drag one of its handles. To move the chart, position the mouse pointer over the chart (not on a handle), and drag the chart to the desired location. To delete the chart and start over, select the chart and press the **Delete** key. If the chart is on a separate worksheet, delete the worksheet.

So Now You Want to Print It?

After you create a chart, your first impulse is to click the Print button to see what your printer spits out. Resist the urge. Unless you have some great beginner's luck, the printout probably won't live up to your expectations. It might have some overlapping text, data that's all scrunched together, and a few other minor problems. Work through this chapter to find out how to give your chart an adjustment.

 When your chart is ready for the printer or when you think it's ready, click the chart and then click the **Print Preview** button (or select **File**, **Print Preview**) to check it out. You don't want to waste paper printing a second-rate chart.

 No, don't click that Print button just yet. If you want to print a full-page version of a chart that's embedded on a worksheet without printing the cell entries, select the chart first, and then click the **Print** button. To print the entire worksheet, including the chart, click somewhere in the worksheet, but outside the chart, to deselect the chart, and then click the **Print** button. (For additional instructions on how to use Excel's printing options, see Chapter 15, "Printing Wide Worksheets on Narrow Pages.")

Changing Your Chart with Toolbars, Menus, and Right-Clicks

Before you get your hands dirty tinkering with the many preferences that control the appearance and behavior of your chart, you need to know where you can find these options. The first place to look for options is the Chart menu. If you don't see the Chart menu, you haven't selected a chart yet. Click a chart, and the Chart menu appears. This menu contains options for changing the chart type, selecting different data to chart, adding data, and even moving the chart to its own page.

A quicker way to access these same options is to right-click a blank area of the chart to display a pop-up menu. Why a blank area? Because if you right-click a legend, an axis, a title, or another element in the chart, the pop-up menu displays options that pertain only to that element, not to the entire chart.

The third way to format your chart is to use the Chart toolbar. To display it, right-click any toolbar and click **Chart**. The Chart toolbar offers the following formatting tools (if a button you want to use is not on the toolbar, click the **Toolbar Options** button, on the right end of the toolbar, and then click the desired button):

Chart Objects. Displays a list of the elements inside the chart. Select the item you want to format from this list, and then click the **Format *Selected Object*** button. (The name in place of *Selected Object* varies depending on the object. If you selected the legend, the button's name is Format Legend.)

 Format Chart Area. Displays a dialog box that contains formatting options for only the specified chart object, so you don't have to view a bunch of formatting options you can't apply to the selected object.

 Chart Type. Enables you to change the chart type (bar, line, pie, and so on).

Legend. Turns the legend on or off.

Data Table. Turns the data table on or off. A data table displays the charted data in a table right next to (or on top of) the chart, so you can see the data and chart next to each other.

Series in Rows. Charts selected data by row. (Again, when choosing to chart by row or column, trial by error is the best method. Click **By Row.** If the chart doesn't look right, click **By Column.**)

Series in Columns. Charts selected data by column.

Angle Clockwise. Enables you to angle text entries so they slant down from left to right. Angled text not only looks cool, but it's great for cramming in a bunch of axis labels when you're running out of space.

Angle Counterclockwise. Enables you to angle data labels so they slant up from left to right.

Now that you know the various paths to the chart options, you're ready to tackle some hands-on formatting.

Bar Charts, Pie Charts, and Other Goodies

Choosing the right chart type for your data is almost as important as choosing the right data. To see how your salespeople are doing relative to each other, a bar chart clearly illustrates the comparisons. To show the percentage of the total sales revenue that each salesperson is contributing, however, a pie chart is better. Excel offers a wide selection of charts, enabling you to find the perfect chart for your data.

To change the chart type, right-click your chart and click **Chart Type**. The Chart Type dialog box appears, providing a wide selection of chart types. Click the **Standard Types** or **Custom Types** tab (the Custom Types tab offers special chart types, most of which are combinations of two chart types, such as a bar chart and a line chart). Select the desired chart type from the **Chart Type** list. On the Standard Types tab, pick the desired chart design from the **Chart Sub-type** list. When you're finished, click **OK** to apply the new settings.

Formatting the Elements That Make Up a Chart

The Chart Wizard is pretty good about prompting you to specify preferences when you first create a chart; but you might have skipped some of the options or chosen to omit some objects, such as the legend and chart title. Whatever the case, you always can add and format chart objects later.

The easiest way to add objects to a chart is to use the Chart Options dialog box, shown in Figure 14.3. (The tabs and options in this dialog box vary depending on the chart type; a pie chart, for instance, has no axes or gridlines.) To display this dialog box, right-click your chart and click **Chart Options**. You can then add or remove the following items:

➤ **Chart Title**—Click the **Titles** tab and type a title in the **Chart Title** text box. The title appears above the chart, providing a general description of it.

➤ **Axis Titles**—Click the **Titles** tab to type a title for the vertical (Y) axis, the horizontal (X) axis, or the depth (Z) axis (in 3D charts). (Axis titles describe the data that's charted along each axis.)

➤ **X and Y Axes**—Bar, column, line, area, and stock charts all have two axes (X and Y); 3D versions of these chart types include a third axis (Z). You can hide the values or labels for any of these axes by clicking the **Axes** tab and removing the check next to the axis whose values or labels you want to hide. This tab is not available for charts that do not use axes, such as pie charts.

➤ **Gridlines**—Every chart that has X and Y axes displays hash marks along the axes to show major divisions. You can extend these hash marks to run across the chart (sort of like graph paper). Click the **Gridlines** tab and turn on any gridlines you want to use.

➤ **Legend**—This tab enables you to add a legend to your chart and specify its location. Legends display a color chart matching each color in the chart to the data that the color represents. This chart feature is particularly important if the chart is printed in black and white, using patterns or shades of gray.

➤ **Data Labels**—The Data Labels tab enables you to add text entries from your worksheet above the various bars or lines that graph specific data. These labels usually make the chart more cluttered than it already is.

➤ **Data Table**—This tab enables you turn on a data table to display specific values alongside the graph. This is another option that can make your chart overly cramped.

Run the Chart Wizard Again

If you love the Chart Wizard, you can use it to add items to your chart. Click your chart to select it, and then click the **Chart Wizard** button. This displays the Step 1 through Step 4 dialog boxes you used to create the chart in the first place.

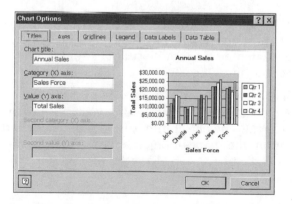

Figure 14.3

The Chart Options dialog box enables you to add items to your chart.

To dazzle your boss and impress your friends, try the following chart tricks:

➤ If you have a three-dimensional chart, select **Chart**, **3-D View**, and use the options in the 3-D View dialog box to rotate the chart. You can even provide an aerial view of your chart.

➤ Right-click a series (for example, the bars representing the sales for one of your salespeople) and click **Format Data Series**. Use the resulting dialog box to change the color and shape used for the series.

➤ Don't like that dingy white chart background? Change it. Right-click the background, select **Format Chart Area**, and select the desired color. To give your chart a matching background, right-click the chart, select **Format**, **Plot Area**, and enter your preferences.

My Context Menu Doesn't Have the Options You Mentioned!

The context menu options vary depending on the chart object you select. If you intend to click the plot area but click a bar in the chart instead, the context menu displays the Format Data Series option rather than Format Plot Area. Try clicking various objects that make up the chart and keep an eye on the selection handles that appear. This will give you a clearer picture of the objects that make up your chart.

Adding Text, Arrows, and Other Objects

You have a chart decorated with all sorts of embellishments, but it's still missing something. Maybe you want to stick a starburst on it that says "Another Record Year!" or point out to your business partner that the new product he developed five years ago is still losing money.

You can add items to your chart by using the Drawing toolbar. Click the **Drawing** button in the Standard toolbar to turn on the Drawing toolbar. (For details on using the Drawing toolbar's tools, see "Sketching Custom Illustrations" in Chapter 7, "Spicing It Up with Graphics, Sound, and Video.")

If you're too lazy to flip back to Chapter 7 (I don't blame you), just rest the mouse pointer on a button to figure out what it does. In most cases, you can draw an object by clicking a button and then dragging the object into existence on your chart. When you release the mouse button, the shape or object appears. You can then drag the object to move it, or drag a handle to resize it. Figure 14.4 shows some of the objects you can add to your chart.

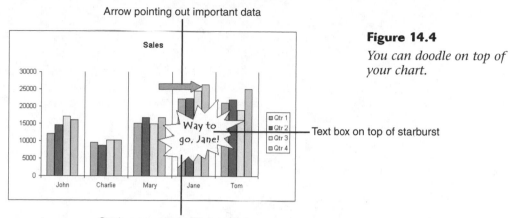

Arrow pointing out important data

Figure 14.4

You can doodle on top of your chart.

Text box on top of starburst

Starburst created with AutoShapes

The Least You Need to Know

The Chart Wizard makes creating charts so easy that you can forget almost everything in this chapter, as long as you can do the following:

➤ To initiate the Chart Wizard, drag over the data you want to chart and then click the **Chart Wizard** button.

➤ To print only a chart, click the chart and then click the **Print** button. To print a chart along with the worksheet data, make sure the chart is NOT selected, and then click the **Print** button.

➤ To display the Chart toolbar, right-click any toolbar or the menu bar in Excel and click **Chart**.

➤ To change the chart type, right-click your chart and click **Chart Type**.

➤ To further customize your chart, right-click your chart and click **Chart Options** (this displays the Chart Options dialog box).

➤ To enhance your chart with other graphic objects, such as arrows and lines, click the **Drawing** button in the Standard toolbar.

Chapter 15

Printing Wide Worksheets on Narrow Pages

In This Chapter

➤ What to do before you print

➤ Formatting tricks to make your worksheet fit on one page

➤ Repeating column headings on every page

➤ Playing hide-and-seek with columns and rows

➤ Designating print areas

Printing worksheets is Excel's version of two pounds of baloney in a one-pound bag. Worksheets are typically too wide for standard 8.5-by-11-inch paper and often too wide for legal paper, even if you print them sideways on a page. You almost need to print some worksheets on banner paper to get them to fit.

Fortunately, Excel is quite aware of the limitations you face when trying to cram wide worksheets on narrow pieces of paper; and it offers several features that can help. In this chapter, you learn how to use these features.

Preprinting: Laying the Groundwork

Before you even think about clicking that Print button, check your page setup and take a look at how Excel is prepared to print your worksheets. Nine times out of ten, Excel will insert awkward page breaks, omit titles and column headings from some of the pages, and use additional settings that will result in an unacceptable printout.

To check your worksheet before printing, click the **Print Preview** button (or select **File, Print Preview**). This displays your worksheet in Print Preview mode, as shown in Figure 15.1, so you can at least see how Excel is going to lay out your worksheet on pages. When you are finished previewing your pages, click the **Close** button to return to the main Excel screen.

Click the Zoom button to zoom in or out.

With Margins on, you can drag margin and column markers to adjust the margins and column widths.

Figure 15.1

Preview your worksheet before you print it.

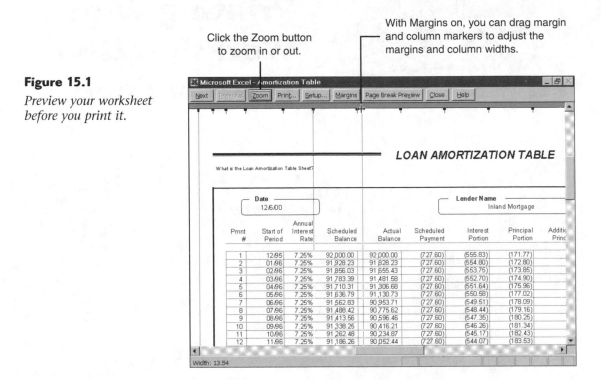

Portrait or Landscape: Setting the Page Orientation

If you have a close fit, you usually can adjust the left and right margins to pull another column or two onto the page. If the worksheet still doesn't fit, your best bet is to change to landscape orientation. This prints the worksheet sideways on the page, giving you about three more inches for your columns. To change the page orientation, take the following steps:

1. Open the **File** menu and select **Page Setup**.
2. In the Page Setup dialog box, click the **Page** tab and select **Landscape**.
3. Click **OK**.

Checking and Moving Page Breaks

As you create your worksheet, Excel displays dotted lines to indicate where it is going to divide the pages. You can insert your own page breaks by using the **Insert, Page Break** command. However, Excel has a feature called Page Break Preview that displays page breaks more clearly and enables you to easily move page breaks by dragging them.

To turn on Page Break Preview, either open the **View** menu and select **Page Break Preview** or click the **Page Break Preview** button in Print Preview. Excel displays page breaks as thick blue lines and displays the page number in big gray type on each page. You can then drag the lines with your mouse to move them, as shown in Figure 15.2. Although this does not help you fit the worksheet on a page, it does give you control over how Excel divides the columns and rows that make up your worksheet. When you're done, open the **View** menu and select **Normal**.

Page number

Figure 15.2

You can drag the blue lines in Page Break Preview to move the page breaks.

Page break

To insert a new page break, click the cell below and to the right of where you want the new page break inserted. Open the **Insert** menu and select **Page Break**. Excel inserts a horizontal page break above the selected cell and a vertical page break to the left of the cell. The page breaks appear as dotted lines. (To insert only a horizontal page break, click the cell that's below the point where you want the page break inserted in column A. To insert only a vertical page break, click the cell to the right of where you want the page break inserted in row 1.)

Insider Tip

Resizing Charts

Page Break Preview is excellent for resizing charts to make them fit on a page.

To remove a page break that you inserted, right-click the cell below the horizontal page break or to the right of the vertical page break, open the **Insert** menu, and select **Remove Page Break**.

Repeating Titles and Column Labels

If your worksheet gets chopped in half by an errant page break, page two omits the row and column labels that indicate the contents of each row or column. This can make it difficult to make sense of any values on page two or subsequent pages. To have Excel repeat the row and column labels on each page, take the following steps:

1. Open the **File** menu and select **Page Setup**.
2. In the Page Setup dialog box, click the **Sheet** tab, as shown in Figure 15.3.
3. To have column labels repeat, click the button next to the **Rows to Repeat at Top** text box. This hides the dialog box, so you easily can select the rows that contain the desired column labels. A small toolbar appears, displaying a button for redisplaying the dialog box.
4. Drag over the rows that contain the column labels that you want repeated, and then click the button to bring the dialog box back into view.
5. To have row labels repeat, click the button next to the **Columns to Repeat at Left** text box. This hides the dialog box.
6. Drag over the columns that contain the row labels you want repeated, and then click the button to bring the dialog box back into view.
7. Click **OK**.

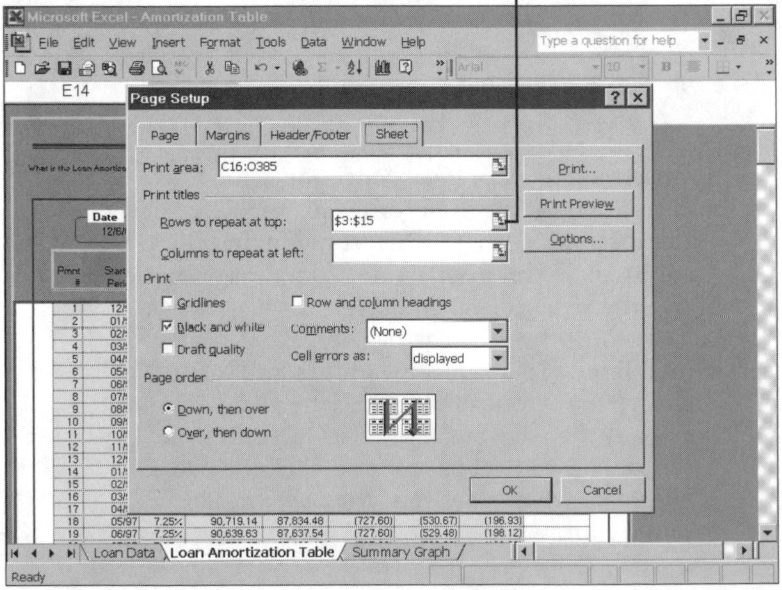

Click this button to hide the dialog box so that you can drag over the desired rows.

Figure 15.3

You can choose to have row and column labels printed on every page.

Adding Headers and Footers

Excel can print a footer (on the bottom of each page) or a header (at the top of each page) that automatically numbers the worksheet pages for you and prints the file's name, the worksheet title, the date and time, and other information. To include headers and footers on your worksheets, take the following steps:

1. Open the **View** menu and select **Header and Footer**. The Page Setup dialog box appears with the Header/Footer tab in front.

2. To use a header, open the **Header** drop-down list and click the desired header.

3. To use a footer, open the **Footer** drop-down list and click the desired footer.

4. Click **OK**.

Whoa!

Printing Row Numbers and Column Letters

You might think that the Row and Column Headings option in the Page Setup dialog box would print the labels from your rows and columns. Actually, turning on this option tells Excel to print the row numbers and column letters.

To create your own header or footer (for example, to include your name or company's name), click one of the **Custom** buttons on the Header/Footer tab. This displays a dialog box that enables you to create a header or footer consisting of three sections. Type the desired text in each section, and use the dialog box buttons to format the text and insert codes for the date, time, filename, worksheet name, and page numbers. To insert "Page 1 of 5," "Page 2 of 5," and so on, type **Page**, press the spacebar, click the # button, press the spacebar, and click the ++ button. # inserts the number of the current page, and ++ inserts the total number of pages.

Setting the Page Order

Earlier in this chapter, you saw that Excel divides long, wide worksheets into pages using both horizontal and vertical page breaks. By default, Excel prints pages from top to bottom, printing all pages to the left of the vertical page break and then pages to the right of the vertical page break. In most cases, this is how you want your pages printed, so you can easily read each column from top to bottom. If, however, you typically read the worksheet data from left to right, you want Excel to print the pages from left to right. To change the page order, open the **File** menu, select **Page Setup**, and click the **Sheet** tab, as shown in Figure 15.4. Under **Page Order**, select **Over, Then Down**. Click **OK**.

Figure 15.4

If your worksheet has both horizontal and vertical page breaks, select the desired page order.

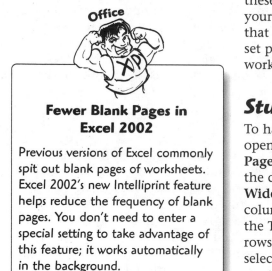

Print pages from top to bottom. ——— Print pages from left to right. ———

When It Just Won't Fit

You adjusted the column widths, changed the page orientation, fiddled with the margins, and maybe even cranked down the font settings. Short of selecting a one-point font, you've done everything you could, and the darn thing still doesn't fit on a page. Lucky for you, Excel has a couple more printing tricks tucked up its sleeve. With these tricks, you can have Excel automatically reformat your worksheet to make it fit on a page, hide columns that contain nonessential or confidential data, or even set print areas to selectively print sections of your worksheet.

Fewer Blank Pages in Excel 2002

Previous versions of Excel commonly spit out blank pages of worksheets. Excel 2002's new Intelliprint feature helps reduce the frequency of blank pages. You don't need to enter a special setting to take advantage of this feature; it works automatically in the background.

Stuff It with "Print to Fit"

To have Excel scale your worksheet to fit on a page, open the **File** menu, select **Page Setup**, and click the **Page** tab. Under **Scaling**, select **Fit To**, and then enter the desired number of pages wide and tall. Use the **Wide** spin box if your worksheet has one or more columns that run past the vertical page break, and use the **Tall** spin box if your worksheet runs one or more rows beyond a horizontal page break. Alternatively, select **Adjust To** and enter the desired scaling percentage to reduce the overall width and height of the worksheet. Click **OK**.

Selective Printing with Print Areas

Worksheets commonly contain much more data than you need to print, so Excel enables you to print selected sections of your worksheets. To print a selection, you mark it as a *print area*. When Excel prints the worksheet, it prints only the area marked as a print area.

To mark a print area quickly, first select the cells that contain the data you want to print. Open the **File** menu, point to **Print Area**, and select **Set Print Area**. To remove the print area later, open the **File** menu, point to **Print Area**, and select **Clear Print Area**.

Hiding Columns and Rows

Another way to print selectively is to hide columns or rows that contain data not required in the printout. To hide columns or rows and prevent Excel from printing them, take the following steps:

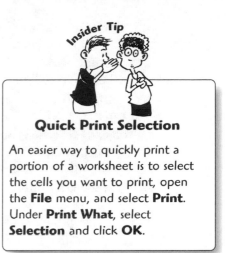

Quick Print Selection

An easier way to quickly print a portion of a worksheet is to select the cells you want to print, open the **File** menu, and select **Print**. Under **Print What**, select **Selection** and click **OK**.

1. Drag over the column or row headers for the columns or rows you want to hide.

2. Open the **Format** menu and select **Column, Hide** or **Row, Hide**. (Alternatively, right-click and select **Hide** from the context menu.) A dark line appears on the worksheet to indicate that rows or columns are hidden.

3. Click the **Print Preview** button. Excel displays the worksheet, omitting the hidden columns or rows.

Bringing hidden rows or columns back into view isn't the most intuitive operation. First, drag over the column or row headings before and after the hidden columns and rows. If columns C, D, and E are hidden, for example, drag over column headings B and F to select them. Open the **Format** menu and select **Columns, Unhide** or **Rows, Unhide**.

Finally! Printing Your Worksheets

 Your worksheet is looking pretty good in Print Preview, and you're just itching to print it. The quickest way to print is to click the tab for the worksheet you want to print and then click the **Print** button. This sends the worksheet off to the printer, no questions asked. To print more than one worksheet or set additional printing preferences, take the following steps:

1. Click the tab for the worksheet you want to print. Ctrl+click tabs to print additional worksheets. (To print all the worksheets in the workbook, you can skip this step.)

2. Open the **File** menu and select **Print** (or press **Ctrl+P**). The Print dialog box appears, as shown in Figure 15.5.

3. To print all the worksheets in the workbook, select **Entire Workbook**. Excel prints all worksheets that contain entries.

4. To print one or more pages of the selected worksheets, select **Page(s)** under **Print Range** and enter the page numbers to specify the range.

5. To print more than one copy, specify the desired number of copies under **Copies**.

6. You can click the **Properties** button to enter additional printer settings, including the print quality. After entering the desired settings, click **OK** to return to the Print dialog box.

7. Click the **OK** button to start printing.

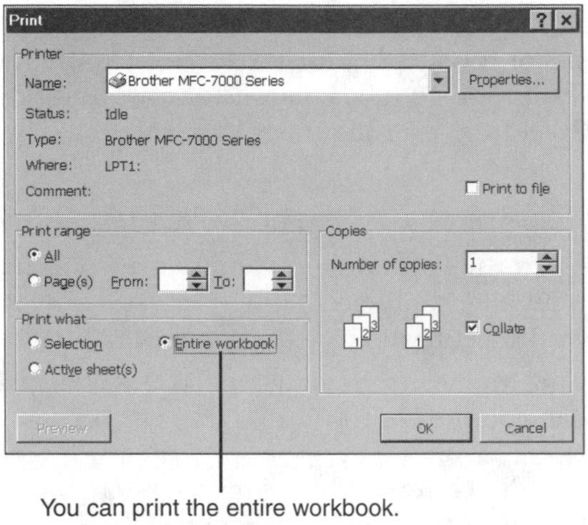

Figure 15.5

Enter the desired printing preferences and click OK.

You can print the entire workbook.

The Least You Need to Know

With all the printing tools and tricks described in this chapter, you should now be able to fit your longest, widest worksheets on 8.5-by-11-inch sheets of paper. Just remember to have plenty of tape and make sure you've mastered these printing basics:

➤ Before you print your worksheets, click the **Print Preview** button to inspect them.

➤ To print sideways on a page, open the **File** menu, click **Page Setup**, click the **Page** tab, click **Landscape**, and click **OK**.

➤ To inspect page breaks, open the **View** menu and select **Page Break Preview**.

➤ To make your spreadsheet title and column labels print on every page, select **File**, **Page Setup** and enter your preferences on the **Sheet** tab.

➤ To have Excel scale your worksheet to fit on a page, select **File**, **Page Setup**, click the **Page** tab, select **Fit To**, and then enter the desired number of pages wide and tall.

➤ To mark a print area quickly, select the cells that contain the data you want to print, and then select **File**, **Print Area**, **Set Print Area**.

➤ To print one or more worksheets, open the **File** menu, click **Print**, enter your printing preferences, and click **OK**.

Part 4

Snapping Slide Shows in PowerPoint

You've seen business presentation programs in action. Some suit stands in front of a group of other suits—usually in a cramped boardroom with a big oak table—and flips through a series of slides, pitching a new product or showing how profitable the company is. Each slide is packed with graphs, illustrations, and bulleted lists, carefully designed to drive home the speaker's point.

Now, with PowerPoint and the chapters in this part, you get your chance to play a high-powered executive. You learn how to create a professional-looking slide show; add graphs, pictures, and lists; and display your slide show on your computer screen or output it on paper, 35mm slides, or even overhead transparencies. You even learn how to make a slide show that runs on any PC, even if the PC is not running PowerPoint!

Chapter 16

Slapping Together a Basic Slide Show

In This Chapter

➤ Using PowerPoint's ready-made slide shows

➤ Changing the overall design of your slides

➤ The five faces of PowerPoint

➤ Controlling all your slides by changing one master slide

You don't have to be a media expert to create the perfect slide show. PowerPoint enables you to start with a predesigned slide show. All you have to do is select a background color and design for the slide show, and then insert a few objects (pictures, bulleted lists, charts, sounds, and video clips) on each slide. Then, just dim the lights, and you're ready to go! In this chapter, you learn slide show basics. Later chapters in this part show you the fancy stuff, including how to present your slide show.

Start from Scratch? Never!

Most applications greet you with a blank screen, daring you to create something. PowerPoint is different. Whenever you start PowerPoint (**Start, Programs, Microsoft PowerPoint**), the New Presentation task pane appears, as shown in Figure 16.1, providing you with a list of options for creating a new presentation. You have several choices: Start with a blank presentation, select a design template to control the overall appearance of your slides, use the AutoContent Wizard to help you design a slide show based on the content of your presentation, pick up a design from an existing presentation (which you or a colleague created), or base your presentation on a template (a PowerPoint template or a template on your Web site or Microsoft's Web site).

Assuming you don't have a presentation and you don't want to start from scratch, create your presentation using the AutoContent Wizard or a template. The following sections provide instructions for each method.

The new New Presentation task pane

Figure 16.1

When you start PowerPoint, the New Presentation task pane displays your options.

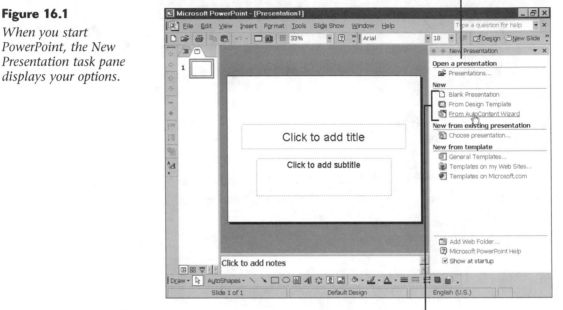

You can choose to start with a blank presentation, a design template, or the AutoContent Wizard.

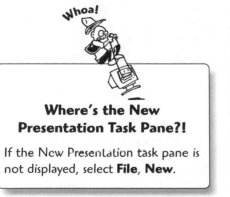

Using the AutoContent Wizard

Do you need to pitch a marketing strategy? Sell a product? Train new employees? Advertise your company on the World Wide Web? Whatever you need to do, just tell the AutoContent Wizard and let it lead you through the process of creating your slide show. The wizard picks the template you need, enables you to specify the desired output type (35mm slides, overhead transparencies, and so on), and creates a standard presentation that you can customize.

Where's the New Presentation Task Pane?!

If the New Presentation task pane is not displayed, select **File**, **New**.

To use the AutoContent Wizard, start PowerPoint and click the **From AutoContent Wizard** link. The first wizard dialog box appears on your screen. Follow the wizard's onscreen instructions, entering preferences for your presentation. Click the **Next** button to advance from one dialog box to the next. You can display the previous dialog box at any time during this process by clicking the **Back** button.

You will encounter a couple of confusing areas. First, when the wizard lists the type of presentations from which you can choose, a dialog box appears within the wizard dialog box with several buttons, including Add and Remove. Don't click either button. Just click the button for the desired presentation category and click the specific presentation you want to create; then, click the wizard's **Next** button. The second tricky part is the choice of output:

➤ **On-screen presentation**—Designs the presentation to be played on a computer. Select this option if you plan to have your audience play the presentation on a computer or plan to give the presentation using special equipment connected to a computer (such as a projector and speakers).

➤ **Web presentation**—Converts the slides into Web pages that your audience can view using a standard Web browser, such as Internet Explorer or Netscape Navigator. Select this option to create a presentation to be stored on a Web server.

➤ **Black and white overheads**—Provides slide designs that are optimized for black-and-white output on overhead transparencies. Select this option if you don't have a color printer or if you want to cut costs by printing in black and white.

➤ **Color overheads**—Optimizes the slide show design for color output. If you have a color printer, select this option.

➤ **35mm slides**—Transfers your presentation to 35mm slides to create a slide show such as those used in the old days. If you don't have the proper equipment, you can send your slide show on disk or via modem to a company that has the required equipment. (See Chapter 18, "Shuffling and Presenting Your Slide Show," for details.)

When you reach the final dialog box, click the **Finish** button. The wizard creates the slide show and displays it in Normal view, as shown in Figure 16.2. (Each slide contains instructions that you must replace with your own text.)

Quick Slide Navigation

PowerPoint 2002 features an Outline/Slide pane on the left that enables you to view an outline of your presentation or thumbnail images of each slide. To display a specific slide, simply click the desired slide heading or thumbnail. See "Changing Views to Edit and Sort Your Slides," later in this chapter, for details on how to view slides and navigate your presentation.

Figure 16.2

PowerPoint displays your presentation in Normal view.

Click this tab to view an outline of the entire presentation.

Thumbnail views of the slides

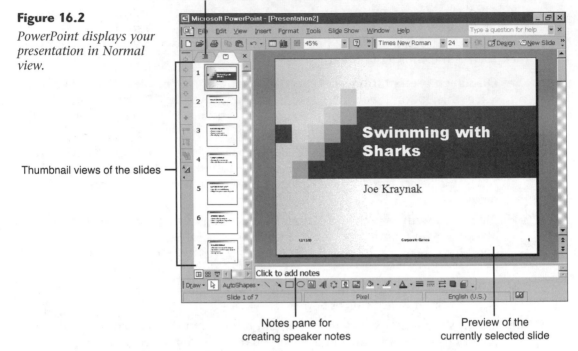

Notes pane for creating speaker notes

Preview of the currently selected slide

Starting with a Design Template

No wizardry is involved in creating a presentation from a template. After you start PowerPoint, click the **From Design Template** link in the New Presentation task pane and click the thumbnail for the desired design in the **Apply a Design Template** list. If the New Presentation task pane is not shown, open PowerPoint's **File** menu and select **New**.

After you click the thumbnail for the desired design, PowerPoint creates a one-slide presentation using the default slide layout, design, and color scheme. On the right is the Slide Design task pane, where you can change the overall appearance of the slide show. Simply click one of the links at the top of the pane (**Design Templates**, **Color Schemes**, or **Animation Schemes**), and then click the desired design template, color scheme, or animation scheme in the list below the links.

After entering your preferences for the overall slide show appearance, you can start inserting new slides, as explained later in this chapter.

Changing Views to Edit and Sort Your Slides

Assuming that all has gone as planned, you now have a slide show (or at least one slide) onscreen. PowerPoint enables you to display your slide show in four views so you can work more easily on various aspects of your presentation. Before you start modifying your slide show, familiarize yourself with these views:

➤ **Normal**—A combination of Slide, Outline, and Notes views, Normal view displays your presentation outline in the left pane, the selected slide in the right pane, and a notes area in the lower-right pane. This is the default view, as you saw in Figure 16.2. The notes area is useful for creating speaker notes. You can close the outline pane on the left by clicking its **Close (X)** button. To bring it back into view, open the **View** menu and click **Normal (Restore Panes)**.

➤ **Slide Sorter**—Great for rearranging the slides in your presentation. Slide Sorter view displays a thumbnail sketch of each slide, which you can drag to move the slide. (Slide Sorter view is explained in greater detail in Chapter 18.)

➤ **Notes Page**—Displays speaker notes pages, should you choose to create them. A copy of the slide appears at the top of the page, and your notes appear at the bottom. (To view the Notes page, open the **View** menu and select **Notes Page**.)

➤ **Slide Show**—Displays your slides as they will appear in an actual slide show. It enables you to check the transitions from one slide to another and test any animation effects that you might have added. (See Chapter 18 for details.)

The easiest way to change from one view to another is to click the button for the desired view in the lower-left corner of the window (see Figure 16.3). You can also select the desired view from the View menu.

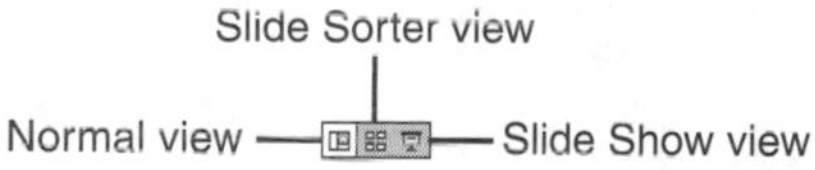

Slide Sorter view

Normal view ——— Slide Show view

Figure 16.3

Use the view buttons to change quickly from one view to another.

Working on Slides

If you created a slide using the AutoContent Wizard, you might have one or more slides that have a box telling you to "double-click" to add something (such as a graphic image or recorded message). Simply double-click where PowerPoint prompts you to double-click and follow the onscreen instructions. (Chapter 17, "Adding Text, Graphics, and Sounds to a Slide," shows you how to place additional text boxes and other objects on your slides.)

Black and White View

 If you're planning to print your slide show using a black–and–white printer, it's a good idea to change to Black and White or Grayscale view. Open the **View** menu, point to **Color/Grayscale**, and click **Grayscale** or **Pure Black and White**, or click the **Color/Grayscale** button in the Standard toolbar and click **Grayscale** or **Pure Black and White**. (You might need to click the **More Buttons** icon on the right end of the Standard toolbar to display the Color/Grayscale button.)

To edit text directly on a slide, click the text. When you click a text object, a box appears around it with several selection handles (small circles). To work with these text boxes, use any of the following techniques:

➤ To move a text box, position the mouse pointer over an edge of the box until it turns into a four-headed arrow, and then drag the box. (When the box is selected, you can use the arrow keys to position it more precisely.)

➤ To resize a box, position the mouse pointer over one of the handles (the mouse pointer turns into a two-headed arrow). Drag the handle.

➤ To edit text inside a box, drag over the text and type new text.

Organizing Your Presentation

To rearrange your presentation using the outline, display the Outlining toolbar by right-clicking any toolbar and selecting **Outlining**. You can then use the following buttons to restructure your presentation:

 Promote. Raises the selected items one level in the outline. If you select a bullet that's directly below a slide title and click Promote, for example, the bullet becomes the title of a new slide.

 Demote. Lowers the selected items one level in the outline. If you click an item in a bulleted list and click Demote, the bullet becomes part of a bulleted sublist.

 Move Up. Moves any items you select up in the outline. You can use this button to rearrange items on a slide or move items from one slide to another. (Before using the Move Up or Move Down button to move slides, click the **Collapse All** button as explained later in this list.)

Move Down. The same as the Move Up button, but in the other direction. You can also move items up or down by selecting them and then dragging their icons or bullets: up or down.

Collapse. Displays less detail on a slide. Select the slide's title before clicking this button to hide any bulleted items or other subtext.

Expand. Redisplays the detail on a slide that you hid using the Collapse button.

Collapse All. Hides all the bulleted text in your slide show so that only slide titles are displayed.

Expand All. Redisplays bulleted text that you hid by clicking Collapse All.

Summary Slide. Inserts a slide that pulls titles from other slides in the show to create an overview of the presentation. You can then transform these titles into hyperlinks and use the summary slide to jump to different slides or slide show sequences.

Show Formatting. Turns the character formatting for the slide show text on or off. (Sometimes you can focus more effectively on the content if you don't have to look at the formatting.)

Inserting and Deleting Slides

PowerPoint's prefab presentations are great, but they either stick you with a bunch of slides you don't need or leave you short, providing you with one solitary slide. In other words, you're going to have to either delete slides or insert them. Deleting slides is easy. In the outline or in Slide Sorter view, click the slide you want to nuke and press **Delete**. In Normal view, display the slide, open the **Edit** menu, and select **Delete Slide**.

Inserting slides is a little more challenging. Select the slide after which you want the new slide inserted. Open the **Insert** menu and select **New Slide**, or click the **New Slide** button in the Formatting toolbar. Don't confuse the New Slide button (on the Formatting toolbar) with the New button (on the Standard toolbar). The New button creates a new presentation. The New Slide button, on the other hand, creates a new slide in the current presentation.

When you enter the New Slide command, PowerPoint immediately inserts a new slide and displays the Slide Layout task pane, which prompts you to select an overall layout for the

Whoa!

Crisis Management with Undo

If you mistakenly delete a slide that you just spent the last half hour creating, click the **Undo** button to get it back.

slide. These predesigned layouts contain text boxes for titles and bulleted lists, graphic boxes for inserting clip art or charts, and additional objects that you must alter to create your slide. Click the desired layout to apply it to the new slide. PowerPoint gives the new slide the same background and color as all the other slides in the presentation.

Changing the Background, Color Scheme, and Layout

When you use a wizard or a template to create your presentation, PowerPoint gives all the slides in the presentation the same overall appearance, which is usually what you want; however, the color scheme and background design are not carved in stone. You easily can change them for one slide or for all the slides in the presentation.

To change the background, color scheme, or layout for a *single* slide, first select the slide. (You don't have to select a slide if you're changing the background or color scheme for the whole show.) After you select a slide (or choose not to select a slide), read the following sections to learn how to change the background, color scheme, and layout for the slide(s).

Applying a Different Design to the Entire Presentation

When you first created your slide show, you picked an overall design for your presentation. If you have since changed your mind, open the **Format** menu and select **Slide Design**, or click the **Slide Design** button in the Formatting toolbar. The Slide Design task pane appears, displaying links for changing the design template, color scheme, and animation scheme. Click the **Design Templates** link, and then click the desired design. (To apply the design to only selected slides, point to the desired design, click the button that appears to the right of the design, and click **Apply to Selected Slides**.)

Lifting a Design from a Presentation

If you or someone else has already created a custom design for a presentation, you can apply that design to the current presentation. Click the **Browse** link (near the bottom of the Slide Design task pane). Change to the drive and folder where the presentation is stored. Click the desired presentation and then click the **Apply** button.

Changing the Background

Behind every slide is a color background. You can change the background color and pattern and even use a picture as the background. To change the background, open the **Format** menu and select **Background** to display the Background dialog box. Open the **Background Fill** drop-down list and select the desired color swatch. To use a custom color, click **More Colors**, and then use the Colors dialog box to pick a color or create your own custom color.

Colors are swell, but if you want to jazz up a slide show, you need to give your slides a background pattern or texture. To do this, display the Background dialog box, open the **Background Fill** drop-down list, and select **Fill Effects**. The Fill Effects dialog box appears, as shown in Figure 16.4, offering four tabs packed with options for adding shading styles, textures, patterns, or a background picture to your presentation. The best way to get a feel for these options is to experiment while keeping an eye on the Sample area.

Think Ahead

When choosing colored or textured backgrounds, think about how you plan to output your slides. A textured background might look great on 35mm slides but awful in print or on transparencies. If you're planning to publish your presentation electronically on the Web, keep in mind that the background might look fine in your Web browser but terrible when displayed in other browsers.

Picking a Different Color Scheme

Every template is set up to display the various elements on a slide in a different color. Slide titles are one color, bulleted items are another color, and fills are another color. You can change the colors used for the various elements. Open the **Format** menu, select **Slide Design**, and then click the **Color Schemes** link in the Slide Design task bar.

The Slide Design task pane displays a list of predesigned color schemes. To stay on the safe side, select one of the prefab color schemes to ensure that you won't have clashing colors or a weird text/background mix. To apply the color scheme to all your slides, click the color scheme. To apply the scheme to only the selected slide, move the mouse pointer over the desired color scheme, click the button to the right of the color scheme, and click **Apply to Selected Slides**.

Textures provide
a sort of bathroom
Formica look.

Figure 16.4

Experiment with the background fill effects to give your background a unique look.

Keep an eye on
the Sample area.

Restructuring Your Slides

🖼 To quickly rearrange objects on your slide, select the slide and then open the **Format** menu and click **Slide Layout**. Point to the desired slide layout, click the button that appears to the right of the layout, and click **Apply to Selected Slides**.

If you're feeling a little daring, click the **Edit Color Schemes** link and select a color for each element. When you're done, select **Apply** (to save your settings and apply the scheme to all slides in your presentation).

Taking Control with the Master Slide

Behind every good slide show is a Master slide, which acts as the puppet master, pulling the strings that make the other slides behave the way they do. The Master slide controls the font style and size for the slide titles and bulleted lists, and it contains any graphics that appear on all the slides. In addition, it inserts the date, slide number, and any other information that you want to display on *all* slides in the presentation.

To display the Master slide, open the **View** menu, point to **Master**, and click **Slide Master** (or hold down the **Shift** key while clicking the **Normal View** button in the lower-left corner of the window). The Master slide appears, as shown in Figure 16.5. In this view, you can make any of the following changes to the Master slide that you want to affect all the slides in the presentation:

➤ To change the appearance of the slide titles, drag over the slide title on the Master slide, and then use the **Font** and **Font Size** drop-down lists in the Formatting toolbar to change the font and text size. For additional font options, open the **Format** menu and select **Font**.

➤ To change the appearance of the text in bulleted lists, drag over the bullet level, and then use the **Font** and **Font Size** drop-down lists to change the font. Right-click a bullet level that you'd like to change, select **Bullets and Numbering** from the context menu, and change the bullet style to something you like better—for instance, little plants, hearts, or big orange diamonds.

➤ You can place additional text or graphics on the Master slide just as if you were placing them on any slide in the show. (See Chapter 17.)

➤ If the Master slide has a text box that inserts the date or slide number on every slide, you can edit the text in the box or change its font and alignment.

Office

Multiple Masters

Microsoft's new version of PowerPoint now features multiple masters, allowing you to store several slide shows in one file or use a different slide master for separate sections of a single presentation. To insert a master, click the **Insert New Slide Master** button in the Slide Master View toolbar.

When you're finished fooling around with the Master slide, click the **Close** button in the Master toolbar (to return to Normal view) or click the desired view button in the lower-left corner of the PowerPoint window.

The Masters Tour

PowerPoint offers additional Master views, including Title Master, Handouts Master, and Notes Master, which are all listed on the View, Master submenu. Title Master enables you to control the formatting for all titles and subtitles on your slides.

Although the Master slide initially controls all aspects of every slide in your slide show, any changes you make to an individual slide override the formatting of the Master slide. You can, for example, change the font used for the title on one slide. If you decide later that you want to use the formatting from the Master slide, select the slide that contains the special formatting, open the **Format** menu, and click **Slide Layout**. Point to the desired layout in the Slide Layout task pane, click the button that appears to the right of the layout, and click **Reapply Layout**.

If you add a graphic, such as a company logo, to the Master slide, it appears on all slides in the presentation. To prevent any image (including images that are part of the original template) from appearing on a particular slide, select the slide, open the **Format** menu, select **Background**, click **Omit Background Graphics from Master**, and click **Apply**.

Figure 16.5

Format the Master slide to control the appearance of all slides in the presentation.

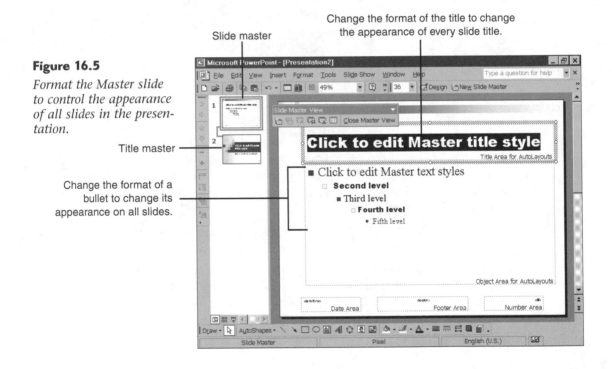

The Least You Need to Know

With the AutoContent Wizard and PowerPoint's templates, you should never have to create a presentation from scratch, but it helps to know your way around PowerPoint. When you're first starting out, make sure you have mastered these basics:

➤ To run the AutoContent Wizard, select **File**, **New**, and then click the **From AutoContent Wizard** link.

➤ To create a new presentation using a template, select **File**, **New**, and click the **From Design Template** link.

➤ To quickly change from one view to another, click the button for the desired view in the lower-left corner of the PowerPoint window.

➤ To insert a new slide in your presentation, select the slide after which you want the new slide inserted, and then click the **New Slide** button.

➤ To change the overall appearance of your presentation, enter the **Format**, **Background** or **Format**, **Slide Design** command and then enter your preferences.

➤ To display the master slide, open the **View** menu, point to **Master**, and click **Slide Master**.

Chapter 17

Adding Text, Graphics, and Sounds to a Slide

In This Chapter

➤ Adding boxes for titles, lists, and other text

➤ Presenting data graphically with charts

➤ Spicing up your presentation with clip art and line drawings

➤ Exploring the third dimension with sound and video

Starting a presentation with a design template or even with the AutoContent Wizard doesn't give you much to work with. These tools provide you with a background design and color scheme, and they might give you some direction on what to include in your presentation; but overall they're pretty drab. If you decide to go with this arrangement, your audience will be nodding off long before the grand finale.

To hook your audience and keep your presentation lively, you need to spice it up with graphics, sound, video, and any other media that reduces the time you have to speak and cuts down on the amount of reading required from your audience. In this chapter, you learn how to add various media objects to your slides.

As If You Didn't Have Enough Text

I know. I just said that your slides probably have *too* much text, and now I'm going to tell you how to add even more text. The problem is that the text boxes on your slides might not be the text boxes you want to use.

Managing Existing Objects

Throughout this chapter, you will place new objects on your slides, which might obstruct existing objects. To learn the basics of working with layered objects, see "Working with Layers of Objects" and "Working with Two or More Objects as a Group" in Chapter 7, "Spicing It Up with Graphics, Sound, and Video."

To insert a text box on a slide, display the slide and then open the **Insert** menu and select **Text Box**. Drag the mouse pointer over the slide where you want the text box positioned, and then release the mouse button. Type your text. If you type more text than the text box can hold, the box automatically expands. To move the text box, simply drag its outline; to resize the text box, drag one of its handles.

The Amazing Shrinking Text

The Slide Master has text boxes that display *text placeholders* on the slides in your presentation. If you type more text than fits in a placeholder box, PowerPoint automatically bumps down the type size to make it fit! (This doesn't work with the text boxes that *you* draw on your slides.) To prevent the Slide Master from bumping down your text size on this slide, click the text box; select **Format**, **Placeholder**; click the **Text Box** tab; click **Resize AutoShape to Fit Text**; and click **OK**. To change this option for all slides, make the change to the text box on the Slide Master.

Jazzing Up Your Slides with Clip Art and Other Pictures

Office comes with a Clip Art gallery that works for all your Office applications. You might have met the gallery in Chapter 7. You can insert clip art from the gallery into your slides. Take the following steps to do just that:

1. Display the slide on which you want to insert the clip art.

2. Open the **Insert** menu, point to **Picture**, and click **Clip Art**. The Insert Clip Art dialog box appears. (If the Add Clips to Gallery dialog box appears, click **Later** to import additional clip art at another time.)

3. Click in the **Search Text** text box, type a brief description of the type of image you're looking for (for instance, "animal"), and click **Search**. The Insert Clip Art task pane displays thumbnail versions of all the images that match your search instructions.

4. Click the image you want to insert, as shown in Figure 17.1. PowerPoint places the image on the currently selected slide and displays the Picture toolbar, which contains tools you can use to edit the picture.

5. You can drag one of the handles that surround the image to resize it, drag the image to move it to the desired location, or drag the green handle to rotate the image.

Drag the green handle to tilt (rotate) the image.
Drag a handle to resize the image.

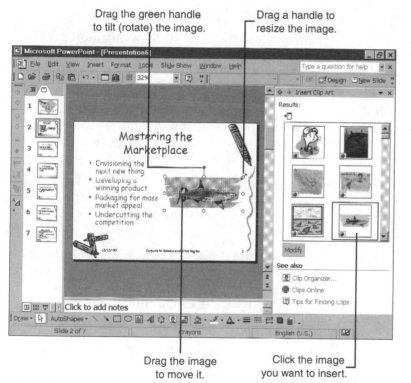

Drag the image to move it.
Click the image you want to insert.

Figure 17.1

You can decorate your slides with predrawn art from the Clip Art gallery.

The Insert, Picture submenu also enables you to insert graphics files you might have on your hard drive. Open the **Insert** menu, point to **Picture**, and select **From File**. In the Insert Picture dialog box, pick the graphics file you want to insert.

Adding Shapes, Lines, and WordArt

If none of the predrawn images works for you, you can use the Drawing toolbar to create your own drawings, insert AutoShapes, add lines and arrows, and do much more. This is the same Drawing toolbar you saw in Word. (To learn more about using this toolbar, see Chapter 7. To insert a WordArt object, see "Inserting WordArt Objects" in Chapter 5, "Giving Your Text a Makeover.")

Backing Up Your Claims with Charts

The staple of most effective presentations is the graph (or *chart*, as Microsoft likes to call it). Charts provide a great way of conveying numerical information visually so that your audience doesn't have to think about the numbers to grasp their significance.

If you created slides with the AutoContent Wizard or with the Slide Layout dialog box, the slide might already have a space for the chart. You should see something such as **Double click to add chart**. Double-click the chart icon. If no designated space exists for the chart, click the **Insert Chart** button on the Standard toolbar.

Either way you do it, the Datasheet window appears, as shown in Figure 17.2, displaying some sample data. To enter the data you want to graph, click inside the cell (the box) where you want to insert the data, type your entry, and press **Enter** or use one of the arrow keys to move to the next box.

Inserting Excel Charts

If you've already created a chart in Excel, there's no sense wasting your time re-creating it in PowerPoint. Simply copy the chart in Excel, and then paste it on a slide in PowerPoint.

Initially, data is graphed by rows, so the column headings appear below the horizontal (X) axis in the chart. To graph by column (so the row headings appear below the axis), click the **By Column** button in the Standard toolbar. (If the By Column button is not on the toolbar, click the **Toolbar Options** button on the right end of the toolbar and click **By Column**.) To learn more about customizing your chart, see Chapter 14, "Graphing Data for Fun and Profit." When you're done playing around with your chart, click anywhere outside the Datasheet window and outside the chart area.

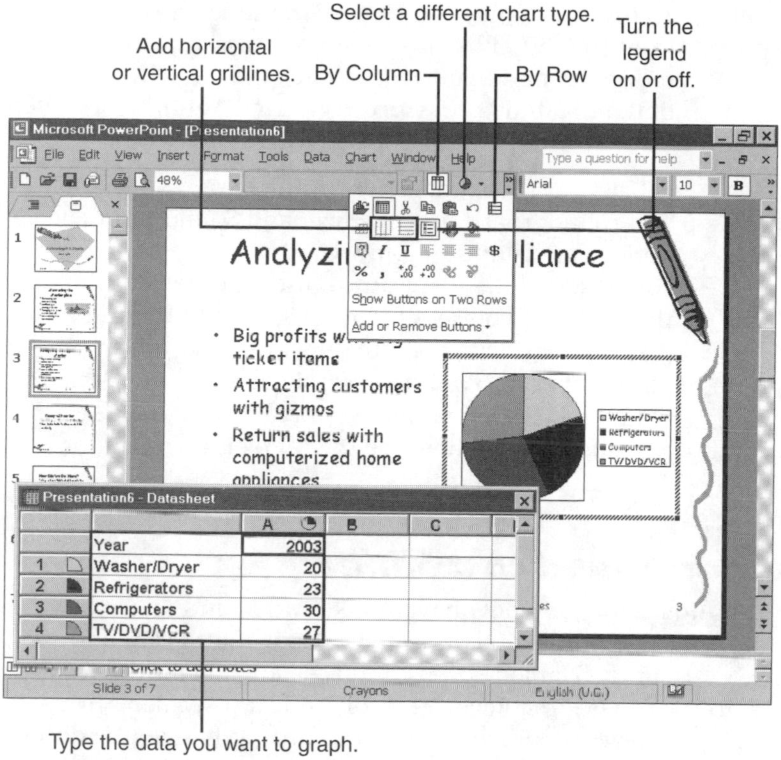

Select a different chart type.

Add horizontal
or vertical gridlines.   By Column

Turn the
legend
on or off.

By Row

Figure 17.2
*The Datasheet window
prompts you to enter the
data you want to chart.*

Type the data you want to graph.

Adding Sounds to Your Slides

Does your voice shake when you speak in front of a group? Does your mouth go dry? Do you have a bad case of Tourette's syndrome? Instead of dealing with the cause of the problem, just avoid public speaking altogether! You can do it in PowerPoint by attaching sounds and recordings to your slides—assuming, of course, that you are creating an onscreen presentation and that your system is equipped with a sound card and speakers. The following is a list of the types of sounds PowerPoint enables you to use:

➤ **Sounds from the Microsoft Clip gallery.**

➤ **Sounds recorded and saved in files on your disk.**

➤ **CD audio tracks**—You can tell PowerPoint to play a specific track from an audio CD in the background while the slide show is playing. Just make sure you have the right CD in the drive when you're presenting your slide show.

➤ **Microphone input**—PowerPoint can record your voice or whatever else you want to input and display an icon for it on the slide. You can make PowerPoint play the sound automatically during the slide show or whenever you click the icon for the sound.

215

Don't Forget Your CDs!

If you choose to play an audio CD track during your presentation, don't forget to load the CD before you start your presentation.

To insert a sound, first display the slide on which you want the sound to play. Open the **Insert** menu, point to **Movies and Sounds**, and click the desired sound option: **Sound from Clip Organizer**, **Sound from File**, **Play CD Audio Track**, or **Record Sound**.

What you do next depends on the option you selected. The Sound from Clip Organizer and Sound from File options are fairly straightforward: You select the audio clip or sound file you want to use and then confirm the action. If you select Play CD Audio Track, use the Play Options dialog box to select the track on which you want PowerPoint to start playing and the track on which PowerPoint should stop playing. If you select Record Sound, the process is a bit more complicated (see the following section for details).

Attaching a Recorded Sound to a Slide

If you select the Record Sound option, you now have the Record Sound dialog box onscreen. First, make sure your microphone is connected to your sound card and is turned on. Drag over the entry in the **Name** text box and type a name for the recording. When you are ready to speak, click the **Record** button and start speaking into the microphone (or making whatever sound you want to record). When you're done recording, click the **Stop** button and click **OK**. PowerPoint inserts a little speaker icon on the slide. Drag it to the position where you want it to appear. You can double-click the speaker icon to play the recorded sound.

Assuming that you present your slide show onscreen (instead of with 35mm slides, overhead transparencies, or handouts), whenever you advance to a slide on which you have placed a sound, the speaker icon appears. To play the sound, double-click the icon.

You can make PowerPoint play your sound automatically whenever you advance to the slide. You do this by adding animation effects, as explained in Chapter 18, "Shuffling and Presenting Your Slide Show."

Narrating an Entire Slide Show

You can use the Record Sound option as described in the previous section to narrate your slide show. Just add a separate recorded sound to each slide. An easier way to narrate an entire slide show is to use the Narration feature. You advance through the slide show while speaking into your microphone. PowerPoint records your voice and attaches your narrative to the correct slides. Turn on your microphone and follow these steps to get started:

1. Go to the first slide in your presentation. (If you don't select the first slide, a dialog box appears after you perform step 3, asking whether you want to start recording with the first slide or the currently selected slide.)

2. Open the **Slide Show** menu and click **Record Narration**. The Record Narration dialog box appears, showing how many minutes of recording time you have based on the free space on your hard drive.

3. Click **OK**. PowerPoint changes to Slide Show view, as shown in Figure 17.3.

4. Start narrating your slide show by speaking into your microphone. Click anywhere on the slide to advance to the next slide. Keep talking. Although it looks as though PowerPoint is doing nothing, it is actually recording your voice. At the end of the show, a message appears, asking whether you want to save the timing of the slide show along with your narration.

5. To save the slide timing along with the narration, click **Save**. To save the narration without the timing, click **Don't Save**. PowerPoint changes to Slide Sorter view; the amount of time each slide appears during the presentation is displayed below each slide.

When you run the slide show, the narration automatically plays with the show. To run the slide show without narration, open the **Slide Show** menu and click **Set Up Show**. Select **Show Without Narration** and click **OK**.

Figure 17.3

Flip through the slides and keep talking.

To pause the recording, right-click and select Pause Narration.

217

Going Multimedia with Video Clips

Even though computer video isn't quite top quality, everyone seems to think that no presentation or Web page is complete without a video clip. PowerPoint has followed this lead by enabling you to insert video clips into your slide show.

To insert a video clip, display the slide into which you want to insert the clip. Then open the **Insert** menu, point to **Movies and Sound**, and click **Movie from Clip Organizer** (you need to insert the Microsoft Office CD-ROM) or **Movie from File**. If you selected the Movie from Clip Organizer option, the Insert Clip Art task pane appears, presenting you with a list of movie clips. Click the desired clip. If you select the Movie from File option, use the Insert Movie dialog box to pick a flick from your disk. PowerPoint supports most movie clip formats, including AVI, MPG, MPE, and VDO; so anything you lift off the Web (with permission, of course) should work.

The Least You Need to Know

When you break a slide show down into its component parts, as we have in this chapter, it becomes clear that a slide show isn't all that complicated. To control a slide's layout, just make sure you've mastered these basics:

➤ To insert a text box on a slide, click **Insert**, **Text Box**, and then drag the text box into existence.

➤ To display the Insert Clip Art task pane, select **Insert**, **Picture**, **Clip Art**.

➤ To move an image, drag it. To resize an image, drag one of its handles.

➤ To add a chart to a slide, click the **Insert Chart** button and type the data you want to chart in the Datasheet window.

➤ To complement your visuals with audio recordings, open the **Insert** menu, point to **Movies and Sounds**, and click the desired sound option: **Sound from Clip Organizer**, **Sound from File**, **Play CD Audio Track**, or **Record Sound**.

➤ To narrate your slide show, switch to the first slide, select **Slide Show**, **Record Narration**, and follow the onscreen instructions.

Chapter 18

Shuffling and Presenting Your Slide Show

In This Chapter

➤ Shuffling your slides in Slide Sorter view

➤ Animating an onscreen slide show with special effects

➤ Making your own interactive presentations

➤ Rehearsing and giving onscreen presentations

Before you unveil your presentation, leave it for a day or two and then come back and try to look at it from the perspective of your audience. Maybe you need to tweak one or two slides, move a bulleted list, fix a chart, or perform some other minor maintenance.

You also might need to make some more substantial changes, such as rearranging your slides or animating your slides to make your presentation more active. Before you take the stage, you should also consider drawing up some speaker notes, preparing handouts for your audience, and even rehearsing your presentation. This time spent in preparation will help you perfect your slide show and become more comfortable presenting it. In this chapter, you learn how to use PowerPoint's powerful presentation tools to do all this and more.

Rearranging Your Slides

When creating a slide show, you usually focus on individual slides, making each slide the best it can be. When you step back, however, you notice less of what's on each slide and more of how the slides are arranged in your presentation. From this bird's-eye perspective, you might notice that you need to rearrange the slides in your presentation.

The best view for arranging slides is Slide Sorter view, which displays a small version of each slide. To change to Slide Sorter view, click the **Slide Sorter View** button. To move a slide, drag the slide to the desired location. As you drag, a vertical line appears, showing where PowerPoint will insert the slide, as shown in Figure 18.1. When you release the mouse button, the slide moves to the new position. To copy a slide instead of moving it, hold down the **Ctrl** key while dragging.

Figure 18.1

In Slide Sorter view, you can move slides by dragging them.

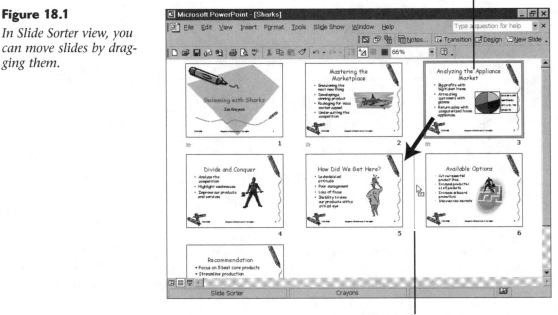

Drag a slide to move it.

This line shows where the slide will be placed.

Although Slide Sorter view offers the most graphical way to shuffle your slides, the presentation outline provides a better view for evaluating the content and flow of your presentation. To move a slide in the outline, simply drag the slide icon up or down to the desired position.

Adding Special Effects

Adding special effects to your presentation can really jazz up the message and keep your audience awake. For example, if you plan to present your slide show using a computer, you can animate the transitions from one slide to the next. Perhaps you want one slide to fade out while the next fades in. The following sections show you how to add these special effects.

Special Effects on the Slide Sorter Toolbar

First, let's finish looking at all the details found in Slide Sorter view. Switch to Slide Sorter view by clicking the **Slide Sorter View** button in the lower-left corner of your screen. Each slide in your presentation appears onscreen (refer to Figure 18.1). PowerPoint also displays the Slide Sorter toolbar. As you begin working with slide effects in the following sections, you'll have occasion to use the Slide Sorter toolbar to assign special effects. Table 18.1 provides a brief description of each button.

Table 18.1　Slide Sorter Toolbar Buttons

Toolbar Button	Name	Description
	Transition	Opens the Slide Transition task pane, which offers options for animating the transition from one slide to the next.
	Hide Slide	Hides the currently selected slide so it will not appear in the show. This is useful when you want to present different versions of one show to different audiences or keep backup material at hand.
	Rehearse Timings	Switches to Slide Show view and provides a dialog box that lets you set the amount of time each slide remains on the screen.
	Summary Slide	Pulls titles from other slides in the presentation to create a new slide. You can transform the slide titles into hyperlinks, so you can click the titles of the other slides to quickly jump to them.
	Speaker Notes	Displays a dialog box that lets you type notes you can refer to during your presentation.

Speaker Notes and Audience Handouts

To create notes, simply type your text in the box that appears below the slide in Normal view. To print slides for your audience or speaker notes for yourself, select **File**, **Print**, and then open the **Print What** list and select **Handouts** or **Notes Pages**. (Audience handouts consist of printouts of the slides, one to nine per page; if you choose to print three slides per page, PowerPoint prints lines next to each slide for the audience to take notes. Each speaker notes page has a picture of a slide along with any notes you typed.) Enter any other print settings, as desired, and click the **Preview** button to check your work.

Animating Transitions from Slide to Slide

If you're using a computer to display your slide show on a monitor or using a special projector connected to your computer, you can time the transitions and add interesting animation effects. Here's what you do:

Consistency and Conformity

In most cases, you should apply the same transition effect to all slides in the presentation. However, you can apply a transition to a single slide or to a group of slides. To select several slides, click one and then Ctrl+click the others.

1. Click the slide to which you want to apply an animated transition. (To use the same transition for all your slides, click any slide in the presentation. You can choose to apply the transition effect to all the slides in the last step.)

2. In Slide Sorter view, click the **Slide Transition** button. The Slide Transition task pane appears, as shown in Figure 18.2, displaying your transition options.

3. In the **Apply to Selected Slides** list, click the desired transition. Look at the currently displayed slide to see a demonstration of the transition. (If you missed the demonstration, click the **Play** button at the bottom of the task pane.)

4. Open the **Speed** list and click **Slow**, **Medium**, or **Fast** to set a speed for the transition.

5. To add a sound to the transition, open the **Sound** drop-down list and select the desired sound. (To use a sound not found on the list, select **Other Sound** at the bottom of the list and locate the sound file you want to use.) To have the sound continue to play until the next sound starts, click **Loop Until Next Sound**.

6. Under **Advance Slide**, select **On Mouse Click** to advance slides whenever you click the mouse. You also can select **Automatically, After ___** to have PowerPoint automatically display the next slide for you after the specified time period and then enter the desired amount of time.

7. To apply the transition effect to all slides in your presentation, click **Apply to All Slides**. If you don't click Apply to All Slides, PowerPoint applies the transition to only the selected slide(s).

Automatic Pilot Isn't Always the Best

If you plan to present your slide show to a live audience, make sure On Mouse Click is selected. You never know when a question is going to pop up, and you don't want your slide show running automatically while you field questions.

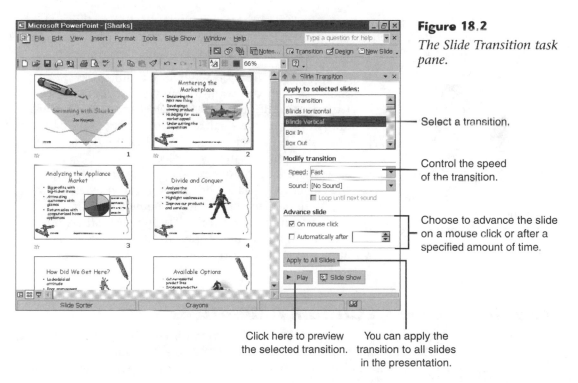

Figure 18.2

The Slide Transition task pane.

Select a transition.

Control the speed of the transition.

Choose to advance the slide on a mouse click or after a specified amount of time.

Click here to preview the selected transition.

You can apply the transition to all slides in the presentation.

223

Using Animated Builds

Slide transitions are cool, but you can use them only on entire slides. PowerPoint also offers animation effects for objects on the slide. For example, you can make your slide title bounce into place from the left side of the slide or have each bulleted list item fade in.

Build It!

The effect of having your slide items appear at different times and in different ways onscreen is called a *build*. PowerPoint includes a wide selection of builds, such as bulleted items appearing one bullet at a time when you click the slide or a graphic flying in from the side of the screen.

PowerPoint offers these options via the Slide Design task pane. To display the available animation effects, first change to Normal view; then click the **Design** button in the Formatting toolbar and click **Animation Schemes** in the Slide Design task pane.

Choose Your Mood

The animation schemes are categorized into three groups: Subtle, Moderate, and Exciting. If you're looking for bold animations, scroll down the list.

To apply an animation scheme to a slide, first click the slide to which you want to apply the scheme—Ctrl+click additional slides to select them. (To apply an animation scheme to all slides in your presentation, any slide can be selected.) Next, click the desired animation scheme. When you select a scheme, PowerPoint automatically "plays" the animation on the currently selected slide, so you can preview it. To apply the selected animation scheme to all slides in your presentation, click the **Apply to All Slides** button. If you don't click Apply to All Slides, PowerPoint applies the animation scheme to only the selected slide(s).

Designing Your Own Custom Animations

PowerPoint also enables you to create your own custom animations. For example, you might want the slide title to fade in when you first display the slide and then have each item of the bulleted list "fly in" from the left side of the screen when you click your mouse. You can even animate some charts to bring the entire chart or certain elements of the chart to life.

To apply a custom animation to an object, first click the object (title text box, list text box, image, chart, and so on). Then, open the **Slide Show** menu and click **Custom Animation**. The Custom Animation task pane appears, as shown in Figure 18.3. Click the **Add Effect** button, point to the desired type of effect (Entrance, Emphasis, Exit, Motion Paths), and click the desired effect. Enter any additional preferences to specify how and when you want the effect to execute. For instance, you might want the effect to execute when you click the mouse button or when the previous effect is complete. You also can select the speed at which the animation proceeds.

2. Click the Add Effect
button and select
the desired animation.

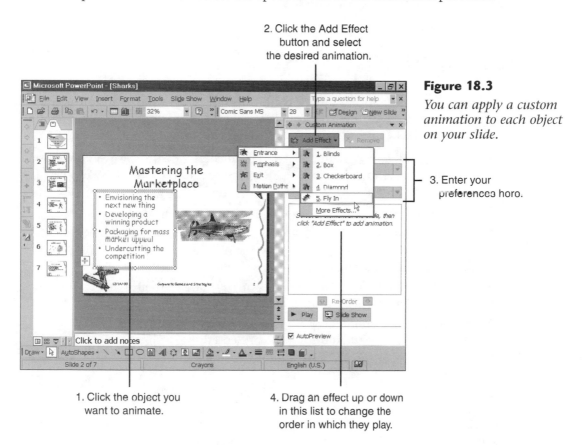

Figure 18.3

You can apply a custom animation to each object on your slide.

3. Enter your
preferences here.

1. Click the object you
want to animate.

4. Drag an effect up or down
in this list to change the
order in which they play.

Making an Interactive Presentation with Action Buttons

If you are creating an online presentation to train individual workers or an information kiosk for online users, you can give your audience control over the presentation by adding *action buttons* to your slides. A simple action button might allow the user to click it to advance to the next slide. Another button might prompt the user to click it to play a video.

To add an action button to a slide, open the **Slide Show** menu, point to **Action Buttons**, and click the desired button. The mouse pointer transforms into a crosshair pointer. Click where you want the button to appear. The selected action button appears on the slide, and the Action Settings dialog box prompts you to assign some action to the button. Enter your preferences and click **OK**.

This feature is particularly useful for creating slides that jump directly to other slides. For example, you can add an action button to jump directly to a slide containing backup figures for a chart. The user can jump to that slide if desired, or just ignore the button.

It's Show Time!

This is it—the moment you finally get to see how your presentation looks and runs. I'll tell you how to show your presentation electronically, give you tips for stopping and adding notes, and even show you how to write on your slides during the presentation. Places, everyone! Cue monitor…lights, camera, action!

Display the first slide in your presentation, and then click the **Slide Show View** button or select **View**, **Slide Show**. Your first slide appears in full-screen view. You can now do the following:

➤ To progress to the next slide or advance the animation, click anywhere on the screen, or press the right-arrow or down-arrow key on the keyboard.

➤ If you set up a specific transition time (as described earlier in this chapter), the slide show progresses automatically.

➤ If you selected a build effect for your slide or any slide elements, click your screen to "build" each effect (unless, of course, you timed the builds).

➤ If you've inserted any sound clips, movie clips, or other special effects, you can click their icons to start them during the presentation.

➤ To quit the show at any time, press **Esc**.

Ready for dress rehearsal? You can rehearse your slide show while specifying the amount of time each slide is to appear onscreen. Open the **Slide Show** menu and select **Rehearse Timings**. PowerPoint displays the Rehearsal dialog box, showing the number of seconds the slide has been onscreen. When you are ready to advance to the next slide, click the **Next** button (the one with the right-pointing arrow on it). If someone bursts into your office during rehearsal, you can click the **Pause** button (the one with the double vertical lines). To change the timing for a slide, edit the numbers displayed in the time text box. When you reach the end of the show, PowerPoint asks whether you want to save your slide show timings. Click **Yes**.

Broadcast Your Presentation Via the Web

With PowerPoint's new broadcast feature, you can present your slide show on the Web (you'll need access to a Netshow server if you are broadcasting your presentation to more than 16 computer locations). To set up and record a broadcast, open the **Slide Show** menu, point to **Online Broadcast**, click **Record and Save a Broadcast**, and follow the onscreen instructions. To schedule a broadcast (and notify your audience members via e-mail), select **Slide Show**, **Online Broadcast**, **Schedule a Live Broadcast** and follow the onscreen instructions. When you're ready to give your presentation, select **Slide Show**, **Online Broadcast**, **Start Live Broadcast**. (Tip: Rehearse your broadcast ahead of time by using yourself as the sole member of your audience.)

Take a gander at PowerPoint's slide show controls by clicking the control button in the lower-left corner of the screen, as shown in Figure 18.4, or right-clicking anywhere on the screen. This opens a menu from which you can select controls for moving to the next slide, turning the arrow pointer into a pen that writes onscreen, and even ending the show.

Here's what each menu item controls:

➤ **Next**—Takes you to the next slide or the next build effect. (Using the arrow keys or just clicking a slide is easy.)

➤ **Previous**—Takes you back to the previous slide or build effect. To flip back a slide, press the P (previous) key. To forge ahead, press N (next).

➤ **Go**—Opens a submenu that lets you select the name of a specific slide you want to view.

➤ **Meeting Minder**—Lets you stop your slide show and compose notes, comments, and other observations made by your audience. Meeting Minder even lets you type the meeting minutes during the presentation, so you can quickly review the meeting at a later date.

➤ **Speaker Notes**—Enables you to add notes about a specific slide or view notes you've already typed.

➤ **Pointer Options**—Displays a submenu with options for hiding the mouse pointer, displaying the pointer as an arrow, or turning the pointer into a pen you can use to scribble on the slides during the presentation. (The scribbles are not saved as part of your presentation.)

Figure 18.4

A slide during the course of the slide show.

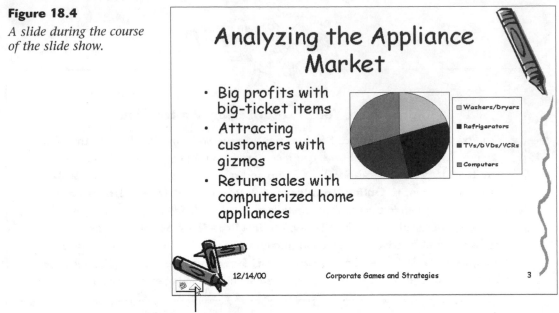

Click here to view a menu
of slide show controls.

➤ **Screen**—Opens a submenu for blacking out your current slide, pausing the show, or erasing your pen scribbles.

➤ **End Show**—Puts a stop to your slide show.

If you want to package your presentation on a floppy disk or CD (assuming you have a CD drive that can record CDs), open the **File** menu, click **Pack and Go**, and follow the onscreen instructions. This creates a version of your presentation that can be played on any PC, whether it has PowerPoint installed on it!

Preview Your Slides Before Printing

Before you take the stage, consider printing your speaker notes and audience handouts. But before you commit your presentation to paper, preview them with PowerPoint's new Print Preview feature. Simply open the **File** menu and click **Print Preview**. Open the **Print What** list and choose the item you want to preview: **Slides**, **Handouts**, **Notes Pages**, or **Outline View**. Open the **Options** list to check out additional settings, such as grayscale and color output. When you're ready to print, click the **Print** button.

The Least You Need to Know

Now that you know the fancy stuff, you're a certified presentation professional. Before you can claim bragging rights, however, make sure you can do the following:

➤ To rearrange your slides, click the **Slide Sorter View** button and then drag the slides to the desired position.

➤ To apply animated slide transitions to your presentation, switch to Slide Sorter view, click the **Slide Transition** button, and enter your preferences.

➤ To animate objects on a slide, display the slide in Normal view, click the **Design** button, click the **Animation Schemes** link, and enter your preferences.

➤ To add an action button to a slide, open the **Slide Show** menu, point to **Action Buttons**, click the desired button, click the slide where you want the button to appear, and enter your preferences.

➤ To preview your presentation, click the **Slide Show View** button and then click the slide to advance it.

➤ Before creating a timed slide show, rehearse the timings by selecting **Slide Show**, **Rehearse Timings** and then proceeding through your slide show as you would present it.

Part 5

Mastering the Information Age with Access

Information is power; however, too much information, if not managed properly, can cripple your intelligence and derail any train of thought. Fortunately, we people of the early twenty-first century have computerized databases that can manage the information for us. We input the data (in the proper form), and the database does the rest: sorting it, summarizing it in reports, and helping us pull it into our other documents.

Although databases can be complicated beasts, Access provides a complete, yet simple, set of tools designed to make working with databases easy. In this part, you learn how to use these tools to create and manage your own databases.

SHE'S GOT YOUR EYES.

Chapter 19

Making Your First Database

In This Chapter

➤ Five-minute database primer

➤ Creating a database step by step with the Database Wizard

➤ Making a database from scratch (only if you have to)

➤ Customizing the database form

➤ Using the Database toolbar

Our society thrives on information. Magazines and TV news shows broadcast results of the latest polls. Telemarketers and junk mailers pay for lists of names, addresses, and phone numbers of prospective customers. People call and show up at our doors asking survey questions. And television networks use the Nielsen Ratings to figure out which shows to create (or kill).

We collect this data and pour it into computers, but then what? Someone (or something) has to tally the results and arrange the data in some meaningful format so we can use it. This something is a *database*. In this chapter, you learn how to create your own database so you can start dumping data into it and generating reports that make your data meaningful.

What Is a Database, Anyway?

A *database* is a collection of data. A phone book is a database. Your collection of cooking recipes is a database. Even your summer reading list is a database.

You can create databases in Excel by typing entries in worksheet cells and in Word by creating a table. In fact, if you need a simple database to create a mailing list or keep track of your worldly possessions, Excel can handle the job.

So why use Access? Because it provides superior reporting tools and lets you create a *relational database* that can pull entries from several tables into a single report. For example, if you need a complex database for keeping track of products, customers, and suppliers, you can create a database consisting of several tables. When you need an invoice, you then create an invoice report that pulls entries from the customers and products tables. This lets you organize the data in smaller units and gives you more flexibility with using that data. But let's slow down and approach this relational database thing with the fear and trepidation it deserves.

What About My Access 2000 Files?

If you have some experience with the previous version of Access (Access 2000), you might have a few old database files floating around on your hard drive. Fortunately, Access 2002 is *backward–compatible* with Access 2000, enabling you to open your old Access 2000 files without having to go through a messy conversion process. In fact, Access is set up, by default, to save any new files you create in the Access 2000 format. To change the default file format, open the **Tools** menu and click **Options**. Click the Advanced tab, and then open the **Default File Format** list and click **Access 2002**. Click **OK**.

Database Lingo You Can't Live Without

Before you dive in and start creating a database, you should familiarize yourself with some basic database terminology. Of course, you can proceed in ignorance; but then you wouldn't know what I was talking about when I told you to "create a field" or "select a record." Here's a quick rundown of the terms you should know and their definitions:

➤ **Form**—A fill-in-the-blanks document you use to type entries into your database. This is just like a form you would fill out to apply for a new credit card.

➤ **Field**—On a fill-in-the-blanks form, fields are the blanks. You type a unique piece of data (such as last name, first name, or middle initial) into each field.

➤ **Record**—A completed form. Each record contains data for a specific person, thing, or other being or nonbeing. In a recipe database, for example, each recipe is a record.

➤ **Table**—Another way to display records in a database. Instead of displaying data on separate forms, you can have Access display the data in a table. Each row displays a record. Each column represents a separate field. A teacher's grade book, for example, would be stored as a table.

➤ **Query**—To pull data from one or more databases. If you have one database that contains customer names and addresses and another database that contains a record of bills you have sent out, you can use a query to pull information from both databases and create a list of customers who owe you money. You'll learn more about queries in Chapter 21, "Finding, Sorting, and Selecting Records."

➤ **Report**—A document that pulls data from one or more databases and arranges it in various ways to present the data in a meaningful context and help you analyze it.

Cranking Out a Database with the Database Wizard

Now that you know the essential (and hip) database lingo, you're ready to create your own database. If you need to create a standard database, such as an inventory list, an address book, or a membership directory, your job is going to be easy. The Access Database Wizard can lead you step by step through the process:

1. Start Access. (Click **Start**, point to **Programs**, and click **Microsoft Access**.) The New File task pane appears on the right, providing options for creating a new database or opening an existing database.

2. Under New from Template, click **General Templates**. The Templates dialog box appears, prompting you to specify the desired type of database.

3. Click the **Databases** tab (if it is not already selected), and click the wizard icon for the type of database you want to create. The preview area shows a graphic representation of what you can do with the selected type of database.

4. Click **OK**. The File New Database dialog box appears, prompting you to name your database file.

Whoa!

No New File Task Pane?

If the Microsoft Access dialog box is not displayed, open the **File** menu and select **New**.

5. Type a name for your new database file in the **File Name** text box and select the drive and folder in which you want to store the file. Click the **Create** button. As Access creates the database file, it displays a Database window and then the first Database Wizard dialog box.

6. Read the information in the first Database Wizard dialog box to find out what the wizard is going to do. Click the **Next** button. The Database Wizard displays a list of tables it will create for your database and a list of fields on each table.

7. In the **Tables in the Database** list, shown in Figure 19.1, click the table whose fields you want to change (if any). The Fields in the Table list box shows the available fields; optional fields appear in italics.

8. Click a field name to turn it on or off. A check mark next to a field name indicates that the field will be included in the table. Repeat steps 7 and 8 to specify which fields you want included in each table.

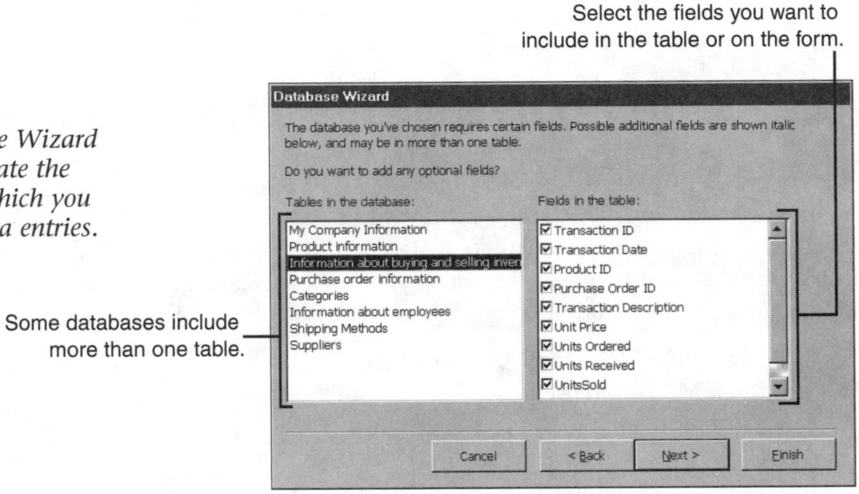

Select the fields you want to
include in the table or on the form.

Figure 19.1

*The Database Wizard
helps you create the
tables into which you
type your data entries.*

Some databases include
more than one table.

9. Follow the wizard's remaining instructions to complete the process, clicking **Next** to move from one dialog box to the next.

10. When the wizard displays the final dialog box, click the **Finish** button. Access creates the database and then displays the Database window, which contains icons for the various elements that make up your database: Tables, Queries, Forms, Reports, Macros, Pages, and Modules.

Access might display a window called the Main Switchboard, which provides buttons for performing the most common tasks related to this database. To work on your database, you can click a button in the Switchboard or minimize the Switchboard and restore the Database window (which is minimized and in the lower-left corner of the screen). The instructions in this chapter assume you are working with the Database window, as shown in Figure 19.2.

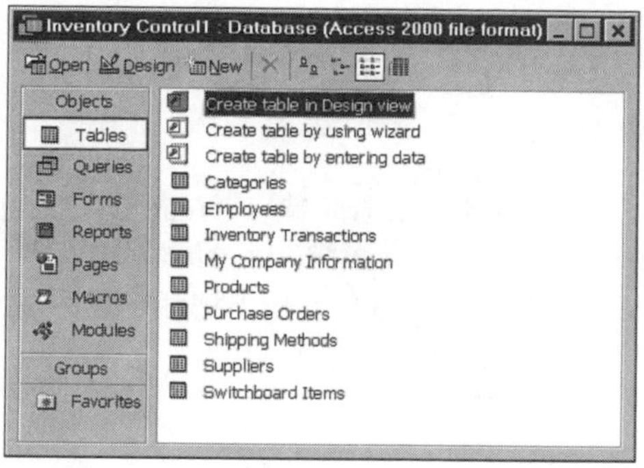

Figure 19.2

The Database window offers access to forms, tables, and reports.

The toolbar near the top of the Database window contains buttons for adding and controlling objects in the selected category. To open a form so you can start entering data, click the **Forms** icon (in the bar at the left), click the form you want to use, and click the **Open** button. You can click the Design button to customize the form, table, report, or other object. The New button lets you create a new object, such as a table or form.

Creating and Customizing Tables

The central element in any database is the *table*. This is the structure that stores all the data you enter and supplies that data when you create a query or report, or choose to flip through your records using a form. Before you start entering data into your tables, make sure you have all the tables you need and that each table contains fields for the required data entries. The following sections show you how to take control of existing tables and create new tables from scratch.

Configuring Tables: Pick a View

You can display tables in either of two views to configure them: Datasheet view or Design view. Datasheet view displays the table as if it were an Excel worksheet. Design view displays a list of all the fields in the table and specifies the data type of each field. To open a table, click the **Tables** icon on the left side of the Database window and double-click the name of the table you want to open. To switch views, open the **View** menu and select **Design View** or **Datasheet View**.

In either view, you can move or delete fields or insert new fields. To select a field in Datasheet view, click the field name at the top of the column, as shown in Figure 19.3. You can then perform the following tasks:

➤ To move a field, drag it to the left or right.

➤ To widen a field, drag the line on the right side of the field name to the right. To make the field narrower, drag the line to the left.

➤ To delete a field, right-click it and select **Delete Column**.

237

➤ To insert a field, select the column to the left of which you want the new column (field) inserted, open the **Insert** menu, and click **Column**.

➤ To rename a field, double-click the column name and type a new field name.

As you're doing all this editing, keep in mind that the Undo feature is a little less reliable in a database program. Because Access saves your data automatically as you enter it, the database has a little more trouble recovering from mishaps. However, unlike its predecessor (Access 2000), Access 2002 does support multiple undo actions. If you make a mistake, open the **Edit** menu and select **Undo**.

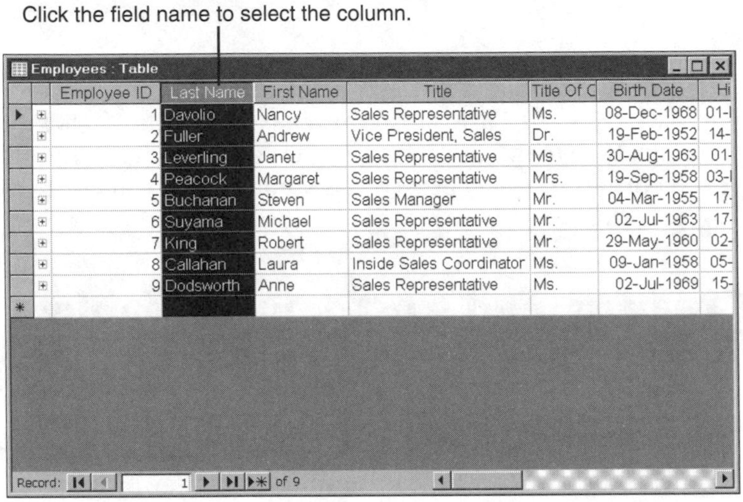

Click the field name to select the column.

Figure 19.3

In Datasheet view, a table looks and acts like an Excel worksheet.

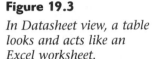

You can perform the same actions in Design view, but the layout is a little different. Design view does not show the data in the table. Instead, it shows the field names and the settings that control each field. Figure 19.4 shows you how to move and delete fields in Design view. To insert a new row (add a new field), select the **Insert, Rows** command.

Changing the Field Properties

Whenever you create a new field, you must type two entries for the field: the field name and the data type. The *field name* appears at the top of the column in the table and tells you what is stored in that field. The *data type* specifies the type of data you can enter into the field. For example, if you set a field's data type as Number, you can't type a regular text entry in that field. This feature helps prevent your data-entry clerk from typing the wrong information in a field.

To change the data type for a field, change to Design view. Click the **Data Type** box for the field whose data type you want to change. A button appears inside the box; click the button to open the **Data Type** drop-down list. Select the desired data type from those described in Table 19.1.

Click the button next to a row to select it;
drag the button up or down to move a row.

Type or change field names in this column.

Figure 19.4

Design view displays a list of field names and their types.

Field Name	Data Type	Description
EmployeeID	AutoNumber	Number automatically assigned to new employee.
LastName	Text	
FirstName	Text	
Title	Text	Employee's title.
TitleOfCourtesy	Text	Title used in salutations.
BirthDate	Date/Time	

Field Properties

General | Lookup

Field Size	20
Format	
Input Mask	
Caption	Last Name
Default Value	
Validation Rule	
Validation Text	
Required	Yes
Allow Zero Length	No
Indexed	Yes (Duplicates OK)
Unicode Compression	Yes
IME Mode	No Control
IME Sentence Mode	None

A field name can be up to 64 characters long, including spaces. Press F1 for help on field names.

Select a field and press the Delete key to remove it.

Insider Tip

Inserting Fields That Take Data from Other Tables

To insert a field that can copy data from another table in your database, you should create a Lookup field. Instead of selecting **Insert, Rows**, select **Insert, Lookup Field**. This runs the Lookup Wizard, which leads you through the process of connecting this field to the corresponding field in the other table.

Table 19.1 Access Data Types and What They're Good For

Data Type	What It's Good For
Text	Text entries or combinations of text and numbers: names, addresses, phone numbers, ZIP codes, Social Security numbers, and any other text or number that doesn't have to be sorted numerically or included in a calculation. (Text fields hold up to 255 characters.)
Memo	Lengthy descriptions over 65,000 characters.
Number	Any number except a dollar amount. Use the Number data type for numbers you might include in calculations or for numbers you want to sort, such as record numbers or part numbers. Don't use this data type for numbers you want to treat as text, such as addresses and phone numbers.
Date/Time	A calendar date or a time.
Currency	Dollar amounts.
AutoNumber	A field that automatically inserts a number for you. Excellent for numbering records sequentially.
Yes/No	True/False or Yes/No entries. As in: Did we get a Christmas card from them last year? Yes/No.
OLE Object	A picture, sound, spreadsheet, document, or other file created using some other application. (You can insert an object as large as 1GB!)
Hyperlink	A link to another file on your hard drive or the network, or to a Web page.
Lookup Wizard	Entries from other tables in the database. Selecting this data type runs the Lookup Wizard, which prompts you to pick the table from which you want to insert data. If you create a combo box (a text box with an arrow button that opens a drop-down list), you can then select entries from a drop-down list instead of typing them into the table.

At the bottom of the Design view window are additional options for changing the properties of fields. For the Currency data type, for instance, you can specify that you want no decimal places used so that amounts are shown only in dollars, or you can specify that this field is required (so Access won't accept the record unless you type an entry in the required field). When you click a field name in the upper half of the window, the options in the lower half show the settings for that field. You can then change the settings, as shown in Figure 19.5. When you click a setting, some options display an arrow button to open a drop-down list. In any case, watch the big box on the right for details and suggestions on using the setting.

As you work in Design view, save your changes every 5 minutes or so, using the standard **File**, **Save** command. You don't want to spend your entire day fiddling with field properties and then lose it all when your system locks up.

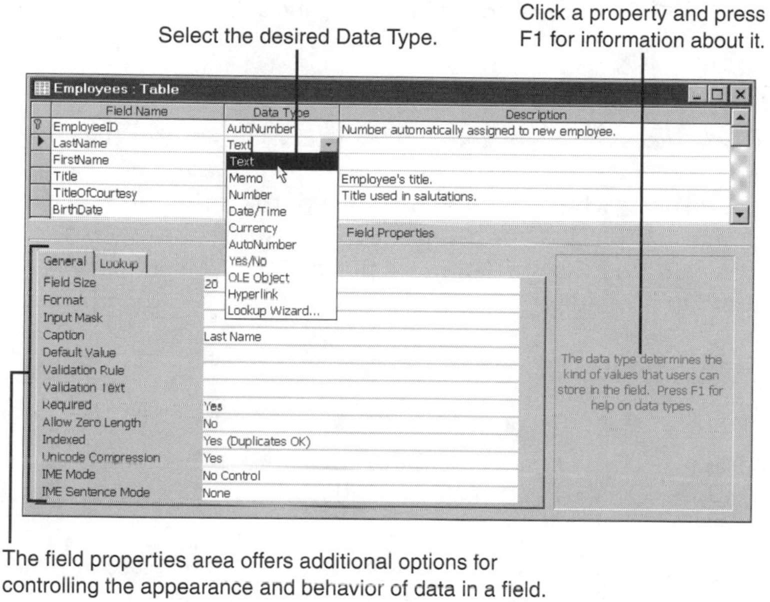

Select the desired Data Type.

Click a property and press F1 for information about it.

Figure 19.5

In Design view, you can change the data types and enter additional field properties.

The field properties area offers additional options for controlling the appearance and behavior of data in a field.

Creating New Tables

So far, you've been rearranging the fields and changing field data types in *existing* tables. But what if your database needs another table? How do you create one? First, return to the Database window, and click the **Tables** icon. The right pane in the Database window provides three options for creating a new table:

➤ **Create Table in Design View**—Displays a blank table in Design view, so you have to start from scratch—not the best option for a rank beginner.

➤ **Create Table by Using Wizard**—Runs the Table Wizard, which leads you step by step through the process of creating a new table using fields from existing tables.

➤ **Create Table by Entering Data**—Displays a blank table in Datasheet view, so you can immediately start typing entries. Before you start entering data, consider renaming the column headings (field names), as explained previously in this chapter.

241

Creating and Customizing Data Entry Forms

If you created a database using the wizard, you already have some forms you can start using. If, however, you changed your table in the previous section or created a new table, you might need to customize your data entry forms or create a new form. The following sections provide the instructions you need to get started.

Restructuring a Form

If you open a form and find that it does not contain the fields you want or that the fields are not in the correct order, you can restructure the form in Design view. In the Database window, click the **Forms** icon and click the name of the form you want to restructure. Click the **Design** button. The form appears in Design view, as shown in Figure 19.6, displaying the various controls that make up the form. When you click a control, handles appear around it, indicating that it is selected. You can then perform the following tasks:

➤ To move a control, drag it.

➤ To resize a control, drag one of the control's handles.

➤ To change the appearance of the text inside the control, select the control and then select a font, a font size, or an attribute (bold, italic, underline) from the toolbar.

➤ To delete a control, select the control and press the **Delete** key. (Be careful about deleting controls. Controls link the form to your table. If you delete a control, you won't be able to use the form to enter that piece of data into the table.)

➤ To change a label, drag over the existing text in the label box, and type new text. (This label should match the field name in the table or at least resemble it.)

➤ To change the control source (the field into which you type your entries), see the next section, cleverly titled "Changing the Control Source and Other Control Properties."

➤ To add a field or control, see "Adding Controls to a Form," later in this chapter. (You can also change the control type.)

➤ You can change the overall appearance of the form by using AutoFormat. Open the **Format** menu and select **AutoFormat**, or click the **AutoFormat** button in the Form Design toolbar.

Changing the Control Source and Other Control Properties

The *control source* links the field into which you type your entries to the table in which the entries are inserted. Say your form has text boxes into which you type a contact's last name and first name. The control sources for these text boxes are the LastName and FirstName fields in the table. If you created your database using the

Database Wizard, you probably don't want to mess with the control source settings. If you're creating a new form, however, you might need to specify the control source for a field.

Drag a handle to resize the control.

Drag the control to move it.   You can change the control source for a field.

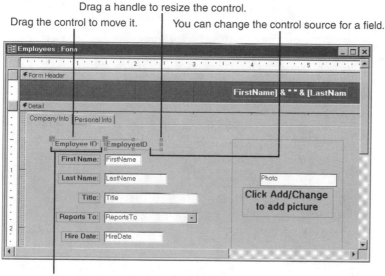

Figure 19.6

In Form Design view, you can change the appearance and arrangement of the controls.

You can change the text of a label.

To change a control source, first right-click the field whose control source you want to change and click **Properties** (or double-click the field). Click the **Data** tab, open the **Control Source** drop-down list, and click the name of the field into which you want the data from this control inserted.

Adding Controls to a Form

If you added any fields to a table earlier in this chapter, you must add controls to the corresponding form. You do this by using the Toolbox toolbar and by "drawing" the controls on the form in Design view. You can add controls such as text boxes, check boxes, option buttons, drop-down lists, and images boxes to your form.

To draw a control, click the button in the Toolbox toolbar for the desired control, as shown in Figure 19.7. (If the Toolbox is not displayed, click the **Toolbox** button.) Position the mouse pointer over the form and drag the mouse pointer to draw a box where you want the control to appear. When you release the mouse button, the control appears, and you can change its properties as explained in the previous section. With some controls, a dialog box appears after you create the control, asking you for more information.

In most cases, the control is accompanied by a box that enables you to type a label describing the control. If a label text box does not appear next to the control, you can use the **Label** button to add a Label control to the form.

Figure 19.7

You can add controls to your form that correspond to fields in the table.

Use this dialog box to set the properties of the new control.

Click the button for the type of control you want to add.

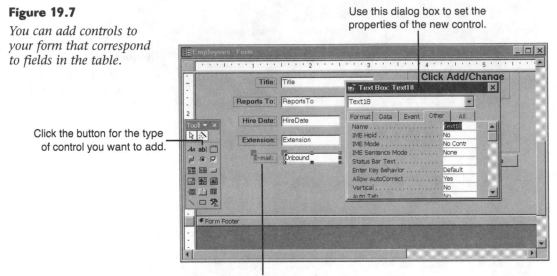

Drag the mouse pointer to draw a box where you want the control to appear on the form.

Creating a New Form

After you have all the tables you need for your database, creating forms for entering data into those tables is easy. The Form Wizard can lead you step by step through the process. All you have to do is tell the wizard which table fields you want included on your form and the order in which you want the fields placed.

To run the Form Wizard, click the **Forms** icon in the **Database** window and double-click **Create Form by Using Wizard**. The first Form Wizard dialog box asks you to select all the fields you want included on the form from the various tables in your database. You can select fields from more than one table. Try to insert the fields in the order in which you want them to appear on the form; you can change the order later, but doing it right the first time is easier.

After you select the fields, click the **Next** button and follow the wizard's instructions to select the layout and style for the form and to give the form a title. Click the **Finish** button when you reach the last dialog box. Congratulations, you're the proud parent of a new form!

The Least You Need to Know

This chapter introduced you not only to basic database concepts and tasks, but also to a lot of customization options you might not need right now. Just make sure you understand the following databasics:

➤ A database is a collection of records.

➤ A record is a collection of data entries that pertain to a single person, place, or object.

➤ To create a new database using the Database Wizard, select **File**, **New** and then click **General Templates** in the New File task pane.

➤ To view a list of tables in your database, open the **Database** window and click the **Tables** icon.

➤ To switch to Design view, click the **Design View** button or select the desired view from the **View** menu.

➤ To create a new table, return to the **Database** window, click the **Tables** icon, double-click **Create Table by Using Wizard**, and follow the wizard's instructions.

➤ To create a new form, return to the **Database** window, click the **Forms** icon, double-click **Create Form by Using Wizard**, and follow the wizard's instructions.

Chapter 20

Entering Data:
For the Record

In This Chapter

➤ Filling out forms when you can't find a data-entry clerk

➤ Entering data in a table

➤ Understanding a little more about the relationships between tables

➤ Selecting data entries from drop-down lists

Now that you have all your tables and forms in place, you're ready to start typing data and entering the records that make up your database. This is the boring work behind database creation, the kind of job that can give you a bad case of carpal tunnel syndrome and make you wish you had stayed in school.

You can enter data in three ways: by filling out pages full of forms, by typing entries in a table, or by entering the data in a query. This chapter shows you how to enter data using a form and a table. In Chapter 21, "Finding, Sorting, and Selecting Records," you learn more about queries.

How Forms, Tables, and Datasheets Differ

Before you start entering data into your database, you should understand the differences between Datasheet view, forms, and tables so you can make an educated decision about how to enter data. The following list will help you decide:

➤ **If you create a form that matches one table blank for blank, you can use either the form or the table to enter data**—You are filling in the same blanks, so it really doesn't matter.

➤ **A form can have blanks that correspond to fields in more than one table—** In such a case, it makes a big difference whether you type the data on a form or use a table. I strongly recommend that you use the form in this case, to ensure that you don't omit any data.

➤ **Datasheet is a *view* that is available for both tables and forms—**A table in Datasheet view is very similar to a form displayed in Datasheet view, but the function of a form differs from that of a table. Even though a form in Datasheet view *looks* like a table, remember that you're still working with a form.

Filling Out Forms

We are all accustomed to filling out forms. You do it in your checkbook, at the license bureau, when you apply for a job, and even when you fill out an application for a credit card. Because you know how to fill out forms, the most intuitive way to enter data in your database is to use a fill-in-the-blanks form.

To complete a form, first display the form you want to fill out. In the Database window, click the **Forms** icon and double-click the name of the form you want to use. Either way you do it, the form pops up onscreen, as shown in Figure 20.1.

If you have any records in the database, the form displays the data that makes up the first record. To display a blank form for entering a new record, click the button that has the asterisk (*) on it.

Figure 20.1

The Form window displays records and lets you edit them or create new records.

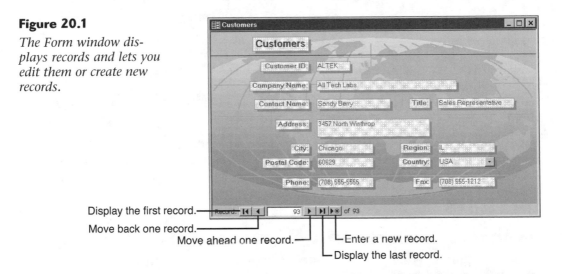

Display the first record.
Move back one record.
Move ahead one record.
Enter a new record.
Display the last record.

If you choose to create a new record, a blank form appears, prompting you to fill in the blanks. How you fill in the blanks depends on the blanks you're filling. Some blanks are drop-down lists that contain entries from other tables. To enter data, you open the drop-down list and select the desired entry. Other blanks are text boxes: You type an entry in the text box. Still other blanks might require that you insert a picture. In such a case, follow the instructions on the form to insert the object.

To move from one blank to the next, press the **Tab** or **Enter** key, or point and click with the mouse. To move back one blank, press **Shift+Tab**. (If a blank is too short for the entry you're typing, press **Shift+F2** to display the Zoom dialog box, and then type your entry.) Some blanks scroll to the left on their own. If the form has another page, you can view the page by scrolling down or by clicking the desired page button at the bottom of the form.

After you have entered all the data for a record, click the **New Record** button (the one with the asterisk). This transfers all the data you entered into the corresponding table(s) and displays a new, blank record for you to fill out. You can also create a new record by pressing **Ctrl** and the plus sign (**Ctrl++**).

Insider Tip

Editing Records

You perform the same steps to edit your records as you perform to type new entries. However, when you press Tab, Enter, or arrow keys to move from one blank to the next, Access highlights the entire entry in that blank. If you want to replace the entry, go ahead and start typing. To edit the entry, click the entry to move the insertion point to the position where you want to type your change. After you have clicked in the text to edit it, you can use the left and right arrow keys to move the insertion point.

Entering Data in a Table

Although forms provide a more intuitive way to enter records into your database, a table might be more efficient. A table also enables you to focus on a single set of data, whereas a form might contain data fields for several tables.

To enter records in a table, click the **Tables** icon in the Database window, and then double-click the name of the table in which you want to add records. Scroll down to the bottom of the table, as shown in Figure 20.2, where you'll find a blank row just waiting for you to create a new record. Just start typing; press the **Tab** key to move from one field to the next. After you type an entry in the last field in the row and press the **Tab** key, Access creates a new row into which you can type entries for the next record.

You can also create a new record by clicking the **New Record** button or selecting **Insert**, **New Record**. Access always creates a new record as a new row at the bottom of the table. After you enter the record, Access automatically rearranges the records to sort them in the proper order (for instance, alphabetically by last name). To move to the first record, press **Ctrl+Home**. To move to the last record, press **Ctrl+End**.

Figure 20.2

Datasheet view lets you type records in a table.

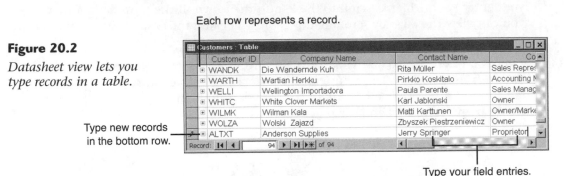

Each row represents a record.

Type new records in the bottom row.

Type your field entries.

What Are These Drop-Down Lists For?

As you enter data in tables and forms, you'll start to notice that some of the blanks are actually drop-down lists from which you can select an entry. You also might notice that you can't type any entries into these blanks unless they're on the list. Why? Because these fields, called *foreign keys*, are linked to fields called *primary keys* in other tables.

Let's pretend we have a restaurant supply business that distributes various foods and beverages. Figure 20.3 shows a database form for entering a record of each item our company ships. The Categories field lets us categorize our products as beverages, condiments, produce, meat/poultry, and so on. The entries in this field come from another table, the Categories table, which enables us to keep track of the various categories of consumables we ship.

Now, say we start selling a product that doesn't fit in any of our existing categories; for example, we might start shipping salmon and lobster, both seafood. To keep track of the category, we first must enter it in the Categories table. Then, when we enter salmon and lobster in the Products table, we can simply select Seafood from the drop-down list in the Products table.

One exception exists to these drop-down lists. If you created a Lookup Data table (using the Lookup Wizard), the second wizard dialog box lets you create the table on your own (by selecting **I Will Type in the Values**). If you select that option, you can type any entry; you're not locked into the entries on the list. If you select **I Want the Lookup Column to Look Up the Values in Another Table or Query**, the table from which you are extracting entries restricts your entries.

Key field supplies data to the foreign field.   Foreign field

Figure 20.3

Access relates data in two or more tables by using matching fields.

Insider Tip

Creating Relationships Between Tables

The easiest way to create relationships between tables is to use the Database Wizard to set up your tables. If you need another table, use the Table Wizard to create the new table. These wizards display a list of existing tables from which to choose, ensuring that the tables are properly linked.

The Least You Need to Know

After you have all the tables and forms set up, data entry is a breeze, assuming you can do the following:

➤ If you have a form for entering data into two or more tables, use the form (rather than a table) to enter your data.

➤ If your form contains fields for only one table, you can enter data more quickly in Table view.

➤ In Datasheet view, a form looks like a table but acts like a form.

➤ To create a new record in a form, click the button that has an asterisk on it.

➤ To create a new record in a table (or in a form that's displayed in Datasheet view), type the record in the last row.

➤ If a field has a drop-down list, open the list and select the desired entry.

Chapter 21

Finding, Sorting, and Selecting Records

In This Chapter

➤ Taking control of your records

➤ Sorting records by name, date, and other criteria

➤ Pulling selected records out of the database with queries

➤ Making it easy with the Query Wizard

Now that you have this oversized filing cabinet sitting in your computer, how do you go about getting at those records? You didn't enter all that information just to give your computer something to do. Now you can answer the pressing questions of your business life: "How many kerflibbles did we sell last year and to which customers? Did we sell more after the Christmas promotion, or was that pretty much just another tax write-off?"

You have at least three options: You can browse through the records one at a time (which you already learned how to do in the previous chapter), list the information in every record according to field name, or create a query that pulls records that match certain criteria out of the database. In this chapter, you learn how to use the latter method to take control of your records.

Sorting Your Records by Number, Name, or Date

Access can sort records based on any field entry in the records. For example, you could sort a list of invoices by date, company name, the amount of the order, the payment overdue date, or even by the ZIP codes. Access offers two sort options: Sort

Ascending and Sort Descending, which you can find on the Records, Sort submenu or as buttons in the toolbar. Sort Ascending sorts from A to Z or 1 to 10. Sort Descending sorts from Z to A or 10 to 1.

You can sort records in either Datasheet view or Form view, although Datasheet view displays the results of the sorting operation more clearly. Take one of the following steps:

➤ In Form view, click inside the field you want to use to sort the records, and then click the **Sort Ascending** or **Sort Descending** button.

➤ In Datasheet view, click the column whose entries you want to use to sort the records. Click the **Sort Ascending** or **Sort Descending** button.

Filtering Records to Lighten the Load

Sometimes you want to look at a distinct group of records. Maybe you work for a collection agency and need to prioritize a list of people who owe money to one of your clients, and you need to know who has owed the most money for the longest period of time. To extract a select group of records, *filter* the records, as explained in the following sections.

Filtering the Easy Way

The easiest way to filter records in Access is to use a technique called *filter by selection*. To use this technique, select the entry on a form that you want to use as the filter. For example, open a record that has "New York" in the City field (in Form or Datasheet view), and then click in the **City** field. Next, click the **Filter by Selection** button. Access displays only those records that have the specified entry in the selected field (in the example, only those records that have "New York" in the City field). Filter by selection is case sensitive, so when you're typing entries, keep this in mind.

If the list of records is still too long, you can filter the list again using another field entry. Repeat the steps using an entry in another field. To remove the filter and return a complete list of records, click the **Remove Filter** button.

When Your Filtering Needs Become More Complex

Filtering by selection is great if you have a specific entry in your record that you can use for the filter and it's easy to find. However, sometimes you need to specify a range of records. You might want a list of clients whom you haven't called for more than a month or a list of records for people whose last name begins with A–K. Filter by selection can't handle anything this complicated.

To create a more complex filter, use the *filter by form* technique. With this technique, you type filter criteria into various fields on a blank form to tell Access which records to pull up. In a billing database, for example, you might type <=#10/25/03# (less than or equal to 10/25/03) in the Date field to find all bills dated 10/25/03 or earlier. Table 21.1 shows some additional sample expressions.

Table 21.1   Filter Criteria Expressions in Action

Field	Sample Expression	Filter Displays
City	"Chicago"	Only those records that have "Chicago" in the City field
City	"Chicago" or "New York"	Records that have "Chicago" or "New York" in the City field
DueDate	Between #10/1/03# and #7/10/03#	Records that have an entry in the Date Due field *between* the dates listed
LastName	>="K"	All records with a last name entry starting with K or a letter after K in the alphabet
LastName	<="J"	All records with a last name entry starting with J or a letter before J in the alphabet
LastName	"K*"	All records with a last name entry starting with K
LastName	"*K"	All records with a last name entry ending with K
State	Not "IN"	Only records that have a State entry other than IN
Customer	Like "L*"	Records for companies whose names start with L

Access is a pretty smart database. You can omit the quotes, and Access will filter the records just as if you had typed the quotes. In addition, whenever you use the asterisk, as in the last example, Access supplies "Like" for you. For example, if you type R*, Access filters the records as if you had typed Like "R*".

To filter by form, open the table or form for the records you want to filter, and then click the **Filter by Form** button. A blank form or a single-row datasheet appears, displaying the names of all the fields. Type a filter criteria expression in each field you want to use to filter the records, as shown in Figure 21.1. (The arrow next to each field displays a list of data, which allows you to perform a quick filter by selection operation.)

You can type a criteria expression in more than one field to further limit the group of records the filter will display. In essence, you are telling Access to show only those records that meet the first condition *and* the second condition. To broaden the filter, you can click one or more **Or** tabs and enter expressions in the fields. For example, you might want a list of customers who owe you money *or* customers to whom you owe money.

 After you've typed your filter criteria expressions, click the **Apply Filter** button (in the Database toolbar). Access filters the records and displays a list of only those records that match the specified criteria. To cancel the filter and show all records, open the **Records** menu and select **Remove Filter/Sort**.

Figure 21.1

Filter by form gives you greater control over the filter operation.

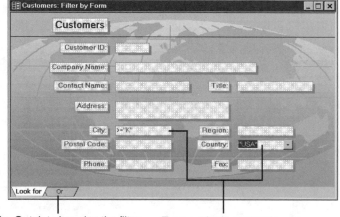

Use the Or tab to broaden the filter.   Type a criteria expression in one or more fields.

Using Queries to Sort, Select, and Calculate

Although filters are powerful tools for extracting records from individual tables, they are somewhat limited. Filters don't really do anything with the records; they don't let you combine information from different tables, and they can't extract only selected fields—they display entire records.

Access provides a more powerful data management tool called a *query*, which can do everything a filter can do and much more. The following sections explain two ways to create and use queries in your database.

Using the Query Wizards

Like all wizards, the Query Wizards are designed to simplify your life. Instead of designing your own query from scratch, you can use the Query Wizards to step you through the process of creating the following four types of queries:

➤ **Simple queries**—Pull data from fields in various tables, place the data in a query table, and (optionally) sort the records. (This is the most common type of query.)

➤ **Crosstab queries**—Pull data from fields, assemble it in a table that's structured like an Excel worksheet, and (optionally) perform calculations using the data. Crosstab queries are excellent for determining totals and subtotals.

➤ **Find Duplicates queries**—Select all records that have the same entry in a specified field. In the Home Inventory database, for example, you could use a find duplicates query to find all possessions located in the living room.

➤ **Find Unmatched queries**—Select all records that have no related records in another table. This type of query is useful for finding records with missing entries. After the query is done, you can enter the missing data.

The following steps lead you through the process of creating a simple query:

1. With the Database window displayed, open the **Insert** menu and click **Query**. The New Query dialog box appears, listing the four Query Wizards.

2. Click **Simple Query Wizard**, and then click **OK**. The first Simple Query Wizard dialog box appears, prompting you to select the fields you want included in the query.

3. Open the **Tables/Queries** drop-down list and select one of the tables whose field(s) you want to include in the query. The Available Fields list displays the names of all the fields in the selected table.

4. In the **Available Fields** list, double-click a field name to move it to the Selected Fields list to include the field in the query. (You can move all the fields from the Available Fields list to the Selected Fields list by clicking the double-headed arrow.)

5. Repeat steps 3 and 4 to add more fields to the query. (You can add fields from more than one table.) When you're done adding fields, click the **Next** button. If you clicked the double-headed arrow in step 4 to include *all* fields, skip to step 8. If you chose fields individually, the next dialog box asks whether you want a detailed query or a summary—move on to step 6.

6. Select **Detail** to display the complete information for each field. (If you want only summary information, such as an average or a sum, click **Summary** and enter your summary preferences.)

7. Click the **Next** button. The next dialog box asks you to either type a title for the query or accept the suggested title and gives you the option of opening the query or modifying the query design.

8. If desired, type a title for the query.

9. To change the query design, click **Modify the Query Design**. To display the results of the query, click **Open the Query to View Information**.

10. Click the **Finish** button. The Simple Query Wizard creates the query and displays it in its own window.

If you chose to view the information (the results of the query), the query appears in Datasheet view. You can click a column heading to select a column and then drag the column to move it. You can also sort the query or filter it as explained earlier in this chapter. (Any changes you make to columns in the query table do not affect the original tables.)

If you chose to modify the query design, the query appears in Design view, where you can enter additional instructions for sorting and filtering the data. When you're finished entering your instructions, change to Datasheet view to display the results.

Sorting a Query in Design View

Instead of using the Sort Ascending or Sort Descending button to sort the records in a query, change to Design view. This view gives you more control over filtering and sorting your records. In some large databases, a single-level sort creates huge subgroups that are as unmanageable as when the records were unsorted. Those subgroups need to be sorted further. So, you sort by State, then by County, then by City.

Creating a Query Without a Wizard

Although the Query Wizards are helpful, they might not create the type of query you need. To make a custom query, take the following steps:

1. In the Database window, click the **Queries** icon.

2. Double-click **Create Query in Design View**. The Show Table dialog box appears, prompting you to select the tables from which you want to extract data.

3. Double-click the name of each table from which you want to extract data. When you double-click the name of a table, the table is added to the **Query#: Select Query** window.

4. Click the **Close** button. The Query window shows the names of all the tables you added, as well as a list of fields in each table (see Figure 21.2).

5. For each field you want to add to your query, click inside the **Field** box at the bottom of the window and double-click the field name in one of the tables at the top of the window. The field names are added to the Field boxes. Table names appear directly below the field names. (Or, you can open the drop-down list and select the field name. Each field name starts with its table name and a colon.)

1. Click a Field box.

2. Double-click
a field name.

3. These fields will appear in the query.

4. Click here to run the query.

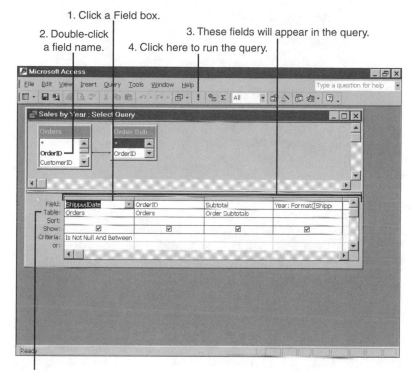

Figure 21.2

*Add the fields from the
tables to your query.*

Table names

6. To sort the records in the query based on the
entries in one of the fields, click in the **Sort**
box for that field, open the drop-down list,
and select **Ascending** or **Descending**.

7. To filter the records based on the entries in
one field, click inside the **Criteria** box in
that field and type a filter criteria expression. See "Filtering Records to Lighten the
Load" earlier in this chapter for details.

8. The **Show** check boxes let you hide or display a field in a query. Remove the check
from the box to hide the field if desired.

9. To run the query, click the **Run** button (the
button with the exclamation point) in the
toolbar. Access runs the query and displays
the results in Datasheet view.

Drag and Drop

You can Shift+click a list of fields
and drag and drop them on the
field's row to add them as a group.
You can Ctrl+click to select non-
contiguous fields.

Totally Cool

You can add a Total row to your query to help group records and include sums, averages, and other operations in your query. To add the Total row, right-click in the query table in Design view and click **Totals**.

Saving, Opening, and Editing Queries

Access does not automatically save queries. To save your query, open the **File** menu and select **Save**. Type a name for the query and click **OK**. Queries are saved with the database. To open a query you saved, first open the database file. In the Database window, click the **Queries** icon and double-click the name of the query you want to open.

Whenever you open a query, Access displays it in Datasheet view. To edit it, you must change to Design view. Open the **View** menu and select **Design View**, or open the **View** drop-down list (on the left end of the toolbar) and click **Design View**. Then, you can add or delete fields, hide fields, move fields, or sort and filter your records.

The Least You Need to Know

After you've entered the data that makes up your database, you can sort, filter, and extract that data in various ways:

➤ To manually flip through your records, open the desired form and use the page controls at the bottom of the Form window to flip from one record to the next.

➤ You can change to Datasheet view to display your records in a table.

➤ To sort records in Form view, click inside the field you want to use to sort the records, and then click the **Sort Ascending** or **Sort Descending** button.

➤ To sort records in Datasheet view, click the field name at the top of the column whose entries you want to use to sort the records, and then click the **Sort Ascending** or **Sort Descending** button.

➤ To quickly sort records, click inside the field that has the entry you want all the other records to match, and then click the **Filter by Selection** button.

➤ Create a query to extract data from various tables. To create a simple query, open the **Insert** menu, select **Query**, click **Simple Query**, click **OK**, and follow the Simple Query Wizard's instructions.

Chapter 22

Giving Data Meaning with Reports

Data is like money: If you don't do something with it, it's useless. Reports do something with your data. You can use a report to transform a membership directory into sheets of mailing labels or a phone list. You also can use a report to pull together a list of contributors, the amount each person contributed to the annual fund drive, and the total amount the fund drive pulled in. Reports can even pull data from one or more tables and graph it.

In this chapter, you learn various ways to create and customize reports; and you learn how to print reports after you've created them.

The Report You Need Might Already Exist!

You can save yourself some time and effort by checking to see if your database already has the report you need. If you used one of the Database Wizards to create your database, you might be in luck. The wizard makes several reports you can use immediately.

 In the Database window, click the **Reports** icon to view a list of reports, as shown in Figure 22.1. Double-click the name of the report you want to view.

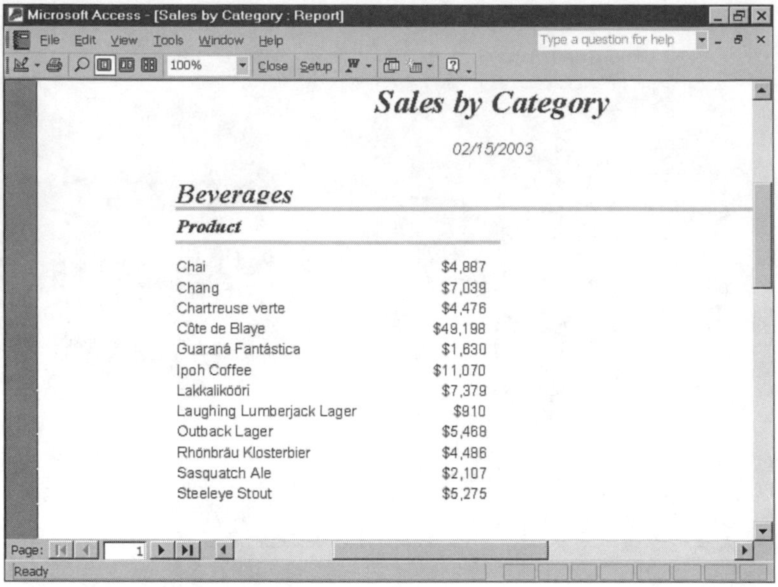

Figure 22.1

The Database Wizard might have created a report for you.

Microsoft Access - [Sales by Category : Report]

File   Edit   View   Tools   Window   Help   Type a question for help

100%   Close   Setup

Sales by Category

02/15/2003

Beverages

Product

Chai	$4,887
Chang	$7,039
Chartreuse verte	$4,476
Côte de Blaye	$49,198
Guaraná Fantástica	$1,630
Ipoh Coffee	$11,070
Lakkalikööri	$7,379
Laughing Lumberjack Lager	$910
Outback Lager	$5,468
Rhönbräu Klosterbier	$4,486
Sasquatch Ale	$2,107
Steeleye Stout	$5,275

Page: 1

Ready

Whoa!

Customize an Existing Report

Even if an existing report doesn't have all the data you need arranged just the way you want it, you might be able to save time by customizing one of the existing reports instead of starting from scratch. See "Customizing the Appearance and Content of Your Report" later in this chapter for details.

Making Reports with the Report Wizard

No matter which task you want to perform in Access, you can be certain that there's some philanthropic wizard waiting in the wings to lend a hand. This is true with reports as well. The following steps walk you through the process of creating a report with the wizard:

1. Open the database file that has the data you want to include in the report.
2. In the Database window, click the **Reports** icon.

3. Double-click **Create Report by Using Wizard**. The first Report Wizard dialog box appears and prompts you to select the fields you want included in the query.

4. Open the **Tables/Queries** drop-down list and select one of the tables or queries that contain a field you want to include in the report, as shown in Figure 22.2. The Available Fields list displays the names of all the fields in the selected table. (You can select fields from more than one table.)

5. In the **Available Fields** list, double-click a field name to include the field in the report. The field moves to the Selected Fields list. (You can move all the fields from the Available Fields list to the Selected Fields list by clicking the double-headed arrow button.)

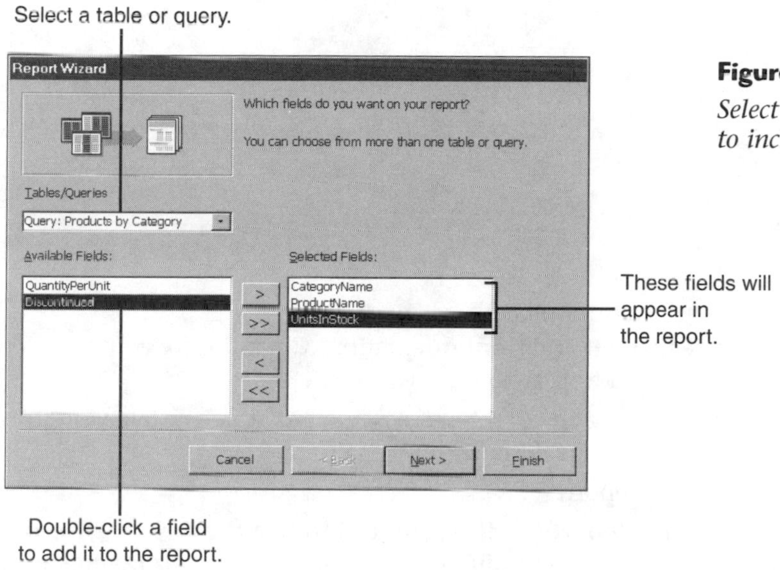

Select a table or query.

Figure 22.2

Select the fields you want to include in the report.

These fields will appear in the report.

Double-click a field to add it to the report.

6. Repeat steps 4 and 5 to add more fields to the report. When you finish adding fields, click the **Next** button. If you included fields from more than one table, proceed to step 7; otherwise, skip to step 8.

7. Click the desired table to use its fields to structure your report. Click the **Next** button. The next dialog box asks whether you want to use any fields to group the data in your report.

8. Double-click a field if you want to use it to group records. If you're creating an inventory of your possessions, for example, you might want to group them by rooms. (You can insert additional fields as group headings by double-clicking their names.) Click **Next**. The next dialog box asks whether you want to sort records using any of the fields.

9. Use the drop-down lists, as shown in Figure 22.3, to select the fields that contain the entries you want to use to sort the records. (For example, you might

263

sort by LastName.) Click the sort button to the right of the drop-down list to change from ascending to descending or vice versa. Click the **Next** button. The wizard now asks you to pick a layout for the report.

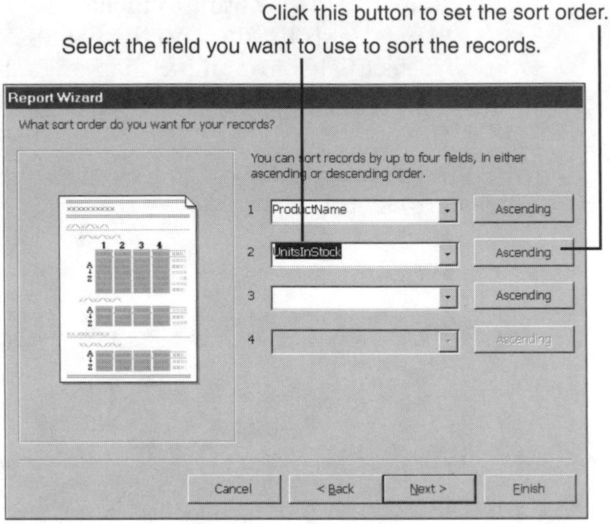

Click this button to set the sort order.

Select the field you want to use to sort the records.

Figure 22.3

You can sort the records using one or more fields.

10. Click the desired layout and print orientation. Click the **Next** button. The wizard asks you to pick a font style for the report.

11. Click the desired style and click **Next**. The final dialog box lets you give the report a title or change its design.

12. Type a title for the report.

13. Select **Preview the Report** (to display it) or **Modify the Report's Design** (to view it in Design view and modify it). Click **Finish**. The wizard creates the report and displays it.

Customizing the Appearance and Content of Your Report

If the Report Wizard just dropped the perfect report in your lap (fat chance), click the **Print** button in the toolbar—and you're done. It's more likely, however, that your report needs a little tweaking before it's ready to present to the general public. The report might need something minor, such as a font change, or some major reconstruction that requires you to move columns or perform some other heavy-duty restructuring.

To make any of these changes, display the report (in the Database window, click the **Reports** icon and double-click the report), and then open the **View** menu and select

264

Design View. Access displays the structure behind the report. In the next few sections, you learn how to work in Design view to modify the report.

Working with a Report in Design View

In Design view, your report looks nothing like the report you just created (see Figure 22.4). For one thing, your report doesn't have those gray bars separating it into sections. The following list explains the various sections in your report and what you'll find in each section:

➤ **Headers**—These print on every page of the report. The report header appears only at the top of the first page. The page header and any additional headers appear at the top of every page. In addition, most reports use a header that contains the field names from one or more tables as column headings. This helps your audience figure out which information goes with which column.

➤ **Detail**—This is used for the data you pull from the various tables in your database. The controls in the Detail section are usually fields that pull data from one or more tables and list it under the column headings.

➤ **Footers**—These appear at the bottom of every page. The Report footer appears on the last page of the report; you can use it to calculate grand totals. The Page footer is useful for including a date or page number on every page. The footer just below the Detail section is useful for subtotals.

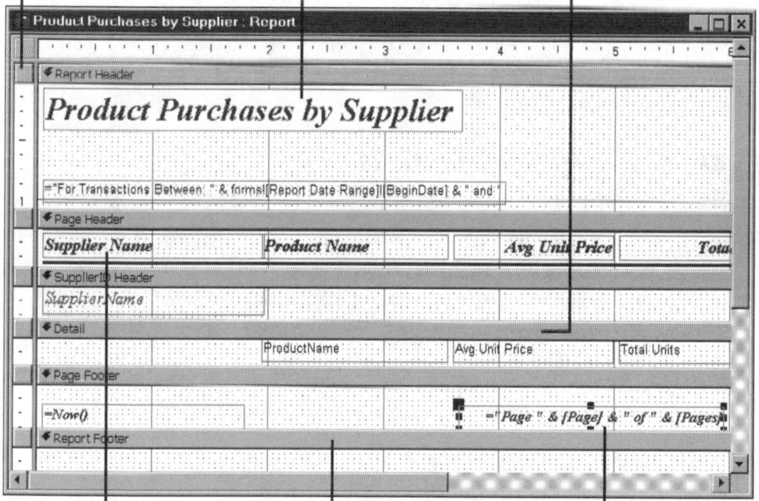

The Report Header contains the title.

The Report Selector button

The Detail area controls the layout of data.

Figure 22.4

A report in Design view.

This header inserts column headings.

This footer inserts the word "Page" followed by the page number.

Drag a section bar up or down to change the size of the section.

You can increase the space used for a particular section of the report by dragging the top of the bar for that section up or down. (Keep in mind that this *will* affect the page breaks in your report.) If there is no space below a section bar, double-click the bar, click the **Format** tab, and type a measurement in the **Height** box (for instance, type **1** to give the section 1 inch of space).

You can change the properties of a section by double-clicking the bar and then entering your preferences. To enter settings that control the entire report, double-click the **Report Selector** button, which appears at the intersection of the two rulers.

AutoFormatting Individual Objects

You can use AutoFormat to change the appearance of individual objects (controls) on the form by selecting the object before running AutoFormat. However, this can give your report an undesirable ransom-note effect.

Changing the Overall Appearance of the Report

The easiest way to change the overall appearance of a report is to use AutoFormat. Click the **Report Selector** button in the upper-left corner of the window (where the horizontal and vertical rulers intersect). A black square appears on the button indicating that it is active. You also can select the entire report (or specific objects on the report) by selecting **Report** (or the object's name) from the **Object** list on the left end of the Formatting toolbar.

Open the **Format** menu and select **AutoFormat**. The AutoFormat dialog box appears, prompting you to select a style for your report. Click the desired style, and then click **OK**. The selected style doesn't appear in Design view. To view the report with the new design, open the **View** menu and select **Print Preview**.

Selecting, Moving, and Aligning Controls

Design view reveals that your report is no more than a collection of text boxes and other controls. Working with these controls is very similar to working with objects in a drawing program. To select a control, click it. Shift+click additional controls to work on more than one at a time. When you click a control, a box and a set of handles appear around the control. You can then move, resize, or delete the control:

➤ To move a control, rest the mouse pointer on the outline of the box that defines the control. When the mouse pointer turns into a hand, drag the box.

➤ To change the size of the control, drag one of its handles.

➤ To delete the selected control, press the **Delete** key.

266

When moving controls, you might want to align one control with another. Access can do this for you. First, select the controls you want to align; you can Shift+click controls or drag a selection box around the desired controls. Then, open the **Format** menu, point to **Align**, and select the desired alignment option: **Left**, **Right**, **Top**, **Bottom**, or **To Grid** (which aligns one edge of the control with an invisible gridline).

Changing Type Styles and Sizes

You learned earlier how to change font styles for the entire report. You can also change font styles and sizes for individual controls. To do so, first select the controls that have the text you want to format. Then, use the tools in the Formatting toolbar to set the desired font and font size, add attributes such as bold and italic, and change the text and background color. You also can add a border, drop shadow, or other special effect to give the control another dimension.

Adding Controls to the Report

In Design view, Access displays a toolbox containing buttons for adding controls, such as Labels, Text Boxes, Check Boxes, and Lines, to your report. If this toolbox is not displayed, select **View**, **Toolbox** or click the **Toolbox** button. The easiest way to add a control is to use a Control Wizard. These steps show you how:

1. Click the **Control Wizards** button to turn it on, if desired. (You don't have to use the Control Wizards; you can create controls without using the wizards.)

2. Click the button for the control you want to create.

3. Move the mouse pointer over the report where you want to insert the control. Drag the mouse to create a box that defines the size and location of the control. When you release the mouse button, the control appears, and the Control Wizard dialog box appears, providing instructions on how to proceed (if the control has a wizard).

4. If a wizard appears, follow the Control Wizard's instructions to create the control. In most cases, you need to supply a name for the control and tell the wizard which field to link the control to. If a wizard does not appear, simply complete the control (the Label control does not have a wizard; simply type in the label).

Calculating Totals, Subtotals, and Averages

Some reports simply present data in an easily digestible format, such as a phone list or an address list. Other reports are designed to help you draw conclusions or determine final results. You might have a report that lists income and expenses to determine profit. If the report simply lists the numbers, it won't do you much good. You need to know a final number—the profit or loss.

267

Inserting Fields

If you want to insert a field in your report, there's an easier way to do it than by using the toolbox. Open the **View** menu and select **Field List**. This displays a list of the available fields. Drag a field from the field list to the desired location on the report; Access then inserts a label box and a text box for the field. Click in the box and change the label, if desired.

To perform such a task, enter a formula into your report. The formula performs calculations using the data the report extracts from various tables. You typically enter a formula inside a text box in a section below the section that contains the numbers you want to total (in other words, below the Detail section). Before you start typing formulas, figure out which section you want the formula to appear in:

➤ To insert a calculation at the end of a row, type the formula at the end of the row that contains the numbers the formula will use in its calculations. For example, a record might include the number of items ordered and the price of each item. You could insert a formula at the end of the row that multiplies the number of items times the price to determine the total cost.

➤ If the report has more than one Detail section, you can enter formulas to perform subtotals on a column of numbers in the section just below the Detail section.

➤ To determine a grand total that appears at the bottom of the last page of the report, add the formula to the Report Footer section.

To enter a formula in a text box, click the **Text Box** button in the toolbox and drag the box where you want to insert the formula. In the **Text** box, type the name of the result (for example, **Total**, **Grand Total**, or **Average**). Then, click inside the **Unbound** text box and type your formula, as shown in Figure 22.5. For example, type **=SUM ([Income])** to total all the values from the Income fields. The following are some other examples of formulas you might use:

=SUM ([Income])–SUM ([Expenses]) determines the total profit.

=[Quantity]*[Price] determines the total cost of a number of items times the price of each item.

=AVG ([Grades]) determines the average of a series of grades.

=[Qtr1]+[Qtr2]+[Qtr3]+[Qtr4] calculates the total profit over the last four quarters.

=[Subtotal]*.05 multiplies the subtotal by .05 to determine a 5% tax on an order.

=[Subtotal]+[Tax] determines the total due by adding the subtotal of the order and the amount of tax due.

The formulas you see here are very similar to formulas you might use in Excel worksheets (except for the funky brackets). The main difference is that instead of using cell addresses in the formulas, you use field names to specify values. For details on using formulas in Excel worksheets, see Chapter 12, "Doing Math with Formulas."

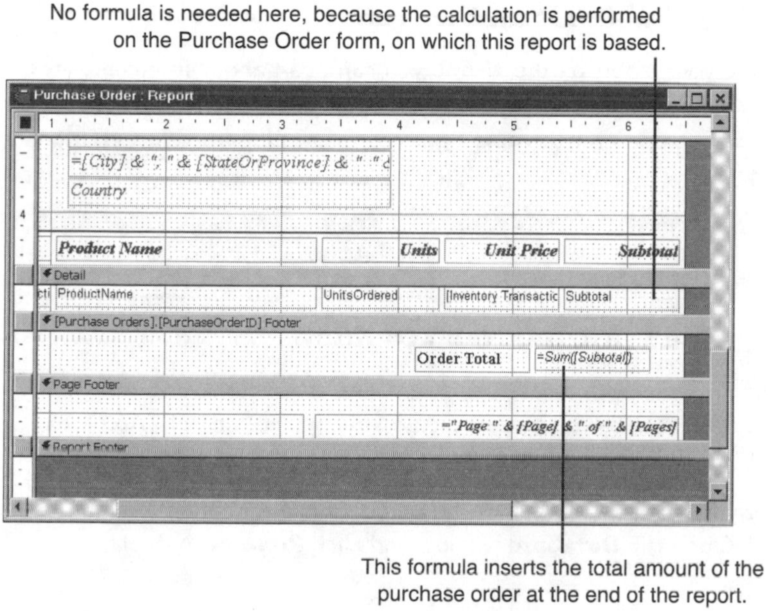

No formula is needed here, because the calculation is performed
on the Purchase Order form, on which this report is based.

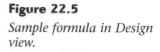

Figure 22.5

Sample formula in Design view.

This formula inserts the total amount of the
purchase order at the end of the report.

After you enter a formula in a text box, you should format the text box. If the formula enters a dollar amount, for example, you should change the Format property of the text box to Currency. To change the property of a control on a report, double-click the control, and then enter your preferences in the Format dialog box.

Saving and Printing Reports

After you've spent a good part of your day designing a report, you don't want to lose it when you shut down, so be sure to save it. In fact, you should save the report regularly as you're designing it to prevent losing any of your work. One little mistake can wipe out your report before you've had a chance to use it. Open the **File** menu and select **Save**, or click the **Save** button in the toolbar. Type a name for the report and click **OK**.

269

To print one copy of the report quickly, make sure your printer is turned on, and then click the **Print** button. If you want to print more than one copy of the report, or if you want to change other printer settings, open the **File** menu and select **Print**. Enter your preferences and click **OK**.

Publish It on the Web!

You might want to place your report on the Web so you can boast about your company's profits and try to attract investors. To save your report as an HTML (Web) document, select **File**, **Export** and then open the **Save as Type** drop-down list and select **HTML Documents**. Click the **Export** button.

The Least You Need to Know

Just when you think you're done with a database, you realize that you have to do something with the data you've entered—you have to create a report. Fortunately, Access has some report tools that can make your job easy:

➤ If you used a wizard to create your database, the wizard might have created the report you need. Open the **Database** window and click **Reports** to display a list of reports.

➤ You can use a Report Wizard to create a new report. In the Database window, click **Reports**, click **New**, and then follow the wizard's instructions.

➤ You usually work with reports in Design view and look at them in Print Preview. To change views, open the **View** menu and select the desired view.

➤ In Design view, you can select the entire report by clicking the **Report Selector** button, which is located where the two rulers intersect.

➤ To change the look of the entire report, click the **Report Selector** button, open the **Format** menu, select **AutoFormat**, pick the desired format, and click **OK**.

➤ To change the look of individual controls on the form, click the control and use the options in the Formatting toolbar.

Part 6

Managing Your Life (and Your E-mail) with Outlook

You've always wanted your own personal secretary to inform you of upcoming meetings, remind you of important dates (such as Secretary's Day), prioritize your list of things to do, filter your mail and memos, and basically run the office while you're out playing golf with prospective clients. Office XP provides you with your own tireless secretary called Microsoft Outlook.

No, Outlook can't arrange a business trip, drive deposits to the bank, or tuck you into bed when your spouse is out of town, but it can help you keep track of appointments and dates, organize your e-mail, and even remind you of the brilliant ideas that popped into your head during the course of a day. In this section, you learn how to use Outlook to do all this and more!

Chapter 23

Keeping Track of Dates, Mates, and Things to Do

In This Chapter

➤ Getting up and running with the Outlook Bar

➤ Scheduling appointments

➤ Having Outlook notify you in advance of upcoming appointments

➤ Never again forgetting a birthday or anniversary

➤ Creating and using an electronic Address Book

A handful of overachievers are ruling our lives. There's the mother who takes her lunch break to help with craft time at school. The father who comes home from a full day's work to organize the neighborhood soccer league. The retired lady, down the street, who starts a membership drive for her philanthropic organization. They quietly force us to pack our calendars with appointments, sell coupon books and candy, and do more than any generation has ever done before, driving us to early graves with hypertension.

To control this madness and preserve your sanity, let Outlook help you manage your life. In this chapter, you learn how to use Outlook to keep track of your appointments, contacts, and all the activities you can't seem to avoid.

Getting Started with Outlook

Before you can take advantage of Outlook, you have to run it. Open the **Start** menu, point to **Programs**, and click **Microsoft Outlook** (or click the **Launch Microsoft Outlook** button in the Quick Launch toolbar). The first time you start Outlook, the Startup Wizard runs and leads you through the process of setting up Outlook to access your e-mail. Follow the wizard's instructions to complete the setup (see "Adding E-mail Accounts" in the next chapter for details).

When setup is complete, the Microsoft Outlook window appears. The Outlook Bar (on the left) is your key to the various features of Outlook. Here you can switch to your Inbox, Calendar, Contacts, Tasks, Notes, or items you deleted. Just click the icon for the desired folder in the Outlook Bar. The Information Viewer (on the right) displays the contents of the current folder. If, for example, you click the Inbox icon in the Outlook Bar, the Information Viewer displays two panes: the top pane shows a list of messages you received (only one sample message the first time you start Outlook), and the bottom pane displays the contents of the currently selected message. You can change the relative dimensions of the Outlook Bar and Information Viewer by dragging the vertical bar that separates them.

Figure 23.1

Outlook makes accessing information easy.

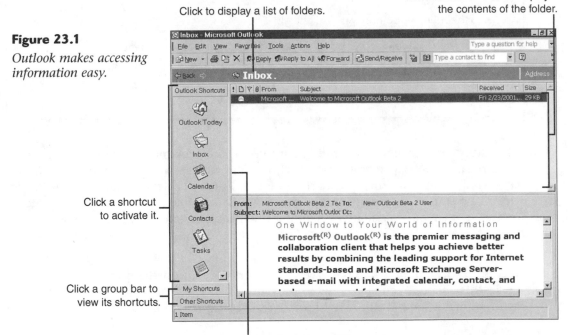

Click to display a list of folders.

The Information Viewer displays the contents of the folder.

Click a shortcut to activate it.

Click a group bar to view its shortcuts.

Drag this bar to change the relative dimensions of the panels.

At the bottom of the Outlook Bar are short gray bars that represent other (hidden) shortcut groups. To see the shortcut icons in any of these groups, click the group (such as My Shortcuts or Other Shortcuts). Also, notice that just above the Information Viewer is a folder banner that displays the name of the current folder. Click that name to display a list of folders. You can then select a folder from the list instead of from the Outlook Bar to view its contents.

Outlook Today

 The Outlook Today icon provides a quick overview of how bad your day is going to be. When you click Outlook Today, the Information Viewer displays a list of your appointments, the number of e-mail messages you've received, and your to-do list. To have Outlook Today appear when you start Outlook, click the **Outlook Today** icon and click **Customize Outlook Today** in the viewing area. Click the check box next to **When Starting, Go Directly to Outlook Today**, and then click **Save Changes** in the upper right of the viewing area.

Using the Standard Toolbar

Like every other Windows application, Outlook has a toolbar you can use to bypass the menu system for commands you frequently enter. Although the toolbar changes depending on what you're currently doing (setting appointments, checking e-mail, jotting down notes), you can count on a couple of things. First, as with all toolbars, Outlook's Standard toolbar displays a ScreenTip when you rest the mouse pointer on a button. The ScreenTip shows the name of the button so you have some idea of what it does. Second, the following buttons are always on the toolbar, no matter what you're doing:

New. Enables you to create a new mail message, new note, new appointment, or some other new item depending on the current view. In the Inbox, for example, this button lets you create a new e-mail message. Although the appearance of the button changes depending on its purpose, the button's location remains the same—it's the leftmost button.

Print. Prints the currently displayed item. If you're working with your calendar and you click the Print button, for example, Outlook prints the calendar.

Move to Folder. Displays a dialog box that contains a list of the Outlook folders, allowing you to move selected items from one folder to another.

Delete. Lets you quickly delete a message, note, or other item.

Find. Displays a new pane at the top of the Information Viewer that can help you find specific messages, contacts, appointments, and other information.

Organize. Displays a new pane at the top of the Information Viewer that contains tools for moving messages from one folder to another and for having Outlook automatically filter incoming messages and place them in a specific folder. (If the Organize button is not displayed, click the Toolbar Options button, on the right end of the toolbar.)

Configuring the Outlook Bar

Outlook is designed to offer you an alternative to the Windows desktop. In addition to keeping track of appointments, dates, and e-mail, Outlook can help you organize your files and run applications. If you click the **Other Shortcuts** group in the Outlook Bar, Outlook displays an icon for My Computer, as shown in Figure 23.2. Click the **My Computer** icon to display a list of icons for disk drives and folders. You can use the Outlook window just like the Windows Explorer window to copy, delete, move, and open files.

You can add folders to the Outlook Bar, in existing groups or in new groups, to give yourself quick access to other resources on your computer or on the network. You also can delete or rename existing groups:

➤ To create a new group in the Outlook Bar, right-click a blank area of the bar, select **Add New Group**, and type a name for the group.

➤ To remove a group, right-click it and click **Remove Group**.

➤ To rename a group, right-click it, select **Rename Group**, and type a new name for the group.

➤ To add a folder to a group on the Outlook Bar, click the group's bar. Right-click a blank area inside the group's bar and click **Outlook Bar Shortcut**. Open the **Look In** drop-down list and select **Outlook** (to add an Outlook folder to the group) or **File System** (to add a folder from your hard drive or network). Use the folder name list to select the desired folder, and then click **OK**.

➤ To remove a folder from a group, right-click it and select **Remove from Outlook Bar**. Don't worry, you're just deleting a shortcut—not the stuff it refers to on the hard disk or in Outlook.

➤ To rename a folder, right-click it and select **Rename Shortcut**. Then type a new name for the folder.

Click Other Shortcuts to view
file-management icons.

My Computer as displayed in Outlook.

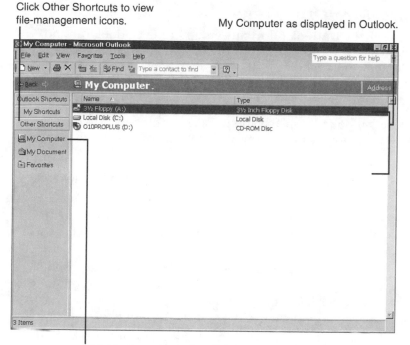

Figure 23.2

The Outlook Bar contains various folders for organizing your work.

Click My Computer to view disk, folder, and file icons.

Keeping Appointments with the Calendar

Outlook offers a calendar that enables you to keep track of appointments and plan your days and weeks. Outlook's Calendar can even notify you of upcoming appointments ahead of time so you won't be late. In the following sections, you learn how to work with the Calendar in various views (by day, week, or month), how to add and delete appointments, and how to set advanced appointment options.

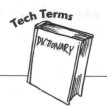

Tech Terms

Appointments, Meetings, and Events

Outlook draws a distinction between appointments, meetings, and events. An *appointment* is something you do on your time, such as getting your teeth cleaned. A *meeting* is something you do with other people; it requires that you coordinate a time block. An *event* is an activity that occurs over one or more days as opposed to a block of time during one day. An *annual event,* such as a birthday or an anniversary, recurs each year.

Daily, Weekly, and Monthly Views

To open the Calendar, click the **Outlook Shortcuts** group in the Outlook Bar and click the **Calendar** shortcut. When you first open the Calendar, it displays three items: a daily schedule, showing the hours of the day; two months, the current month and next month; and the Task List, displaying the names of any tasks you need to accomplish (assuming you've typed them in).

You can change views in Outlook to display various Calendar objects or to display another arrangement. Use the following controls in the Standard toolbar to change the display:

Today	*Go To Today.* Activates today's date as reported by the clock inside your computer.
1	*Day.* The default setting. This option displays an hourly run-down of the current day on the left side of the Calendar window.
5	*Work Week.* Displays a five-day breakdown of your schedule (Monday through Friday). It doesn't leave much room for the hourly breakdown of your days, but it does show just how hectic your schedule will be for the current week.
7	*Week.* Replaces the day list with a list showing the seven days of the current week. This gives you a quick look at what's going on during a given week, including weekends.
31	*Month.* Displays a full-screen view of the currently selected month, showing the names of all appointments scheduled for each day. This is similar to the monthly calendar you have hanging in your home or office. (You might need to click the Toolbar Options button, on the right end of the toolbar, to access the Month button.)

Setting Appointment Dates and Times

You can quickly enter an appointment in the Calendar so the Calendar displays the name of the appointment and sounds an alarm to remind you of the appointment 15 minutes ahead of time. To do this, take the following steps:

1. Click the **Day** button to switch to Day view (if you selected a different view earlier).
2. Drag over the scheduled appointment time. For example, if you have a one-hour appointment that starts at 10:00 a.m., drag over the time blocks for 10:00 and 10:30.
3. Type a description of the appointment. (For example, you might type "Meet with Ned about building plans.")
4. Press **Enter**. The appointment description appears on the Day list, and a bar to the left of the appointment shows the time blocks that the appointment occupies (see Figure 23.3).

The bell indicates that an
alarm will sound prior
to the appointment time.

Scheduled appointments

Figure 23.3

When you set an appointment, it appears on the daily, weekly, or monthly calendar.

This line shows the time you
will be at the appointment.

Setting an appointment by dragging and typing is quick, but it does not enable you to enter special settings, such as whether you want the reminder alarm on or off (it's off by default). To enter additional settings, use the Appointment dialog box to schedule a new appointment. To display the Appointment dialog box, double-click a time block on the daily schedule, or click the **New Appointment** button (at the left end of the Standard toolbar). Use the Appointment dialog box, as shown in Figure 23.4, to enter settings for the appointment.

When you are done entering the appointment, click the **Save and Close** button. The appointment then appears on the daily schedule. If you click the Close (X) button instead of Save and Close, don't worry. Like a good secretary, Outlook reminds you to save the appointment.

Two Places at the Same Time?

Outlook will let you set overlapping appointments, but shoves one appointment box off to the right to provide a visual cue that your schedule might be a little tight. Darn, I guess I can't make it to that quarterly meeting after all.

Enter a name for the appointment.

Type a Location, if desired.

Set the start and end times.

Figure 23.4

The Appointment dialog box provides additional options.

Turn the alarm on or off.

Enter optional notes here.

Specify how you want this time block marked.

If you turned on the alarm, you might be a little surprised the first time it pops up on your screen and starts beeping. If you dozed off, you might instinctively try to hit the snooze button. Well, there is a snooze button! Click **Snooze** to be reminded again in 15 minutes (or whatever number of minutes you specify). Or, you can click **Dismiss** to turn off the reminder altogether.

Color-Code Your Appointments

To display an appointment in color, click the appointment, click the **Calendar Coloring** button, and click the desired color. To have Outlook automatically assign a color to an appointment based on its contents, double-click the **Calendar Coloring** button, select **Automatic Formatting**, and use the resulting dialog box to specify the conditions Outlook should look for to determine the color assignment.

Editing, Moving, and Deleting Appointments

Unless you have a regularly scheduled appointment, you can count on the fact that your appointment will be rescheduled two or three times before the scheduled date.

That's why you need some way to rearrange appointments, delete canceled appointments, and edit the appointment information. The following list provides you with all the instructions you need to perform these tasks:

➤ Double-click the appointment to display its settings in the Appointment dialog box and then enter your changes.

➤ If the appointment is rescheduled for a time on the same day, drag the appointment up or down on the daily schedule to the new time.

➤ To move an appointment to a different day, change to Week or Month view and drag the appointment to the desired day. The time will stay the same, so you might have to adjust that after moving it to the correct day.

➤ You can increase or decrease the scheduled time for the appointment. Drag the top or bottom line of the time block up or down.

Divide Your Day into Shorter Intervals

You can change the default settings for the Calendar to change the times that your day starts and ends and change the days that comprise your workweek. Open the **Tools** menu, select **Options**, and click the **Calendar Options** button (on the Preferences tab). Enter your preferences and click **OK**. To divide your day into different intervals, right-click inside the area that displays the time intervals (8^{am}, 9^{00}, 10^{00}, and so on) and click the desired interval: **60 Minutes**, **30 Minutes**, **15 Minutes**, and so on.

➤ If your computer is on a network and you don't want other people on the network to know about your appointment, right-click the appointment and select **Private**. A key appears on the appointment, indicating that it is hidden from public view. For example, you might want to keep that appointment with the special prosecutor to yourself.

➤ You can drag an item from the Task List to the Calendar to place it on your schedule. When you release the mouse button, the Appointment dialog box appears, prompting you to enter additional details.

➤ If someone cancels the appointment altogether, you can delete it by right-clicking the appointment and selecting **Delete**.

Scheduling a Recurring Weekly or Monthly Appointment

If you have the same appointment at the same time every week or every month, you don't have to enter the appointment into the calendar for each week or month. Have Outlook do it for you by marking the appointment as a *recurring appointment*.

First, double-click the appointment to display the Appointment dialog box. Then click the **Recurrence** button. The Appointment Recurrence dialog box appears. Use it to set the frequency of the appointment, its duration, and the number of times you want Outlook to place it on the calendar. Click **OK** after entering your preferences, and then click the **Save and Close** button to set the appointment.

Insider Tip

Planning a Meeting

If you're on a network, you can set up a meeting with your colleagues using Outlook's meeting planner. Open the **Actions** menu and click **Plan a Meeting**. Click the **Add Others** button and choose to add people from your address book or from a public folder on the network. Select the names of the people who must attend the meeting and click **OK**. Outlook displays the blocks of free time available for all the attendees (assuming they're all on the network and are diligent in keeping their schedules updated in Outlook). Drag the vertical lines to mark the start and end times for the meeting, and then click the **Make Meeting** button to send your invitations.

Keeping Track of Birthdays, Anniversaries, and Other Big Events

Do you have a big family? Have they nearly disowned you because you forget to send birthday and anniversary cards on time? Does your spouse make jokes about how you always forget your wedding anniversary? Well, the Event schedule can help remind you of these big events to avoid embarrassment, save your marriage, and reestablish your family ties.

Scheduling an event is no more difficult than scheduling an appointment. First, display the Calendar, and then open the **Actions** menu and select **New All Day Event**. The Event dialog box appears, looking like the Appointment dialog box's evil twin. In the **Subject** text box, type a brief description of the event. To have Outlook remind you before the big day, select the **Reminder** check box. To have Outlook remind you a few days in advance so you have time to buy a present and a card, open the **Reminder** drop-down list and select the number of days or weeks in advance you want to be warned.

If you want Outlook to mark this as an annual event (so Outlook will remind you every year), click the **Recurrence** button. Click **Yearly** and click **OK**. This returns you to the Event dialog box. Click **Save and Close**.

Removing the Annual Event

You finally record your wedding anniversary in the calendar so you'll never again miss it. You're so proud of yourself. Two months later your wife informs you that you are the one thing in her life getting in the way of her happiness. Now, you *want* to forget. To remove the recurrences, click the entry for the joyous event, click the **Delete** button, select **Delete the Series**, and click **OK**. Now, add recurring entries for alimony and child-support payments.

There's a Rolodex on Your Screen!

Electronic address books used to be only slightly better than their corresponding paper versions. They enabled you to edit entries easily without erasing, and they typically provided search tools to help you find people. The current breed of electronic address books enables you to do much more. For instance, if you have an e-mail connection, you can quickly address e-mail messages from the Address Book. If you have a modem, the Address Book can dial phone numbers for you. And this latest version of Outlook even lets you store your contacts' instant message addresses!

In the following sections, you learn how to add names, addresses, phone numbers, and other information to your Address Book and use that information to simplify your life.

Adding Address Cards to the Contacts List

Before you can use the Contacts List, you must display it. In the Outlook Bar, click **Contacts**. To add a person's name and contact information to your Address Book, click the **New Contact** button in Outlook's toolbar (all the way on the left). The Contact dialog box appears, as shown in Figure 23.5. Use the Contact dialog box to enter the person's name, address, phone number, e-mail address, and other contact information. Click the **Save and New** button to save the address card and display a new blank card, or click the **Save and Close** button to close the window.

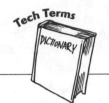

What's an Instant Message?

An instant message (IM, for short) is like an e-mail message with wings. Almost immediately after someone types and sends an instant message to you, it pops up on your screen. You can then carry on a text-based "conversation" by typing messages back and forth. Most instant message programs support audio; with a sound card, speakers, and a good microphone, you can carry on a conversation just as if you were talking on the phone.

Figure 23.5

Outlook lets you add all sorts of contact information for each person.

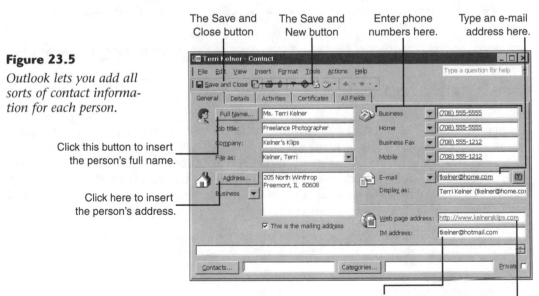

When you switch back to the main Outlook screen, Outlook displays a tiny address card for each contact, arranged alphabetically by last name. If you have gobs of cards, you can click a button on the right side of the screen to display an alphabetical grouping of cards. (This is like using the lettered tabs in a paper address book.) To select a card, click it. To display all the information a card contains or edit the information on the card, double-click it.

Making Your Modem Dial Phone Numbers

If your computer has a modem, you can use Outlook to transform your $3,000 computer into a $100 programmable phone. Your modem should have two phone jacks: one that connects it to the incoming phone line (so it can dial out and talk to other modems) and another one that lets you plug in your phone. First, connect your modem to the phone jack, and then plug your phone into the modem; make sure you have the right wires plugged into the right jacks. Now you're ready to roll.

To dial out, click the address card for the person you want to call. Then open the **Dial** drop-down list in the toolbar and click the number you want to dial. (If you didn't enter a phone number on the person's address card, it won't appear on the Dial drop-down list.) The New Call dialog box appears. Click the **Start Call** button. Outlook dials the phone number (with the help of your modem). Pick up the phone and wait for the person (or answering machine) to answer.

Insider Tip

Using the Speed Dialer

The Dial drop-down list contains a Speed Dial submenu on which you can list the phone numbers of the people you call most often (or emergency numbers). To add a number to the Speed Dial submenu, click the person's card, click the **Dial** button (NOT the arrow next to the button), click the **Dialing Options** button, enter the person's name and phone number, and click **Add**. When you're done adding speed-dial numbers, click **OK**. To dial a number quickly, click the down-arrow next to the **Dial** button and select the number from the Speed Dial submenu.

Sending E-mail Messages to Your Contacts

If you entered an e-mail address for one of your contacts, you can quickly send the person an e-mail message. Click the person's address card and then click the **New**

285

Message to Contact button in the toolbar. This opens a Message dialog box with a new message addressed to the selected contact. Type a description of the message in the **Subject** text box; type the full message in the large message area at the bottom of the dialog box, and click the **Send** button. For more information about sending e-mail messages, see Chapter 24, "Managing Your E-mail."

Check Out Your Contact's Web Site

If you typed a Web page address for your contact's personal or business Web page, you can quickly pull up the page (assuming you have a Web browser installed) by double-clicking the person's address card and clicking the Web page address you entered. Click the person's IM (Instant Message) address to contact the person online.

What Do You Have to Do Today?

If you like to be constantly reminded of what you have to do, get married. Short of that, you can use Outlook's Task List. Click the **Tasks** shortcut in the Outlook Bar. In the Task List, you can type the various tasks you need to perform. Just click the **Click Here to Add a New Task** text box, type a brief description of the task, and press **Enter**.

To enter additional information about the task, double-click it. This displays a Task dialog box, which enables you to change the name of the task, specify a starting date and due date, and turn on an alarm that sounds when the due date arrives. You can also enter billing information and other notes that provide useful information about the task or click Assign Task to delegate the task via e-mail!

After you've completed a task, click the check box next to the name of the task. A check mark appears inside the box, and Outlook draws a line through the task title to indicate you've completed it. This is for management types who need to reward themselves for their minor accomplishments. For the rest of us, there's a Delete button. Click the **Delete** button to remove the task from the list.

The Least You Need to Know

Outlook is a powerful program for managing your life. Even though this chapter merely introduced you to the most important features of Outlook, the information still might be overwhelming. Just make sure you can perform these basic tasks:

➤ Click an icon in the Outlook Bar to view your Inbox, Calendar, Contact List, Task List, or Notes.

➤ Click the **New** button to create a new e-mail message, appointment, contact, to-do item, or note.

➤ To enter an appointment, display the daily calendar, drag over the desired time blocks, type a description of the appointment, and press **Enter**.

➤ To record a birthday, an anniversary, or other recurring event, display the Calendar, open the **Actions** menu, select **New All Day Event**, and enter the required information.

➤ To enter contact information for a friend, relative, or colleague, click **Contacts** in the Outlook Bar, click the **New Contact** button, and enter the required information.

➤ To enter a task in the Task List, click the **Tasks** icon in the Outlook Bar, click in the **Click Here to Add a New Task** text box, type a brief description of the task, and press **Enter**.

Chapter 24

Managing Your E-mail

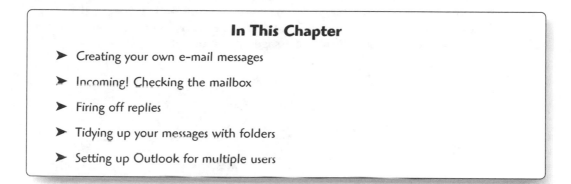

In This Chapter

➤ Creating your own e-mail messages

➤ Incoming! Checking the mailbox

➤ Firing off replies

➤ Tidying up your messages with folders

➤ Setting up Outlook for multiple users

When you are scheduling appointments, keeping track of contacts, and honing your other life management skills, you don't want to have to switch to some other program to manage your e-mail. You need something more convenient. You need Outlook's Inbox.

In this chapter, you learn how to use Outlook's Inbox to check for incoming mail and manage your messages. You also learn how to reply to messages and create and send your own electronic missives.

Nickel Tour of the Inbox

To view the Inbox, click the **Inbox** shortcut in the Outlook Bar. Two panes appear. The top pane displays a list of messages. Initially, the top pane contains a single message from Microsoft, welcoming you to Outlook. The bottom pane displays the contents of the selected message (the message itself). If the two-pane view is not on, open the **View** menu and select **Preview Pane**. Just above the message list, Outlook displays the following Sort By column headings:

➤ **Importance**—Displays an icon that shows whether the sender marked the message as high importance or low importance.

➤ **Icon**—Shows a picture of a sealed envelope. After you double-click a message to read it, the envelope appears opened.

➤ **Flag Status**—Displays a flag if you choose to flag a message. You can use flags to mark messages that you might want to reread or respond to later.

➤ **Attachment**—Shows whether the sender attached a file to the message. If a file is attached, you can open it or save it to your disk.

➤ **From**—Displays the name of the sender.

➤ **Subject**—Displays a brief description of the message.

➤ **Received**—Shows the date and time the message was received.

To sort the messages by the entries in one of the columns, click that column's heading. For example, you can sort the messages by the date and time they were received by clicking **Received**. Clicking the same button again uses the same sort category but reverses the order. For example, if the messages are sorted by date with the most current messages at the end of the list and you click **Received**, Outlook rearranges the messages to place the most current messages at the top of the list.

Customizing Your Columns

You can rearrange or resize the columns in the Inbox by dragging them. Drag the column bar to the left or right to rearrange. To resize a column, point between the buttons until the pointer shows a double-headed arrow, and then drag left or right. To further customize the Inbox, select **View**, **Current View**, **Customize Current View** and enter your preferences.

When you display the Inbox, notice that the toolbar changes to provide e-mail buttons and controls. You can use these buttons to reply to messages, display the address book, or send and receive messages, as shown in Figure 24.1.

Compose a New message.   Display e-mail addresses for your contacts.
    Reply to the selected message.   Search for messages.

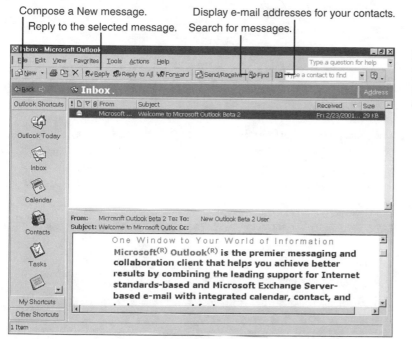

Figure 24.1

The toolbar enables you to quickly enter common e-mail commands.

For additional e-mail folders and options, click **Inbox** in the banner just above the message list. This opens a drop-down list that displays shortcuts for Drafts (messages you are working on and have saved as drafts), Sent Items (messages you have already sent), Outbox (messages you will send in the future), Deleted Items (only if you deleted an item), and Journal (for recording your daily routine).

Adding E-mail Accounts

When you start Outlook for the first time, it displays a series of dialog boxes, leading you through the process of setting up an e-mail account. The settings you enter tell Outlook the address of the mail server you use for sending and receiving e-mail. The settings also provide Outlook with the username and password required for accessing your e-mail account.

If you canceled the e-mail account setup when you first ran Outlook, or if you have multiple e-mail accounts, take the following steps to add an e-mail account now:

1. Open the **Tools** menu and click **E-mail Accounts**. The E-mail Accounts dialog box appears.

2. Click **Add a New E-mail Account** and click **Next**. Outlook prompts you to specify the type of e-mail server you use, as shown in Figure 24.2.

3. Choose the type of e-mail server you use to download your e-mail and click **Next**. (If you're unsure, contact your Internet service provider or network administrator.)

291

New Support for Hotmail

Free Web e-mail accounts, such as those offered by Hotmail (www.hotmail.com), have become very popular for allowing users to access their e-mail on the Web and for allowing various members of a household to have their own, separate e-mail accounts. Outlook now supports these Web e-mail services, allowing you to access your Web e-mail using a standard e-mail program—Outlook.

If your network uses an Exchange server
for e-mail, select this option.

Figure 24.2

*Specify the type of e-mail
server you will use.*

Most Internet service
providers use POP
or IMAP e-mail servers.

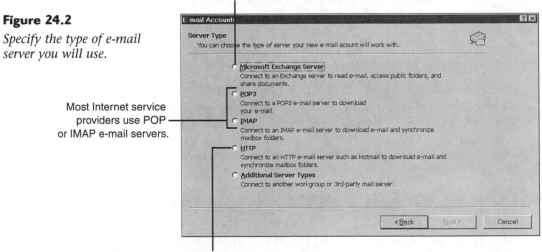

To enter settings for a Hotmail or other type
of Web e-mail account, select this option.

4. Enter the requested information. The information varies depending on the type of e-mail server you selected in step 3, but typically consists of the following:

   Your Name is the name you want to appear as the "sender" in the e-mail messages you send. You can use any name or nickname.

   E-mail is your e-mail address. When someone receives a message from you and clicks the Reply button to respond, this is the e-mail address to which the person's reply will be sent.

User Name is the name your Internet service provider or network uses to identify you. To connect to the mail server, Outlook sends your username and password to log on.

Password is the password your Internet service provider or network uses to prevent unauthorized access to your e-mail.

Incoming mail server is the address of the mail server that stores messages sent to you. (If you're setting up a Web-based e-mail account, you enter a Web site address rather than incoming and outgoing mail server addresses.)

Outgoing mail server is the address of the mail server that processes the messages you send.

5. If a Test Account Settings button appears in the dialog box, click the button to ensure you can connect to your e-mail server. (If the connection fails, click the **Back** button and edit the settings, as necessary.)

6. Click the **Next** button. The final dialog box appears, indicating that you have successfully set up your e-mail account.

7. Click the **Finish** button.

To edit or delete an e-mail account, open the **Tools** menu, click **E-mail Accounts**, click **View or Change Existing E-mail Accounts**, and click **Next**. Outlook displays a list of your e-mail accounts. To delete an account, click its name and click the **Remove** button. To set an account as the default e-mail account, click its name and click the **Set As Default** button. To edit the settings for an account, click its name, click the **Change** button, and enter your changes.

Creating a New E-mail Message

After you've set up at least one e-mail account, sending messages is fairly simple. Click the **New Mail Message** button (at the left end of the toolbar) to display the Message dialog box. In the **To** text box, type the e-mail address of the person to whom you want to send the message. If you entered the e-mail address on the Address card in Contacts, click the **To** button to select the person's name from a list instead of typing it. You can send a copy of the message to other people by entering their e-mail addresses in the **Cc** (carbon copy) text box. If you type more than one address in a text box, separate the addresses with semicolons.

Click the **Subject** text box and type a brief description of the message. Then click the message area at the bottom of the window and type your message. If you want to send only a text message, you're finished; click the **Send** button. If you want to attach a file, set the importance of the message, or perform some other fancy feat, use the appropriate technique described here:

➤ To attach a file to the message, open the **Insert** menu and select **File**. Change to the disk and folder in which the file is stored and double-click the file's name.

293

➤ You can add fancy formatting to the message, as shown in Figure 24.3. Open the **Message Format** drop-down list (on the right end of the toolbar just above the To box), and select **Rich Text** or **HTML**. Drag over the text you want to format, and use the toolbar buttons to select a font, select a font size, and add attributes such as bold and italic.

➤ To apply a design scheme that controls the background, fonts, text color, and the appearance of any links, click in the message area and then open the **Format** menu and select **Theme**.

➤ You can use Outlook's stationery to create a fancier e-mail message, but you must choose to create a new message using the stationery. Open the **Actions** menu (on Outlook's main screen), point to **New Mail Message Using**, and click **More Stationery**. Choose the desired stationery, click **OK**, and then compose your message.

➤ If you have more than one e-mail account, you can choose the account you want to use to send the message. Open the **Accounts** drop-down list (to the right of the Send button) and click the desired e-mail account.

Figure 24.3

Although sending a message is fairly easy, Outlook offers several options for customizing the message.

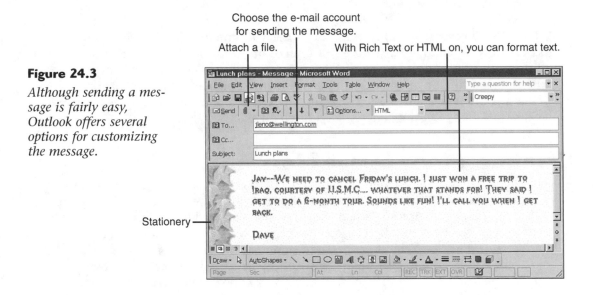

Retrieving and Reading Incoming Messages

Whenever someone sends you an e-mail message, it sits in a special area on the mail server waiting for you to fetch it. To retrieve your messages, click the **Send/Receive** button. Outlook connects to each mail server you set up earlier, retrieves the messages (assuming you have some), and displays a list of the messages in the Inbox. Click the message in the top pane to view a few lines of the message in the bottom pane.

You can then scroll down in the bottom pane to read the rest of the message and click the **Forward** or **Reply** button in the Outlook toolbar to forward the message or send a reply.

To display the message in its own window, double-click the message. Outlook displays the message in a special Message window, where you can use the following toolbar buttons:

Reply. Enables you to reply to the person who sent you the message. If you click this button, a Message window appears, addressing your reply to the sender. Outlook inserts the text of the original message, preceded by `-----Original Message-----` to show where your reply ends and the original message begins.

Reply to All. Click to send a reply to the sender and to any people other than yourself listed in the To, Cc, or Bcc box of the original message.

Forward. Click to pass the message on to someone else, without necessarily adding a reply. You don't need to retype a message when you can just forward it. Besides, this is a great tool for delegating work so you can spend more time at the driving range.

Previous Item or Next Item. Click to view the previous message or the next one. These buttons double as drop-down lists providing additional options; for example, you can view the next or previous message sent by the same person or view the next or previous message concerning this topic.

Organizing Messages in Folders

One e-mail box is enough for most people, but if it gets cluttered and your personal mail gets all mixed up with your business correspondence, you might need additional mailboxes (or folders) to keep your mail organized. You could, of course, simply do a little manic housecleaning and delete everything from the previous nine months, but can you afford to lose those messages? By creating folders and organizing your mail, you have a comprehensive yet manageable message diary.

To create a new folder, take the following steps:

1. Open the **File** menu, point to **New**, and click **Folder** (or press **Ctrl+Shift+E**). The Create New Folder dialog box appears, prompting you to name the folder.
2. In the **Name** text box, type a name for the folder.

3. Open the **Folder Contains** drop-down list and select **Mail and Post Items** to specify the type of folder you want to create.

4. In the **Select Where to Place the Folder** list, select the folder below which you want the new subfolder created (select **Personal Folders** to place the new folder on the same level as the Inbox and Outbox folders).

5. Click **OK**. The **Add Shortcut to Outlook Bar?** dialog box appears, asking whether you want the folder added to the Outlook Bar.

6. Click **Yes**. Outlook creates the new folder and displays a shortcut icon for it in the My Shortcuts group of the Outlook Bar.

You can move messages to the new folder by dragging them from one folder (probably the Inbox folder) to your new folder in the folder list. Another way to regroup your messages is to click the **Organize** button in Outlook's toolbar. This displays a pane at the top of the Information Viewer with controls for reorganizing folders and messages.

Insider Tip

Rules Wizard

To have Outlook automatically move messages from a specific person or messages that contain unique content to a folder when you receive them, use the Rules Wizard. Click the **Rules Wizard** link near the top of the Organize pane, click **New**, and enter the requested settings to create a *rule* that tells Outlook how to handle incoming messages.

Setting Up Profiles for Multiple Users

If you share a computer with other people, either at home or at work, each person should have his or her own mailbox. Of course, you can create a separate folder for each person and then use the Rules Wizard to route the mail to each person's folder, but there's a better way—create a separate *profile* for each user.

A profile acts like a username, allowing each person to log on to Outlook and read his or her e-mail messages. Profiles provide each user with an Inbox, keeping e-mail accounts entirely separate. To create a new profile, take the following steps:

1. Right-click the **Microsoft Outlook** icon on the Windows desktop and click **Properties** (or double-click the **Mail** icon in the Windows Control Panel). The Mail Setup - Outlook dialog box appears, giving you access to your e-mail accounts, Outlook data files, and profiles.

2. Click the **Show Profiles** button.

3. Click the **Add** button. The New Profile dialog box pops up, requesting a name for the new profile.

4. Type a name for the profile (up to 63 characters, including spaces), and click **OK**. The E-mail Accounts dialog box appears, prompting you to add an e-mail account for this profile.

5. Follow the trail of dialog boxes and enter the settings required to access the e-mail account for this profile. See "Adding E-mail Accounts," earlier in this chapter, for details. When you click the Finish button, you return to the Mail dialog box.

6. Click **Prompt for a Profile to Be Used** to turn on this option, and then click **OK**.

The next time you start Outlook, the Choose Profile dialog box appears, prompting you to select a profile. Open the **Profile Name** list, click the desired profile, and click **OK**. Outlook starts and automatically checks for incoming e-mail for the mail account(s) you set up for this profile.

The Least You Need to Know

After you've set up Outlook to work with your e-mail services, sending and receiving e-mail messages is easy:

➤ To enter settings for your e-mail account, open the **Tools** menu, select **E-mail Accounts**, and follow the onscreen instructions.

➤ To check for incoming messages, click the **Inbox** shortcut in the Outlook Bar and click the **Send/Receive** button.

➤ To display the contents of an e-mail message you received, click the description of the message.

➤ To reply to an e-mail message, select the message, and then click the **Reply** or **Reply to All** button.

➤ To send a new message, click the **New Mail Message** button. Type the recipient's e-mail address, a brief description of the message, and the message itself. Click **Send**.

➤ To access settings for e-mail accounts and profiles, right-click the **Microsoft Outlook** icon on the Windows desktop and click **Properties**.

Part 7

Taking Your Office to the Next Level

After you've mastered the Office XP basics, you might start to wonder how you can use advanced features to make the most of your investment, save time, and become more productive.

In this part, you use the Office applications together and on the Web to get the most out of Office. You learn how to share data dynamically between documents created in different applications, create your own Web pages and online presentations, publish your documents electronically on the World Wide Web, and create your own shortcut keys and buttons to automate tasks. And, if you're working with Microsoft Small Business Edition, this part even shows you how to use the new version of Microsoft Publisher!

Chapter 25

Sharing Data Between Applications

Your Office applications actually *like* to share and help one another. Excel nearly jumps out of its seat when a Word document asks to share some worksheet data or a graph. When your Access report looks as dull as Ted Koppel sounds, Word enthusiastically lends a hand, transforming that bland collection of Access data into a beautifully formatted report.

After all, Microsoft Office is a *suite* of applications. Although they take initiative and work independently, they're also designed to work as a unit—all for one and one for all! This chapter shows you various techniques for using the Office applications together in this way to create more dynamic documents and save yourself some time.

Dynamic Data Sharing with OLE

You can usually share data simply by copying it from a document you've created in one application to a document you've created in another. But just how is the data between the two documents related? If you change the data in one document, is it automatically changed in the other? The answer: That depends. It depends on how the two applications are set up to share data, and it depends on how you inserted the copied data. You can share data in any of the following three ways:

➤ **Link**—If you're using Office applications or any other applications that support OLE (pronounced "Oh-lay," and short for Object Linking and Embedding), you can share data by creating a *link*. With a link, the pasted data retains a connection with the source document (the document from which it was copied). Whenever you edit the data in the source document, any changes you make to it appear in the destination document (the document that contains the pasted data). For example, suppose you insert an Excel graph into a Word document as a link. Whenever you change the graph in Excel, those changes appear in the Word document.

➤ **Embed**—With OLE, you can also embed data from one file into another file. With embedding, the pasted data becomes a part of the file into which you pasted it. If you edit the source document, your changes do not appear inside the document that contains the pasted data. The pasted data does, however, retain a connection with the program that you used to create it. So if you double-click the embedded data, Windows automatically runs the application, and you can edit the data.

➤ **Paste**—You can paste data in any number of ways, including as an embedded or a linked object; however, not all applications support OLE. For those applications that do not support OLE, you can still share data between programs by copying and pasting the data. The pasted data, however, has no connection with the source document or the application you used to create it.

Sharing Data with Scraps

When you're working with Office applications, don't forget one of the great data-sharing features built right into Windows—*scraps*. If you select data in a document and then drag it to a blank area on the Windows desktop, Windows creates a shortcut for the data and marks it as a scrap. You can then drag this scrap into another document to insert it.

Embedding an Object with Copy and Paste Special

Think of embedding as using a photocopier to make a copy. With a photocopy, the original remains intact in the original location, and you have an extra copy you can use to create a new document or stick inside another document. You can manipulate the copy in any way you want. You can edit it, delete part of it, highlight it, and so on, all without affecting the original. To embed data in a document, take the following steps:

1. Select and copy the data you want to use.

2. Change to the document in which you want to embed the copied data and position the insertion point where you want the data pasted.

3. Open the **Edit** menu and select **Paste Special**. The Paste Special dialog box appears, as shown in Figure 25.1.

4. To retain a connection between the pasted data and the program used to create it, select the option with "Object" in its name. If you are pasting data copied from Excel, for example, select **Microsoft Excel Worksheet Object**.

5. Click **OK**. The copied data is inserted as an object, and handles appear around it. Word automatically switches to Print Layout view when you insert an object because the object does not appear in Normal view.

Choose the "Object" option.

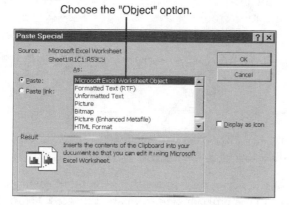

Figure 25.1

You can paste copied data so that the data retains a connection with the program used to create it.

To edit an embedded object, double-click it. The toolbars and menus change to provide options for editing and manipulating the object. If you double-click an Excel chart that's embedded in a Word document, for example, the Excel toolbar and menus appear inside the Word window. Keep in mind that you're not editing the original object in its original document—just a copy. The advantage of this method versus static sharing (described in the following note) is that the copy comes with its own editing tools. Isn't that convenient?

Creating a Link Between Two Files

In many cases, you are creating a document with data from several sources. You can wait until each document is absolutely, completely finished and then copy the appropriate data from the source documents, but things can—and usually do—seem to change up to the last minute. To avoid including outdated information in your final document, you can create a link between the two documents. Then, when copied data in the original document (called the *source* document) is changed, the pasted data in the other document (called the *destination* document) is updated, too. The following are the key points to remember about linking data:

➤ You can link data between Excel, Word, PowerPoint, and any other application that supports OLE by using the **Paste Special** command on the **Edit** menu. If a program does not support OLE, the Paste Special command is not available.

➤ When you link data, you have two separate documents stored in two separate files. If you send someone a file that contains a link, you must also send the linked file.

➤ Linking works only one way. If you edit data from the source document in the destination document, the source document is not changed. (In most cases, Office does not allow you to edit source data in the destination document, but if you paste the link as HTML or RTF data, you might be able to edit the source data right inside the destination document.)

➤ Linking works best when you use the same data in several documents. You can maintain the one source document without having to worry about updating the documents that use information from the source.

Don't Want a Dynamic Link!

If you need to insert data from one document into another without retaining a connection between the pasted data and the program used to create it, select **Edit**, **Paste** to paste the data in the destination document. You can also drag selected data from one document to the other.

Creating a link is almost as easy as embedding. If you remember the words from the preceding section, feel free to sing along:

1. Copy the data.
2. Change to the target document and select **Edit**, **Paste Special**.
3. Click the **Paste Link** option button, as shown in Figure 25.2.
4. Pick the format that has "Object" in its name.
5. Click **OK**. Olé!

Choose Paste link.   Choose the desired format.

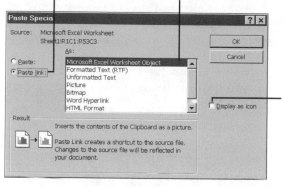

Figure 25.2

To create a link, you must specify how you want the data pasted.

You can have the link displayed as an icon.

If you decide later to break the link between the pasted data and its original file, or if you want to change the way the links are updated, open the **Edit** menu and select **Links**. This displays the Links dialog box that lists all the links in the document. By default, the update method is set to **Automatic Update**. You can change the setting to Manual Update; however, whenever you want your links updated, you have to display this dialog box again, click the desired link, and click **Update Now** (not the most efficient method). To break the links, click the desired link and click **Break Link**.

Embedding a New Object with Insert Object

You can also link or embed with the Insert Object command. You use this command when you know that you want to link or embed something, but you have not yet created the object in the source application. Say you're writing a letter to order some plants and you need a worksheet that lists the items you're ordering and the quantities, prices, and totals. You haven't created the worksheet, and you need it quickly. What do you do? Insert Object.

To insert an object, open the **Insert** menu and select **Object**. The Object dialog box appears, displaying two tabs. Use the Create New tab when you need to create an object to link or embed (and haven't done so yet). The Create from File tab offers options for linking or embedding an entire file.

Whoa!

Be Careful When Moving Files

Because a link points to another file in a folder on your hard drive or on the network, you must be careful when moving, deleting, or renaming your files or folders. If you shuffle around your files and folders, your Office applications will be unable to find them.

To create a new object, select the type of object you want to insert (for example, an Excel worksheet or a PowerPoint slide), as shown in Figure 25.3. Enter any additional preferences and click **OK**. Windows inserts a placeholder for the selected object and runs the application needed to create the object. By looking at the title bar, you might not realize that Windows has changed applications on you; but if you check out the toolbars and menus, you see that you now have options for creating and manipulating the new object. When you finish creating the object, click anywhere outside it to return to your document.

Figure 25.3

You can create a new object and embed it in your document.

Select the type of object you want to insert.

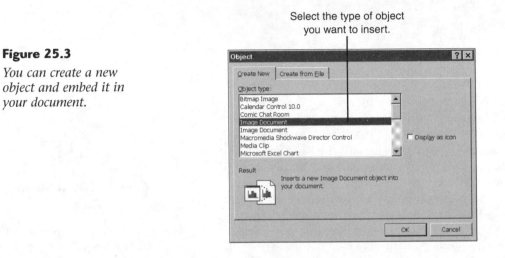

You can also embed or link an entire file created in another application. To do this, click the **Create from File** tab in the Object dialog box. Click the **Browse** button, use the Browse dialog box to select the file you want to insert, and click **Insert**. Select any other options (such as Link to File, Float over Text, or Display As Icon), and click **OK**.

Insider Tip

Display As Icon?

The Display As Icon option can come in handy if you are working with shared files on a network. Instead of pasting lengthy inserts into a document, you can insert an icon that the reader can click to display additional information. This is also useful for sharing files via e-mail.

Transforming Word Documents into Presentations and Vice Versa

Although your marketing department and sales force want you to think that presentations are some sort of magical multimedia event, most presentations are nothing more than an outline on slides. Sure, the outline might contain a few graphical decorations and some audio clips, but it's still an outline. Moreover, knowing that it's an outline, you might find some need to transform it into a full-fledged Word document.

Do you have to retype the outline in Word? No way. Just open the presentation in PowerPoint, open the **File** menu, point to **Send To**, and click **Microsoft Word**. The Send to Microsoft Word dialog box appears, asking how you want the slides and text laid out on Word pages (or if you just want the outline). Select the desired option, as shown in Figure 25.4, and click **OK**.

You can also transform an outline you typed in Word into a PowerPoint presentation. In Word, open the outline you created. Open the **File** menu, point to **Send To**, and click **Microsoft PowerPoint**. Word converts the outline into a presentation and displays it in PowerPoint.

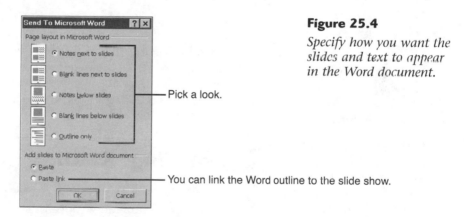

Figure 25.4

Specify how you want the slides and text to appear in the Word document.

Pick a look.

You can link the Word outline to the slide show.

Publishing Access Reports in Word

Access is a great tool for storing and managing data, but its page layout features are grossly inadequate. Access can slap a title on the report and arrange the data in columns, but that's about it. For more control over the look and layout of your reports, consider transforming the report into a Word document.

To convert an Access report to Word format, first open the report in Access. Then open the **Tools** menu, point to **Office Links**, and click **Publish It with Microsoft Word**. Access exports the report to Word, creating a new document. You can now format the document using Word's advanced formatting tools, and you can add graphics and other objects to enhance the document.

Insider Tip

Merging Data with Word Documents

You can also use Access and Word together by inserting field codes in your Word document that pull data from an Access database. (See Chapter 10, "Printing Envelopes, Mailing Labels, and Form Letters," for details on how to merge from Word.)

Insider Tip

Drag and Drop

To copy data quickly from an Access database to an Excel worksheet, simply drag the selected data from a table, query, form, or report in Access and drop it on the Excel worksheet.

Analyzing Your Access Database in Excel

Although Access is the best tool for storing and extracting data, Excel provides superior tools for performing calculations and analyzing data. If you tried entering formulas in your Access report (as explained in Chapter 22, "Giving Data Meaning with Reports"), you know how difficult it can be to enter the correct formula using the right field codes. It's much easier to do it in Excel with cell addresses and the point-and-click method (as explained in Chapter 12, "Doing Math with Formulas").

In addition, Excel offers scenarios that enable you to play What if? with a set of values. You can change one or more values to see how the changes affect the net result, and you can create several scenarios to see how they compare.

To send a table, form, query, or report to Excel, first open it in Access. Then open the **Tools** menu, point to **Office Links**, and click **Analyze It with Microsoft Excel**. Access sends the data to Excel and creates a new worksheet for the data. You can now add formulas, format the data, create graphs, and do anything else that you normally do with an Excel worksheet.

E-mailing, Routing, and Faxing Office Documents

In addition to providing tools for sharing data between your applications, Office features several tools for sharing documents with colleagues and collaborating on projects. If you're on a network or your computer is wired to the Internet, you can send documents to others via e-mail or even route documents to a series of individuals for review. If you have a fax modem and a fax program installed on your computer, you can even fax documents directly from your Office applications using the Fax Wizard. The following sections show you how to accomplish these feats.

E-mailing a Document

In Chapter 24, "Managing Your E-mail," you learned how to attach files to an e-mail message in Outlook to send a file to an e-mail recipient. However, if you're working on the document in Word or Excel, you don't have to switch to Outlook to e-mail the document. Instead, you can e-mail it directly from the application in which you created it.

To e-mail a document, open it in the application you used to create it. Open the **File** menu, point to **Send To**, and click **Mail Recipient** (to send the document as an HTML mail message) or **Mail Recipient (for Review)** (to send a document to a colleague for review) or **Mail Recipient (As Attachment)** (to send the document as an attachment). If you selected Mail Recipient, an e-mail bar appears, as shown in Figure 25.5, displaying text boxes for addressing the message. Type the recipient's e-mail address in the **To** text box, and type a brief description of the message in the **Subject** text box. Click the **Send a Copy** button. Your default e-mail program sends a copy of the document to the recipient as an HTML-formatted message, and the e-mail bar disappears.

If you selected Mail Recipient (for Review), a separate e-mail message window appears with the document listed as a file attachment. Your Office application adds text to the subject and message areas asking the recipient to please review the attached file. Click in the **To** text box, type the recipient's e-mail address, and click the **Send** button.

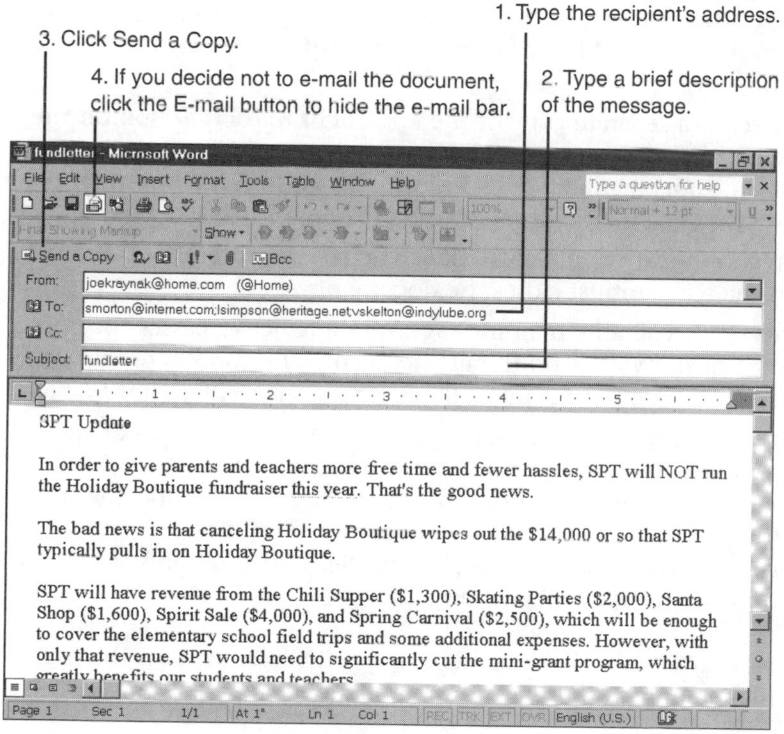

3. Click Send a Copy.

4. If you decide not to e-mail the document, click the E-mail button to hide the e-mail bar.

1. Type the recipient's address.

2. Type a brief description of the message.

Figure 25.5

You can e-mail a copy of a document directly from your Office application.

Routing and Reviewing Documents

If you're team-editing a document, you need tools for tracking changes and determining who entered each change. You also need some way to physically move the document from one reviewer to the next in an orderly fashion. Fortunately, Office provides the tools you need.

To route a document to members of a team, take the following steps:

1. Open the document in the Office application you used to create it.

2. Open the **File** menu, point to **Send To**, and click **Routing Recipient**. The Routing Slip dialog box appears.

3. Click the **Address** button. A list of contacts appears.

4. Double-click a contact's name to add it to the list of routing recipients. (If a desired recipient is not listed, click the **New Contact** button and add the person to your address book.)

5. Repeat step 4 to add each desired recipient to your routing slip, and then click **OK** to return to the Routing Slip dialog box.

6. If desired, edit the entry in the **Subject** text box to provide a clear description of the e-mail message you are about to send.

7. If desired, click in the **Message Text** box and type a message or instructions you think the routing recipients should read before editing the document.

8. Enter your preferences to specify how you want the document routed:

   One After Another routes ,the document from one person to the next on your recipient list, so you have only one document to deal with when the review is complete.

   All at Once sends a separate copy of the document to each person on the list. When you receive the reviewed documents, open the original document, open the **Tools** menu, and click **Compare and Merge Documents** to create a single document with everyone's changes.

   Return when Done automatically e-mails you the document after the last reviewer on the recipient list closes the document.

   Track Status sends you an e-mail message after a reviewer passes the document onto the next reviewer on the list, to keep you informed of the review progress. (This option is unavailable if you select All at Once.)

   Protect For is initially set to **Tracked Changes**, so any changes a reviewer enters are recorded. To allow a reviewer to enter comments to the document but prevent the reviewers from making changes to the document, select **Comments**. If you're routing a form that you want recipients to fill out without changing the form, select **Forms**. Select **(none)** only if you do not want to track changes in the document.

9. Click the **Route** button to send the document to the first recipient on the list or to all recipients (depending on the selection you made in step 8).

Assuming you kept the Protect For setting as Tracked Changes, when you receive the routed document, each reviewer's changes should appear in a different color. Any deleted text appears with strikethrough (so it looks as though it has been crossed out), and any inserted text appears underlined. You can use the buttons in the Reviewing toolbar to move from one change to the next and to accept or reject each change. The following list describes the Reviewing toolbar buttons:

Final Showing Markup ▼	*Display for Review.* Lets you specify whether you want to view the final document with changes, the final document without changes, the original document with changes, or the original document without changes.
Show ▼	*Show.* Gives you the option of hiding insertions and deletions, formatting changes, comments, or the changes made by a particular reviewer.
◄	*Previous.* Highlights the previous change or comment.
►	*Next.* Highlights the next change or comment.
	Accept Change. Makes the change permanent. If the change consisted of deleting text, the deleted text is removed from the document. If the change consisted of inserted text, the text is displayed as normal text (not in a different color or underlined).
	Reject Change. Reverts to the original text. If text was deleted, it is restored. If text was inserted, it is removed. If a comment is highlighted, Reject Change deletes the comment,.
	New Comment. Displays a pane that allows you to type a comment. The comment automatically includes your name (as a reviewer) and the current date and time as recorded on your computer. After you enter a comment, a tiny yellow icon appears in the document at the insertion point. Click the icon to view the comment.
	Track Changes. Toggles the track changes feature. If the feature is on, your changes are marked in a unique color. Inserted text appears underlined; deleted text appears with strikethrough formatting. When the feature is off, you can make changes, but no edit trail appears to show you just what changes you have made.
	Reviewing Pane. Toggles a pane at the bottom of the window that displays reviewers' comments and changes,.

Faxing Documents from Word

If your computer has a fax modem, and a fax program is installed on your computer, you can fax a Word document right from Word. Open the document in Word; then open the **File** menu, point to **Send To**, and click **Fax Recipient**. This starts the Fax Wizard, which leads you through the process. Follow the onscreen instructions.

The Least You Need to Know

The key to making the most of your Office applications is laziness. You should never have to type something in one application that you already entered in another. After you have the right mindset, you can start using the Office applications together:

➤ If two applications support OLE, you can embed or link data created in one application into a document created in the other application.

➤ Embedding places a duplicate of the copied data inside the destination document. The embedded data is still associated with its original application; if you double-click the pasted data, Windows runs the application used to create it.

➤ Linking inserts instructions that pull data from another (source) file into the current (destination) file. Because the linked data is in a separate file, whenever you edit that file, the link is automatically updated.

➤ To paste copied or cut data as a link (instead of embedding it), open the **Edit** menu, select **Paste Special**, and make sure **Paste Link** is selected.

➤ Most Office applications contain commands that enable you to quickly transform data into a format that can be used in another Office application.

➤ To send a document via e-mail or fax, open the **File** menu, select **Send To**, and select **Mail Recipient** or **Fax Recipient**.

Chapter 26

Creating and Publishing Your Own Web Pages

In This Chapter

➤ Churning out Web pages with templates

➤ Saving existing documents as Web pages

➤ Inserting links to other Internet and intranet resources

➤ Transforming PowerPoint presentations into Web pages

➤ Placing your pages on the Web

Nowadays, if you're not on the Web, you're out of the mainstream. Corporations, small businesses, universities, towns, churches, and anyone with an Internet connection and an hour of spare time are flocking to the Web to express themselves and reach out to customers, members, citizens, and anyone else who might be wandering the Web. Using Web authoring tools, these companies and individuals are beginning to move away from paper publications to more interactive electronic publications on the Web.

As you can imagine, the Microsoft Office applications have also been forced to make the transition from printing on paper to publishing electronically on the Web. Microsoft Office features several tools that work together with Microsoft's award-winning Web browser, Internet Explorer, to help you create your own Web pages and navigate the Web. In this chapter, you learn how to use these tools.

Creating Web Pages in Word

For years, you have used desktop publishing programs and word processors to publish on paper. However, when you need to make the transition to publishing on the Web, you might think that you need to learn how to use an entirely new program and fiddle with those complex formatting codes that control the appearance of your Web page.

Fortunately, Microsoft has added some Web page creation tools to Microsoft Word. With these tools, you can easily make the transition from desktop publishing to Webtop publishing without having to learn a new program. Word offers two ways to create Web pages: You can transform existing documents into Web pages or use the Web Page Wizard to create a page from scratch. These techniques are discussed in the following sections.

Internet Explorer Included

Office XP comes with the latest version of Microsoft's Web browser, Internet Explorer 5.5. To run it, click the **Internet Explorer** icon on the Windows desktop or click the **Launch Internet Explorer Browser** icon in the Quick Launch toolbar.

Web Browsing in Office

Assuming that you have an Internet connection and are using Microsoft Internet Explorer as your Web browser, you can open Web pages directly from the Office applications. To turn on the Web toolbar, right-click any toolbar and select **Web**. Even more useful is Internet Explorer's capability to open Office documents. Select **File, Open** to open an Office document, and then click the **Tools** button to turn the Office application's toolbars on or off in Internet Explorer.

Transforming Existing Documents into Web Pages

If you have a document that already contains most of the text you want on your Web page, don't re-create it; just transform it. To transform a Word document into a Web page, first save the document as a normal Word document so you don't mess up the original. Then open the **File** menu and select **Save As Web Page** (this works for Excel workbooks, too). The Save As dialog box appears.

314

Type a filename for the document, and then select the folder in which you want it stored. To give your page a title other than the filename, click the **Change Title** button and enter the desired page title. (The title appears in the browser's title bar when you or someone else opens the page.) Click **Save**. Word saves the document and converts any Word formatting codes into HTML codes. Skip ahead to "Formatting Your Web Pages" to add a little flair to your document.

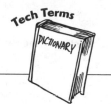

HTML: The Codes Behind the Document

HTML stands for Hypertext Markup Language, which is a coding system used to format documents on the Web. For example, in HTML, you can make text bold by adding the <b> code (start bold) before the text and the </b> code (end bold) after it. Of course, when you're creating a Web page in Word, all you have to do is drag over the text and click the **Bold** button in the formatting toolbar. Word automatically inserts the HTML codes for you. To view the codes, select **View, HTML Source**.

Making Web Pages with a Wizard or Template

The easiest way to create a Web site in Word is to use the Web Page Wizard or a template. This wizard displays a series of dialog boxes that lead you through the process of creating a custom Web site consisting of multiple linked pages. A template merely slaps a ready-made Web page on your screen; you simply edit the text and add your own graphics to customize the page.

To run the Web Page Wizard or use a template, open Word's **File** menu and select **New**. In the New Document task pane, below New from Template, click **General Templates**. In the Templates dialog box, click the **Web Pages** tab and double-click the desired template or double-click **Web Page Wizard**. If you choose the Web Page Wizard, it leads you through the process of creating a multipage Web document, allowing you to add, delete, or rearrange pages. Follow the wizard's instructions and click **Next** after entering your preferences in each dialog box.

Of course, the page(s) you end up with depends on what you selected. Figure 26.1 shows a typical Web site that consists of two columns. On the left is a table of contents for your site, and on the right is the default home page with some placeholder text. (When a user clicks a heading, such as **Section 2**, in the table of contents, on the left, the frame on the right automatically scrolls down to the selected section, no matter how far down the page Section 2 ends up when you're done adding your own text. This helps visitors to your Web site skip to the information that interests them.) The following sections show you how to modify your Web pages.

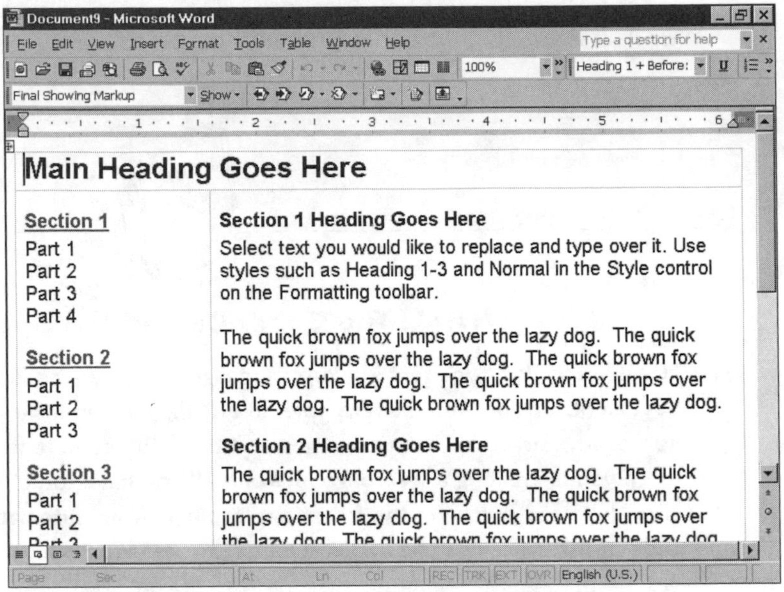

Figure 26.1

Web page templates and wizards provide the overall structure you need to get started.

Formatting Your Web Pages

In most cases, you can format your text just as you would if you were working on a Word document (see Chapter 5, "Giving Your Text a Makeover"). When you apply formatting to selected text, Word inserts the proper HTML codes for you. The following list provides a quick rundown of additional formatting options, plus a few standard options that are easy to overlook when creating Web pages:

➤ Use the Style drop-down list in the Formatting toolbar to apply common Web page styles. For example, apply the Heading 1 style to the page's title.

➤ Don't forget to use tables to align text. You can create and edit tables on a Web page just as you can in any Word document. Word handles all the complicated HTML table codes for you.

➤ The Format, Theme command displays a list of predesigned styles for your Web page. The style controls the background, fonts, graphic bullets, horizontal lines, and the appearance of other objects to give your Web page(s) a consistent look and feel. You can also use the Format, Background options to customize the background.

➤ To insert a horizontal line to divide the contents on your page, position the insertion point where you want the line inserted. Select **Format**, **Borders and Shading** and click the **Horizontal Line** button (at the bottom of the dialog box). Click the line you want to insert and click **OK**.

➤ Display the Web Tools toolbar for access to additional buttons for inserting objects on a Web page, including movie clips, a background audio clip, and scrolling text boxes. To display the toolbar, right-click any toolbar and select **Web Tools**.

Previewing Your Page in Internet Explorer

Assuming you have a Web browser installed on your computer, you should preview your Web page to see how it looks in a browser. (This is sort of like Print Preview for Web pages.) Sometimes, what you see in your Office application is nothing like what you get on the Web. Open the **File** menu and click **Web Page Preview**.

Connecting Your Page to Other Pages with Hyperlinks

No Web page is complete without a few links that kick you out to another part of the page or to another page on the Web. All Office applications have the Insert Hyperlink feature, which enables you to quickly insert links to other documents, files, or pages.

 To quickly transform normal text into a link, drag over the text you want to use as the link and click the **Insert Hyperlink** button in the Standard toolbar. The Insert Hyperlink dialog box appears, as shown in Figure 26.2, allowing you to enter preferences for the link. The Insert Hyperlink dialog box provides the following Link To options:

➤ **Existing File or Web Page**—Lets you point the link to a recently opened file, a page you have recently opened in Internet Explorer, or a Web page address. You can also add a ScreenTip to the link that displays a description of the link when a visitor rests the mouse pointer on the link.

➤ **Place in This Document**—Inserts a link that points to a heading or bookmark that's on the same page as the link. To use this option, first mark the destination point in the document by applying one of Word's heading styles (Heading1, Heading2, and so on) to a heading or by inserting a bookmark. To insert a bookmark, position the insertion point near the destination, select **Insert**, **Bookmark**, and type a name for the bookmark.

➤ **Create New Document**—Inserts a link that points to a document you have not yet created. Type a name for the new document and select the folder in which you want the document stored. Word creates a new blank Web page. You can then insert text, links, and other objects to complete the page.

➤ **E-mail Address**—Inserts a link that points to an e-mail address. A person visiting your page can then click the link to run his e-mail program and quickly send you a message. The message will automatically be addressed to the e-mail address you specify.

After entering your preferences for the link, click **OK**. When you click **OK**, the selected text is transformed into a link and appears blue (or whatever color you chose for displaying links). As you're creating links, test them to make sure they work. You don't want to point your visitors down a dead-end street.

You can select to link to a recently opened file or Web page.

Text that will appear as a link

Add a ScreenTip to describe the link.

Figure 26.2

You can create links that point to different areas on the same page or to different pages.

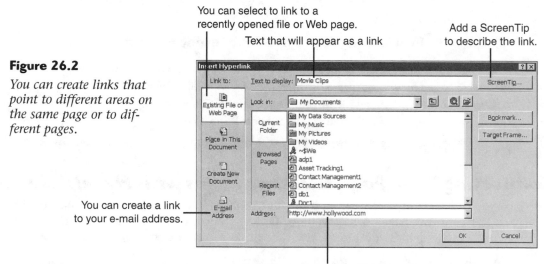

You can create a link to your e-mail address.

Type the address of the Web site or page you want the link to point to.

Placing a Link Bar on Your Web Page

To make it easy for visitors to navigate your Web page, consider adding a link bar to your Web page. A link bar appears at the top or left margin of the page and displays links that point to various locations on the page and to other Web pages or even other sites. The following steps lead you through the process of inserting a link bar. The only drawback is that you first must save your Web page to a special Web server that is running Microsoft FrontPage Server Extensions 2002 or SharePoint Team Services from Microsoft. If you have access to one of these special Web servers, you can take the following steps to insert a link bar:

1. Save your document as a Web page to a Web server that is running Microsoft FrontPage Server Extensions 2002 or SharePoint Team Services from Microsoft. If you don't save your Web page to a supported Web server, Word will insert an error message in your document (instead of inserting a link bar) after you complete step 7. See "Placing Your Pages on the Web," later in this chapter, for details on how to save a Web page.

2. Open the **Insert** menu and click **Web Component**.

3. Under **Component Type**, click **Link Bars**.

4. Under **Choose a Bar Type**, click the desired bar type and click **Next**.

5. Under **Choose a Bar Style**, click the desired bar style and click **Next**. (To make the bar match the theme that's applied to your Web page, click **Use Page's Theme**.)

6. Under **Choose an Orientation**, click the desired arrangement.

7. When you have specified all the settings you want, click **Finish**. The Link Bar Properties dialog box appears.

8. Click **Add Link**.

9. Select the desired link. (If you don't see a link you want, use the **Look In** and **Link To** options to change the settings.)

10. Under **Text to Display**, type the text you want the link bar to display for the link.

11. Click **OK**.

12. Repeat steps 8–11 to insert additional links in the bar. (Use the **Move Up** and **Move Down** buttons to rearrange the links.)

13. Click **Apply** to preview the settings in your document, and then click **OK** when you are done.

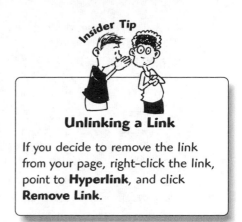

Insider Tip

Unlinking a Link

If you decide to remove the link from your page, right-click the link, point to **Hyperlink**, and click **Remove Link**.

Working with Frames

Frames provide a structure that allows visitors to your Web site to easily navigate the pages that make up your site. The left frame, for example, contains links that point to other pages at your site. When someone clicks a link, the associated page opens in the right frame; but the contents of the left frame remain onscreen, allowing the person to quickly open other pages. Unlike link bars, which require a special type of Web server, the frames feature is available for all Web pages, regardless of the type of server on which the page is stored.

To resize a frame, drag the edge of the bar that separates the frames. (When you move the mouse pointer over the edge of the bar that's used for resizing the frames, the mouse pointer appears as a double-headed arrow.) For more frame options, display the Frames toolbar by selecting **View**, **Toolbars**, **Frames**. Use the following buttons on the Frames toolbar to make your changes:

Table of Contents in Frame. Creates a new frame with links to headings in the current frame. To create a table of contents, first mark headings in your Web page as Heading1, Heading2, and so on. Then, click the **Table of Contents in Frame** button to create the new frame.

New Frame Left. Inserts a blank frame to the left of the current page or frame.

New Frame Right. Inserts a blank frame to the right of the current page or frame.

New Frame Above. Inserts a blank frame above the current page or frame.

New Frame Below. Inserts a blank frame below the current page or frame.

Delete Frame. Removes the current frame. If the Web Page Wizard sticks you with an undesired frame, this is probably the only frame button you'll need.

Frame Properties. Displays a dialog box that allows you to change the size of the frame, specify a different document to display in the frame, and add borders to the frame.

Creating an Online Presentation in PowerPoint

Although Word seems like the most obvious choice for publishing pages on the Web, PowerPoint offers a more graphical approach, enabling you to transform a slide show into individual linked pages. Visitors to your Web page can advance through the slide show by clicking buttons or other types of hyperlinks. PowerPoint offers a couple of ways to create Internet presentations:

➤ If you have already created the presentation you want to use, save it as an HTML file. Open the presentation in PowerPoint, open the **File** menu, and select **Save As Web Page**. In the Save As dialog box, click the **Publish** button. Enter your preferences, as shown in Figure 26.3, and click **Publish**.

➤ Use the AutoContent Wizard to create a new presentation (as explained in Chapter 16, "Slapping Together a Basic Slide Show"). In the third AutoContent Wizard dialog box, the wizard provides five output options for the slide show. Select **Web Presentation**.

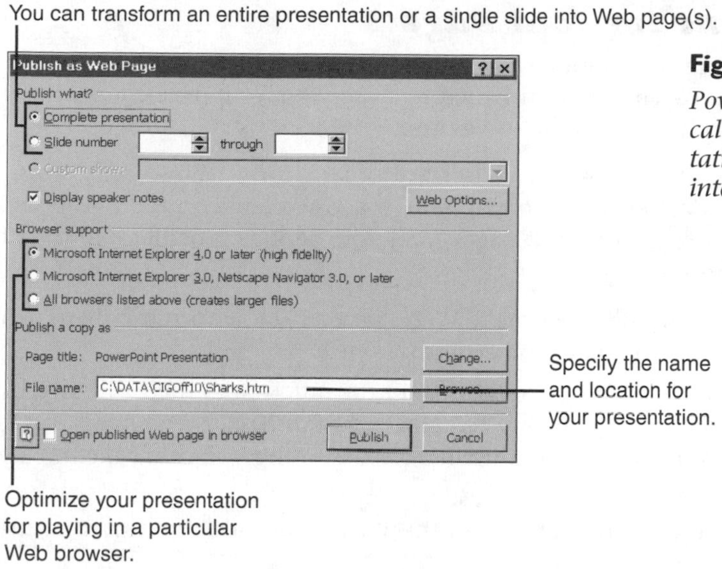

You can transform an entire presentation or a single slide into Web page(s).

Figure 26.3

PowerPoint can automatically convert your presentation into a series of interlinked slides.

Specify the name and location for your presentation.

Optimize your presentation for playing in a particular Web browser.

After you create your Web presentation, you can insert links to other slides in the presentation using the Animation Settings option. Select the object or text that you want the user to click to move to another slide (the next slide or any slide in the presentation). Right-click the selected text or object and click **Action Settings**. The Action Settings dialog box appears. Click the **Mouse Click** tab if it is not already in front. Click the **Hyperlink To** option to turn it on. Open the **Hyperlink To** drop-down list and select the slide to which you want this object or text to point. You can select the first or last slide, select the next or previous slide, or click **Slide** and pick the specific slide to which you want this link to point. (You can also choose to point a link to another file, a page on the Web or another PowerPoint presentation.) Click **OK**. (To learn more about inserting hyperlinks that point to other pages on the Web, see "Connecting Your Page to Other Pages with Hyperlinks," earlier in this chapter.)

Placing Your Pages on the Web

When you have completed your Web page, you must place it on a Web server so that other people can open and view it with their Web browsers. In the past, the only way to place a page on a Web server was to use a separate FTP (File Transfer Protocol) program. Now, Office provides a couple of tools that enable you to save your Web page(s) directly to a Web folder or a folder on the FTP server simply by using the File, Save As command.

The following sections lead you through the process of finding a home for your Web page(s) and setting up Office to upload your Web page and any associated files to the Web.

321

Finding a Home for Your Page

If you work at a big corporation or institution that has its own Web server, lucky you. You already have a Web server on which to store your Web pages. Just ask your Web administrator for the path to the server and write it down.

For the less fortunate, the best place to start looking for a Web server is your Internet service provider. Most providers make some space available on their Web servers for subscribers to store personal Web pages. Call your service provider and obtain the following information:

➤ Does your service provider make Web space available to subscribers? If not, maybe you should change providers.

➤ How much disk space do you get, and how much does it cost (if anything)? Some providers give you a limited amount of disk space, which is usually plenty for several Web pages, including images, assuming you don't include large audio or video clips.

➤ Can you save your files directly to the Web server or do you have to upload files to an FTP server?

➤ What is the URL of the server to which you must connect to upload your files? Write it down.

➤ What username and password do you need to enter to gain access to the server? (This is typically the same username and password you use to connect to the service.)

➤ In which directory (folder) must you place your files? Write it down.

➤ What name must you give your Web page? In many cases, the service requires you to name your opening Web page (your home page) index.html or default.html.

➤ Are there any other specific instructions that you must follow to post your Web page?

➤ After posting your page, what will its address (URL) be? You'll want to open it in Internet Explorer as soon as you post it to check it out.

Setting Up a Web Folder

If you have access to a FrontPage 2000 or a Web server that is running Microsoft FrontPage Server Extensions 2002 or SharePoint Team Services from Microsoft, you should first set up a Web folder in My Computer. If you must upload your files using FTP, skip ahead to the next section. To set up a Web folder, take the following steps:

1. Take one of the following steps, depending on which version of Windows you use:

   In Windows 98, double-click the My Computer icon on the Windows desktop, double-click the **Web Folders** icon, and then double-click the **Add Web Folder** icon to display the Add Web Folder dialog box.

   In Windows Me, double-click the **My Network Places** icon on the Windows desktop, and then double-click the **Add Network Place** icon to display the **Add Network Place Wizard** dialog box.

2. In the **Type the Location to Add** or **Type the Location of the Network Place** text box, type the address of the Web server, complete with a path to the directory in which you want your new folder created (for example, http://www.internet.com/public/).

3. Click the **Next** button.

4. If the Enter Network Password dialog box appears, type your username and password in the appropriate text boxes (and choose to have Windows remember your password, if desired), and then click **OK**.

5. Type a name for your Web folder or network place. This is the name that Windows will use to identify the folder on your computer.

6. Click the **Finish** button.

To save your Web page(s) to your Web folder, select the **File**, **Save As Web Page** command. Then, click the **Web Folders** or **My Network Places** icon, double-click the Web folder you just set up, and click the **Save** button (see Figure 26.4).

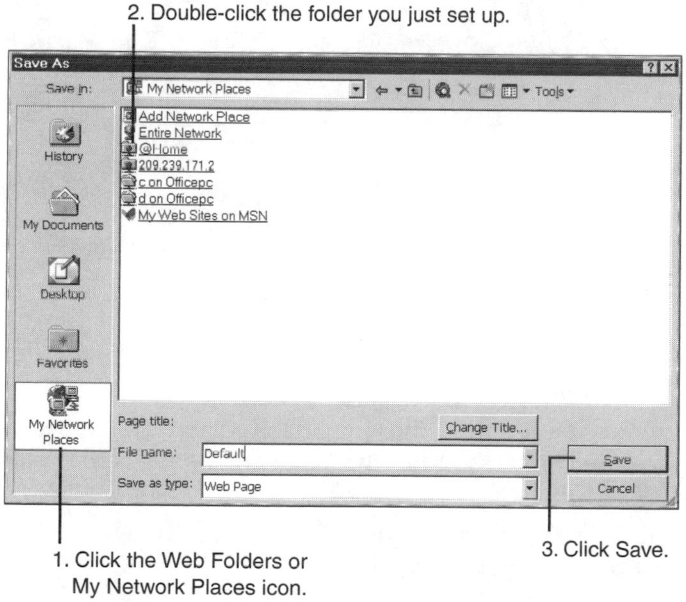

2. Double-click the folder you just set up.

Figure 26.4

You might be able to save your Web page(s) directly to a folder on the Web server.

1. Click the Web Folders or My Network Places icon.

3. Click Save.

Uploading Files to an FTP Server

Many Internet service providers still require that you upload Web pages to an FTP server to place them on the Web. Fortunately, Office simplifies the process, allowing you to perform FTP uploads with the File, Save As Web Page command. Take the following steps:

1. Open the page in the Office application you used to create it.

2. Open the **File** menu and select **Save As Web Page**.

3. In the Save As dialog box, open the **Save In** drop-down list, and select **Add/Modify FTP Locations**. This opens a dialog box prompting you to enter the address of the FTP site, your username, and your password, as shown in Figure 26.5.

4. Enter the address of the FTP site, your username, and your password in the appropriate text boxes and click **Add**. (In the **Name of the FTP Site** text box, type only the address of the FTP site—for example, type **ftp.internet.com**. Don't include the path to the folder and do not type ftp:// before the address.)

5. Click **OK**. This returns you to the Save As dialog box, which now contains the address of the FTP site.

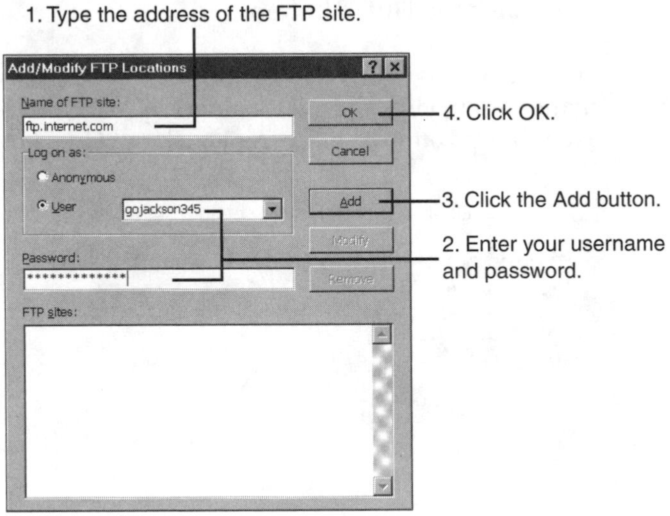

Figure 26.5

You can set up your Office applications to save Web pages directly to an FTP server.

1. Type the address of the FTP site.

Add/Modify FTP Locations	? ✕

Name of FTP site:
ftp.internet.com

Log on as:
○ Anonymous
⦿ User   gojackson345

Password:
●●●●●●●●●●●●●

FTP sites:

OK — 4. Click OK.

Cancel

Add — 3. Click the Add button.

Modify — 2. Enter your username and password.

Remove

6. Click the address and click **Open**.

7. If you are not connected to the Internet, the Connect To dialog box appears; click **Connect**. After you are connected, the Save As dialog box lists the directories (folders) on the FTP server.

8. Change to the folder in which your service provider told you to save the Web page file, and then click the **Save** button.

Managing Your Web Site with FrontPage

Although the Web page creation and publication tools in Word, Excel, PowerPoint, and Access are sufficient for most beginning users, Office XP includes an industrial-strength Web-management program called FrontPage. With FrontPage, you can further customize existing Web pages, create new Web pages, modify linked pages, and control the structure of a complex Web site (which FrontPage refers to as a *web*).

To run FrontPage, click the Windows **Start** button, point to **Programs**, and click **Microsoft FrontPage**. The Microsoft FrontPage window appears, as shown in Figure 26.6. As you can see, it looks very similar to the Microsoft Word window and contains many of the same menus and toolbar buttons. What's unique about the FrontPage window is that it contains a Views bar at the left. This bar contains the following buttons:

➤ **Page**—Displays the current Web page. Use this view to add text and objects to a page, format your page, insert links, and perform other Web-page related tasks. In Page view, three tabs appear below the work area: Normal (for displaying the formatted Web page), HTML (to display the HTML tags that control the layout and formatting), and Preview (to display the page as it will appear in a Web browser).

➤ **Folders**—Displays a list of folders and files that make up your Web site, allowing you to quickly rearrange the folders and files just as if you were using Windows Explorer. As you drag Web pages and other files from one folder to another, FrontPage automatically adjusts the hyperlinks so they point to the correct files.

➤ **Reports**—Displays a site summary that acts as an inventory of the contents of your Web site, including the number of files and their sizes; the number and type of hyperlinks; the number of incomplete tasks; and any problems, such as hyperlinks that point to nonexistent pages or other files.

➤ **Navigation**—Displays a graphic representation of the structure of your Web site, giving you a bird's-eye view of your site and allowing you to quickly restructure the site. In Navigation view, you can even create a navigation bar to place at the top of every page; users can click links on the bar to jump to specific opening pages.

➤ **Hyperlinks**—Shows a list of pages linked to the current Web page, so you can verify that the links on a page are working properly.

➤ **Tasks**—Acts as a project-management tool for your Web site. You can create a list of tasks, assign tasks to individuals or workgroups, check the status of each task, associate each task with a file, and mark a task as completed when it's done.

Figure 26.6

Use FrontPage to fine-tune your Web pages and manage your Web site.

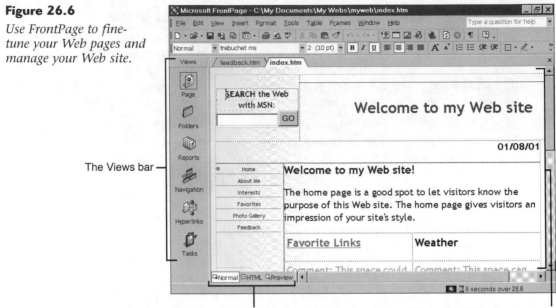

The Views bar —

In Page view, click a tab to specify the desired page view.   Work on individual pages here.

Edit Any Page

You can open a Web page in Internet Explorer and then choose to edit it in FrontPage. First, open the page in Internet Explorer, and then select **File**, **Edit with Microsoft FrontPage**. If Edit with Microsoft FrontPage is not on Internet Explorer's File menu, FrontPage is not set up as your default Web page editor. Restart FrontPage and when it displays a dialog box asking if you want to use FrontPage as your default Web page editor, click **Yes**.

Creating a New Web Site

Although a Web site can consist of a single page, more complex sites can contain dozens of pages stored in related folders or directories on the server. To ensure that you are starting with a sound structure, use one of the FrontPage templates or wizards to create the overall structure for your Web site:

1. Open the **File** menu, point to **New**, and click **Page or Web**. The New Page or Web task pane pops up on the right side of the screen.

2. Under New from Template, click **Web Site Templates**.

3. Click the icon for the type of Web you want to create and click **OK**. If you clicked an icon for a template, FrontPage automatically creates the web. If you clicked an icon for a wizard, FrontPage runs the wizard.

4. If you clicked an icon for a web wizard, follow the wizard's instructions and enter your preferences.

After FrontPage has created the web, click the Page button in the Views bar to start editing the pages that comprise the web. A folder list appears to the right of the Views bar displaying a list of pages. Click the icon for the page you want to view, and then edit and format the page in the Page view window, as shown previously in Figure 26.6.

Making Pages

In addition to helping you manage consist the overall structure of your Web site, FrontPage offers powerful features for creating individual pages and includes a wide selection of Web page templates from which to choose. To create a new Web page using a template, take the following steps:

1. Open the **File** menu, point to **New**, and click **Page or Web**. The New Page or Web task pane appears.

2. Under New from Template, click **Page Templates**.

3. Click the desired icon and click **OK**. FrontPage creates the page and displays it in the Page view window.

4. Edit and format the page as desired.

5. To save the page as its own document file, open the **File** menu and select **Save**.

6. Type a name for the Web page.

7. To give the page a title that differs from the filename, click the **Change Title** button, type a title for the page, and click **OK**.

8. Click the **Save** button. The name of the new page appears at the bottom of the Folder List.

Verifying Hyperlinks

When you create a Web site that consists of multiple pages, it's easy to lose track of the overall structure of the site and how the pages are interconnected. To help, FrontPage can display your Web site in Hyperlinks view, as shown in Figure 26.7. To switch to this view, click the **Hyperlinks** button in the Views bar. In Hyperlinks view, you can perform the following tasks:

➤ Click the plus sign next to a page icon to view pages that link to this page.

➤ Click the minus sign next to a page icon to collapse (hide) the list of pages that link to this page.

➤ To give a page center stage and see more clearly how other pages link to it, right-click the page's icon and select **Move to Center**.

➤ To delete a page and remove any links to it, right-click the page and select **Delete**.

➤ To open a page, double-click its icon or right-click the page and select **Open**.

Formatting and Editing Pages

The tools for editing and formatting pages in FrontPage are very similar to those used in Word. Use the same steps explained earlier in this chapter. To place more complex objects on your Web page, such as a hit counter (to keep track of the number of visitors), table of contents, or scrolling marquee, click the **Web Component** button on the Standard toolbar and select the desired component.

Web Servers Have Some Limitations

Many service providers that offer Web publishing support have strict rules for naming files and creating folders. Before you do much work with FrontPage, make sure you know the rules, so you can work around them.

Publishing Your Web

Perhaps the coolest, most useful feature of FrontPage is that it allows you to transfer your entire Web site from your hard drive to the Web server as a single unit. To publish your web to the server, take the following steps:

1. Open the **File** menu and click **Publish Web**. The Publish Web dialog box appears.

2. Type the address of the Web or FTP server on which you want your web placed or, if you set up a Web folder or network place earlier in this chapter, click the **Browse** button and select the folder you created. If typing the address of a Web server, start with http://. If typing the address of an FTP server, start with ftp://.

3. Click the **Publish** button.

4. Type your username and password, if required to log on, and click **OK**. FrontPage uploads all the folders and files that make up your Web site to the specified Web or FTP server.

Click a plus sign to view pages that link to this page.

Click a minus sign to hide the links for this page.

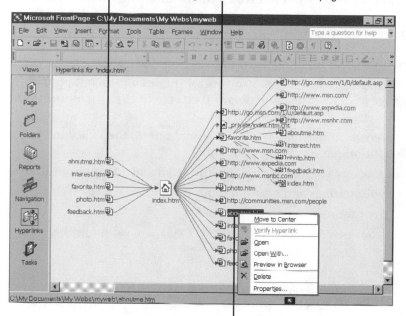

Figure 26.7

In Hyperlinks view, FrontPage provides a graphic representation of how your Web pages are linked.

Right-click a page for additional options.

Creating Your Very Own Photo Gallery on the Web

Whew! That was too much like work. Let's have some fun and create an online photo gallery. All you need is FrontPage and a handful of digitized photos, and you're ready to begin:

1. Open FrontPage's **File** menu, point to **New**, and click **Page or Web**.

2. Under **New from Template**, click **Page Templates**.

3. On the General tab, scroll down the list of templates, click the **Photo Gallery** icon, and click **OK**. FrontPage displays a sample photo gallery (see Figure 26.8).

4. Double-click one of the pictures displayed in the sample gallery. The Photo Gallery Properties dialog box appears.

5. Click the **Remove** button five times to remove all sample photos from the gallery.

6. To add a photo of your own, take one of the following steps:

   Click the **Add** button, select **Pictures from Files**, and use the resulting dialog box to select a digitized image stored on your system.

   Click the **Add** button, select **Pictures from Scanner or Cameras**, and follow the onscreen instructions to insert a scanned image or to download an image from your digital camera.

7. Repeat step 6 to insert additional digitized photos.

8. Under **Thumbnail Size**, use the settings to control the size of the mini-image that your Web page initially displays. (Users will be able to click the thumbnail to view a full-size version of the image.)

9. To add a caption or descriptive text, click the desired photo; then click in the **Caption** or **Description** box, and type your entry.

10. Click the **Layout** tab, and click the setting for the arrangement you want to use.

11. Click **OK** to save your settings and return to your new photo gallery Web page.

12. Edit any text on the page as you normally would.

13. Save and publish your new Web photo gallery, as explained earlier in this chapter.

Click Add to add a photo to the gallery.

Click the Layout tab to specify the desired arrangement of photos.

Figure 26.8

FrontPage's new Photo Gallery template makes creating and publishing your own online photo gallery on the Web easy.

Click a photo to select it.

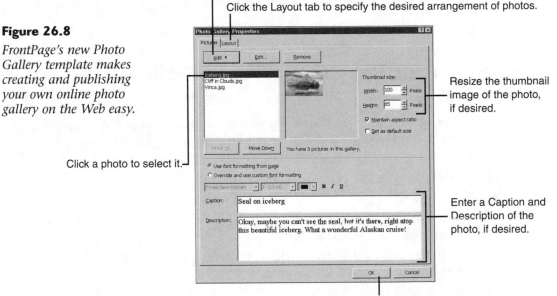

Resize the thumbnail image of the photo, if desired.

Enter a Caption and Description of the photo, if desired.

Click OK when you're done.

The Least You Need to Know

This chapter provided the least you need to know about using Office XP's Web page authoring tools. These tools are too powerful to cover completely in a single chapter. However, we did manage to cover the following important points:

➤ To create a new Web page in Word, run the Web Page Wizard. You can find it in the Templates dialog box, on the Web Pages tab.

➤ To transform an existing Word document or Excel worksheet into a Web page, open the document and use the **File**, **Save As Web Page** command to save it.

➤ To create an online slide show, run PowerPoint's AutoContent Wizard and select **Web Presentation** in the third dialog box.

➤ Use the **Insert Hyperlink** button in the Standard toolbar to insert links that point to other documents, pages, or files.

➤ To place your Web page(s) on the Web, you must upload it to an FTP or a Web server, as instructed by your Internet service provider or Web administrator.

➤ To publish a Web page or a web (a collection of Web pages) from FrontPage, open the **File** menu and click **Publish Web**.

Chapter 27

Macros for Mere Mortals

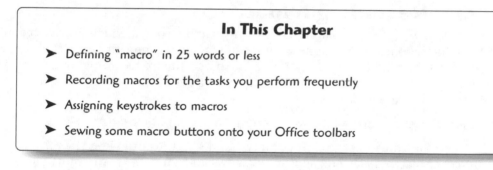

In This Chapter

➤ Defining "macro" in 25 words or less

➤ Recording macros for the tasks you perform frequently

➤ Assigning keystrokes to macros

➤ Sewing some macro buttons onto your Office toolbars

You probably already have a few favorite shortcut keys. You can bypass the Office application menus by pressing Ctrl+S to save a document, Ctrl+P to print, and Ctrl+B to boldface text. But you secretly wish that Microsoft had built in a few more shortcuts for step-heavy operations you perform frequently.

To make your wishes come true, you can create your own shortcut keys and buttons using *macros*. A macro is a recorded series of commands you can play back in Office applications by selecting the macro's name from a list or by pressing a keystroke or clicking a button you assigned to the macro. In this chapter, you learn how to record commands using the macro recorder and how to name and run your macros.

Do You Need a Macro?

Office includes shortcut keys and buttons for the most commonly entered commands. Before creating your own macro to automate a task you commonly perform, check the help system to determine whether Office already offers a shortcut for that task. Also, ask yourself whether you can use an easier feature, such as AutoCorrect or AutoText, instead of using a macro.

Roll 'Em: Recording a Macro

The easiest way to create a macro is to use the macro recorder, which is available in all the Office applications. The steps for recording macros, however, vary slightly among the Office applications. (In Access, the procedure for recording macros is much more complex; check the Access help system for details or ask your Office Assistant to lend a hand.)

The following steps show you how to record a macro in Microsoft Word:

1. Open the **Tools** menu, point to **Macro**, and select **Record New Macro**. The Record Macro dialog box appears, as shown in Figure 27.1, prompting you to name the macro.

2. Type a unique, descriptive, and brief name for your macro, up to 80 characters (no spaces). The macro name must start with a letter—never a number. The macro recorder supplies a default name—Macro1, Macro2, and so on, as you keep recording macros—but nondescriptive names such as this aren't very helpful when you're trying to remember which macro did what.

3. Open the **Store Macro In** drop-down list and choose to store the macro in the current document or in **All Documents (Normal.dot)** to make the macro available in all your documents. At this point, you can assign the macro to a keystroke or create a toolbar button for it. (See "Assigning Shortcut Keys for Quick Playback" and "Making Buttons for Your Macros," later in this chapter, for details.)

4. Click in the **Description** text box and type a brief description of the macro's function (the task it performs).

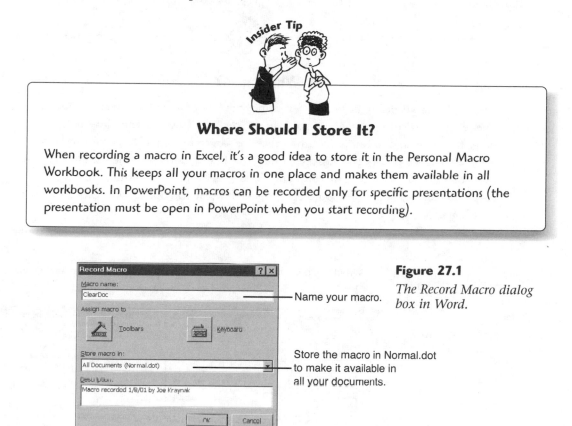

Where Should I Store It?

When recording a macro in Excel, it's a good idea to store it in the Personal Macro Workbook. This keeps all your macros in one place and makes them available in all workbooks. In PowerPoint, macros can be recorded only for specific presentations (the presentation must be open in PowerPoint when you start recording).

Name your macro.

Store the macro in Normal.dot
to make it available in
all your documents.

Figure 27.1

The Record Macro dialog box in Word.

5. Click the **OK** button. A small toolbar appears with buttons for stopping and pausing the recording, as shown in Figure 27.2 (in Excel and PowerPoint, you don't get a Pause button).

6. Perform the task whose steps you want to record. You can select menu commands and press keystrokes to enter commands, text, or objects. You cannot, however, move the insertion point or select text using the mouse; you must use the arrow keys to move text and Shift+arrow keys to highlight text.

7. When you are finished performing the steps, click the **Stop Recording** button.

Why Pause?

Use the Pause Recording button to test commands before recording them. If you're not sure what a particular command is going to do, click the **Pause Recording** button, enter the command to test it, and then click the **Undo** button. If the command did what was expected, click the **Resume Recorder** button and enter the command again to record it. You can also pause recording if you need to refer to another document, check a filename, or perform some other operation that you don't want recorded as part of the macro.

Figure 27.2

As you perform the task, the macro recorder records the commands you enter.

When you are done performing the task, click the Stop Recording button.

Enter commands as you normally would.

Pause Recording button

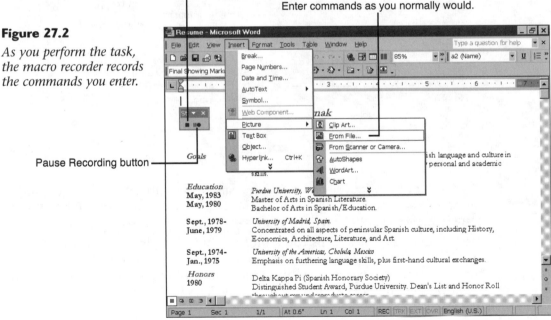

Excel Exceptions

Excel macros automatically record any cell selections using absolute references. If you want to use relative references, click the **Relative Reference** button on the Stop Recording toolbar. You can click this button repeatedly to switch back and forth from absolute to relative references.

Playing Back a Recorded Macro

When you record a macro, its name is added to the list of macros you have recorded. To play the macro (and perform the steps recorded in that macro), open the **Tools** menu, point to **Macro**, and select **Macros**, or press **Alt+F8**. A list of available macros appears, as shown in Figure 27.3. Click the name of the macro you want to run and click the **Run** button.

Click the name of the macro
you want to run.

Click the Run button.

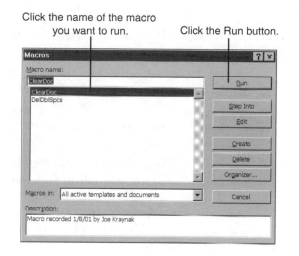

Figure 27.3

You can select the macro you want to run from a list of recorded macros.

Although selecting a macro from a comprehensive macro list is a foolproof way to find and play the macro, it is hardly the most efficient. If you find yourself frequently playing back the macro, consider assigning a shortcut keystroke to the macro or adding a button for the macro to one of your toolbars. The following sections show you just what to do.

What's It Doing to My Document?

Before running your macro for the first time, save your document. If the macro goes whacko and messes up the document, close the document without saving the changes. To stop a macro before it does too much damage, press **Ctrl+Break** and then use the Undo feature to try to recover from the disaster. If, however, the macro includes a File, Save command, you might be out of luck.

Assigning Shortcut Keys for Quick Playback

Shortcut key combinations are by far the most efficient way to enter commands in your Office applications because you don't have to move your fingers from the keyboard to enter the command.

To assign a shortcut key combination to one of your macros in Word, take the following steps:

Hey, Ctrl+P Doesn't Print My Document Anymore!

When assigning shortcut key combinations, be careful not to assign a macro to a keystroke that the application already uses, such as Ctrl+P (for Print) or Ctrl+S (for Save).

1. Open the **Tools** menu and select **Customize**.
2. Click the **Keyboard** button.
3. Under **Categories**, click **Macros**. A list of available macros appears in the Macros list, as shown in Figure 27.4.
4. Click the macro to which you want to assign a shortcut key combination.
5. Click in the **Press New Shortcut Key** text box and press the key combination you want to use for this macro. A message appears below this text box indicating whether the keystroke is already in use. If the keystroke is in use, press the **Backspace** key and press a different key combination.
6. Click the **Assign** button.
7. Click the **Close** button.

What About PowerPoint and Excel?

PowerPoint doesn't support shortcut keys for macros, and Excel has a different method for setting up shortcuts. Select **Tools**, **Macro**, **Macros**. Select the macro and click **Options**. In the **Shortcut Key** box, type the keyboard character to use for the shortcut. You can use **Ctrl+*character*** or **Ctrl+Shift+*character***.

Click Macros.

Click the macro
you want to assign
to a shortcut key.

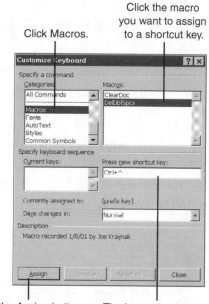

Figure 27.4

You can assign a shortcut key combination to a macro.

Click the Assign button.   The keystroke that you
press appears here.

Making Buttons for Your Macros

The Office toolbars are great time-savers. Instead of having to flip through a series of menus and submenus, you simply click a button in one of the toolbars or select the desired option from one of the drop-down lists. These toolbars can give you quick access to your macros as well. To add a macro to one of the Office toolbars, take the following steps:

Remove a Toolbar Button

To remove a button from a toolbar, display the Customize dialog box and then drag the button off the toolbar.

1. Make sure the toolbar on which you want to place your macro button is displayed. (Select **View**, **Toolbars** to display a list of available toolbars.)

2. Open the **Tools** menu and select **Customize**.

3. Click the **Commands** tab.

4. In the **Categories** list, select **Macros**. A list of available macros appears in the **Commands** list. (Excel provides only two options: Custom Button and Custom Menu Item.)

5. Drag the desired macro (or the Custom Button in Excel) from the Commands list over the toolbar on which you want it to appear, drag it to the desired location (watch for a dark I-beam pointer that shows where the button will appear), and release the mouse button. The button appears on the toolbar. (Leave the Customize dialog box open to perform the next steps.)

6. To change the name of the button, right-click it, drag over the entry in the **Name** text box, and type a new name for the button.

7. To add an image to the button, point to **Change Button Image** and click the desired image. If you want to display the image only, not the button name, right-click the button and select **Default Style**.

8. If you're doing this in Excel, right-click the button and select **Assign Macro**. Select the desired macro from the list and click **OK**.

9. When you are done, click the **Close** button in the Customize dialog box to close it.

Additional Keystrokes

For more keystroke options, hold down a key combination and then release it and press another key. A comma appears after the first keystroke, and the second key or keystroke you pressed is tacked onto the end (for example, Ctrl+Shift+X,L). To enter this keystroke, you press Ctrl+Shift+X, release the keys, and then press L.

Saving Your Macros

When you create a Word macro, the macro is saved automatically when you save or close the document in which you created the macro. If you create the macro in the Normal.dot template, however, so that it's available to all documents, the macro isn't saved with the File, Save command. What if the power goes out before you close Word and save those precious macros? Sorry, they're gone. To save your document and Normal.dot, Shift+click **File** in the menu bar and select **Save All**. This saves all open documents plus Normal.dot.

No Need to Shift When You Click

If you plan to do a lot of customizing in Word, add the Save All command to your File menu so that it will be there even if you forget to hold down the Shift key while clicking File. Select **Tools, Customize**, click the **Commands** tab, click **File** in the **Categories** list, click **Save All** in the **Commands** list, and drag it out of the dialog box and over your File menu. The menu drops open. Position the Save All command where you want it and let go. Then just select **File, Save All** when you want to save all open documents plus Normal.dot.

You face the same problem when you create macros in Excel. The macros are not saved until you save the workbook or exit Excel. If you create your macros in the Personal Macro Workbook, select **Window, Unhide** and unhide Personal.xls. Then select **File, Save** to save the macro workbook. If you don't save Personal.xls as you're going along, Excel prompts you to save it before exiting.

The Least You Need to Know

You can spend weeks learning how to customize Office with macros and program your own macros using the Visual Basic Editor, but you don't need to know everything when you're just starting out. At this point, you should be able to do the following:

➤ To start recording commands, open the **Tools** menu, point to **Macro**, and click **Record New Macro**.

➤ To play a macro you recorded, open the **Tools** menu, point to **Macro**, select **Macros**, click the macro's name, and click the **Run** button.

➤ To stop an errant macro before it does too much damage, press **Ctrl+Break**.

➤ To assign a shortcut key combination to a macro, open the **Tools** menu, click **Customize**, and click the **Keyboard** button.

➤ To add a button for one of your macros to an Office toolbar, select **Tools**, **Customize**, click the **Commands** tab, click **Macros** (in the **Categories** list), and then drag and drop the desired macro onto one of the toolbars.

➤ To save your macros along with your document, Shift+click the **File** menu and click **Save All**.

Chapter 28

No-Brainer Publications with Microsoft Publisher

In This Chapter

➤ The five-second publication

➤ Customizing prefab publications via the task pane

➤ A little customizing goes a long way

➤ Some basic tools you should know about

➤ A few wizardly tricks of your own

Although your local print shop will gladly "fulfill your every publishing need," they will also charge you an arm and a leg to create publications that don't quite match what you had in mind. In addition, they might not be able to meet your tight deadlines—they usually have to "fit you in," which translates to "maybe sometime next week."

To save some money, get the job done on time, and let your own creative vision drive your publications, use Microsoft Publisher. Publisher comes with a coven of publication wizards for creating newsletters, brochures, mailing labels, letterhead, business cards, and even résumés. You just fire up a wizard, answer a few questions, and you have a custom publication, carefully laid out for you. In this chapter, you learn how to use Publisher to "fulfill your every publishing need" on *your* schedule and for a few pennies per printout.

Conjuring Up Quick Publications with Wizards

With Microsoft Publisher, you never have to start with a blank page. On startup, Publisher displays a collection of predesigned publications for creating everything from greeting cards to résumés. You simply click the desired publication and enter your preferences in the task pane and any dialog boxes that appear. If the pre-designed publications are not displayed, select **File, New**. This displays the New from Existing Publication task pane (on the left), along with a selection of Quick Publications (on the right), as shown in Figure 28.1.

2. Click the desired publication.

Figure 28.1

Publisher offers a wide selection of prefab publications.

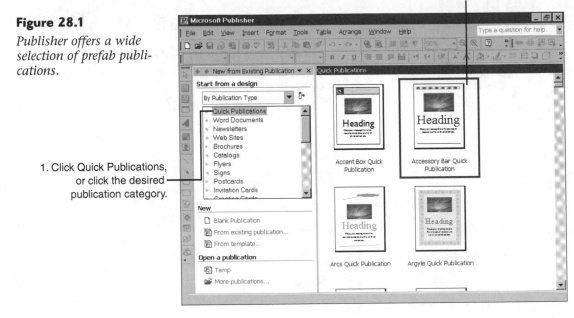

1. Click Quick Publications, or click the desired publication category.

No Publisher?!

Not all versions of Microsoft Office XP include Publisher. If Microsoft Publisher does not appear on the Start, Programs menu, try running the Office installation again to determine whether your copy of Office includes Publisher.

The first time you choose to create a publication, the Microsoft Publisher dialog box appears, indicating that the wizard will add personal information to your publications for you and prompting you to click OK to enter the information. Click **OK**. The Personal Information dialog box appears, providing a fill-in-the-blank form, as shown in Figure 28.2. Under **Select a Personal Information Set to Edit**, click the desired type of information you want to enter: **Primary Business**, **Secondary Business**, **Other Organization**, or **Home/Family**. Then, type your entries in the text boxes, to enter your name, address, phone number, e-mail address, and other contact information. (You can repeat the steps to enter information for two businesses, one organization, and your home.)

1. Click one of these options to change the
form for business or personal information.

Personal Information   [?][X]

Select a personal information set to edit:

Primary Business
Secondary Business
Other Organization
Home/Family

Personal information for this set

Name: Job or position title:

Bill Simpson   Boss

Address: Color schemes

8508 North Stingray Avenue   ☐ Include color scheme in this set
Chicago, Illinois 60629
                                                For print publications:

                                                Prairie   ▢▢▢▢▢ ▼

Phone/fax/e-mail:

Phone: 555-555-5555
Fax: 555-121-4484
Email: bsimpson@Sharkspree.com   Logo

Organization name:

Shark Spree Designs

Tag line or motto:

Beauty with attitude

                        Help on Logos   Update   Cancel

2. Enter your contact information
in these text boxes.

Figure 28.2

Complete this form to enter your name, mailing address, phone number, and other contact information.

Publish Your Own Web Site

To create a page for publication on the Web, click **Web Sites** and select the desired design. You can tweak your Web pages just as you do with standard paper publications. However, Publisher offers a few additional tools for inserting *hyperlinks* (which point to other Web pages and resources), previewing your pages in your Web browser, and publishing your pages electronically on the Web. There are also a few design no-no's you should be aware of when creating your Web pages. See Chapter 26, "Creating and Publishing Your Own Web Pages," for details.

PageWizard or Task Pane?

Publisher's publication wizards are much more subtle than the PageWizards in the previous version. Task panes have taken over most of the work, allowing you to enter your preferences without having to proceed through a long series of dialog boxes.

After you submit the required information, the publication wizard slaps together a sample publication and displays it in the work area on the right. To the left of the work area is the task pane, shown in Figure 28.3, where you can change the overall design, layout, color scheme, and other settings that control your publication. To make a change, click the desired category in the list at the top, and then click the desired setting or enter the requested information at the bottom. You can hide the task pane at any time by clicking the **Close (X)** button on the right end of the task pane's title bar. To back up to a previous task pane, click the **Back** button (on the left end of the task pane's title bar).

At this point, all you need to do is click the **Print** button. However, you might want to replace some of the clip art, add text, or rearrange items before you print. The following sections explain your options.

Figure 28.3

Use the options in the task pane to tweak the publication's overall design and layout.

4. To back up, click the Back button.

3. To hide the task pane, click the Close button.

1. Click the desired category of settings.

2. Follow the onscreen instructions or enter the desired setting.

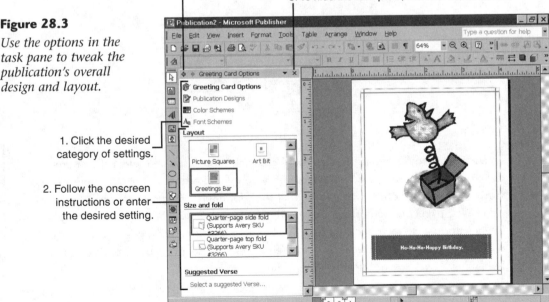

Basic Stuff You Ought to Know

Your first glance at the publication the wizard created might just turn you to stone. The page is dinky, the graphics look sloppy, and the text looks as if the wizard were trying to fit it on the head of a pin. Before you can do anything, you need to know how to zoom in and out and flip from one page to the next.

First, zoom in. Open the **Zoom** drop-down list in the Standard toolbar, as shown in Figure 28.4, and select the desired zoom percentage—75% is usually sufficient. Just below the work area are the page flippers. Click the icon for the desired page to quickly display it. You already know how to use the scrollbars; you'll get plenty of scrollbar practice in Publisher.

Tools for inserting objects

Select the desired zoom percentage.

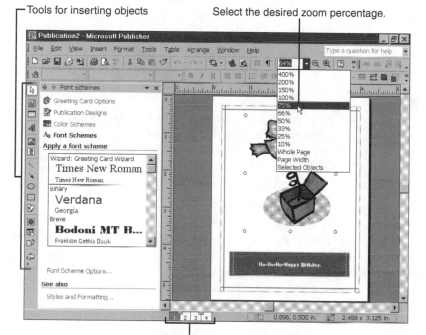

Figure 28.4

Before you can start working, make sure you can see everything.

Use the Page Navigation buttons to flip pages.

After you have everything in plain sight, you're ready to fiddle with the publication. However, there are a few additional things that might not seem obvious at first:

➤ You will encounter two types of text boxes—normal and WordArt—that might look the same. To edit text in a normal text box, click in the text box to position the insertion point and type your changes (just pretend you're working in Word). For WordArt "text boxes," double-click the box to display a dialog box for editing the text. Edit your text and click **OK**.

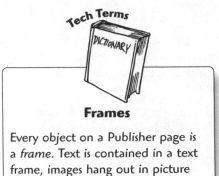

Frames

Every object on a Publisher page is a *frame*. Text is contained in a text frame, images hang out in picture frames, and WordArt objects are held in WordArt frames. Frames make rearranging objects on a page easy.

➤ The dotted lines are page layout guides. They don't print. See "Page Layout Tools You Can't Live Without," later in this chapter, for details.

➤ Some publications have a text frame off to the side that displays information about the publication. This won't print. In fact, nothing placed on the gray area outside the page will print. You can drag objects onto this work area as you lay out your pages.

➤ A greeting card might have a graphic on the first page that looks as though it doesn't fit on the page. Don't worry about it. Publisher does this wrap-around thing with the graphic so it prints on both the front and back of the card. It's actually pretty cool.

Making New Pages

If you created a greeting card, you probably don't want to add any pages to it. It consists of four pages that print on a single sheet of paper; if you fold it correctly, you end up with a greeting card. However, if you're working on a newsletter, résumé, or some other document that might need to spread out on two or more pages, you'll have to add pages to your publication.

To add a page, flip to the page where you want the new page inserted. Open the **Insert** menu and select **Page**. The Insert Page dialog box appears. Enter the desired number of new pages, specify where you want them inserted (Before or After Current Page), and select the desired setting under Options: **Insert Blank Pages**, **Create One Text Frame on Each Page**, or **Duplicate All Objects on Page ___**. Click **OK**, and Publisher slaps in the specified number of pages. (Press **Ctrl+Shift+N** to insert a blank page at the end of the publication, no questions asked.)

Working Faster with Grainy (or No) Pictures

Nothing can slow down your computer more than graphics. They take a great deal of memory and processing power to display correctly and will slow your scrolling and frame work down to a crawl.

To speed things up, you can hide the graphics or display them in a lower resolution. Open the **View** menu and select **Picture**. In the Picture Display dialog box, select the desired option: **Detailed Display** (high-quality, but slow), **Fast Resize and Zoom** (fast, but grainy pictures), or **Hide Pictures** (white placeholders that don't even show the picture). Click **OK** to save your settings.

Customizing a Prefab Publication

Some head hunter just called to inform you of a mind-boggling job prospect—high pay, good benefits, four weeks of vacation, company car. You need a great-looking résumé, and you need it quick. You fired up the résumé wizard and answered all the questions. Now what? Here's a bare-bones list of what you need to know to manually customize your publication:

➤ Click in a text frame (box) to position the insertion point, and then type your additions. You can drag over text to highlight it and then type to replace it.

➤ To format text, highlight it and use the Formatting toolbar buttons or the Format menu options just as you do in Word (although the paragraph formatting options are limited). See Chapter 5, "Giving Your Text a Makeover," for details.

➤ To select a frame, click it. Handles (small black boxes) appear around the frame, as shown in Figure 28.5. Drag a handle to resize the frame, and drag an edge of the frame to move the frame. When you move the mouse pointer over an edge of a frame, the pointer appears as a moving van. Cute, huh?

➤ If you type more than a text frame has room for, an Overflow button (with three dots on it) appears at the bottom of the frame, indicating that the text doesn't fit. You have three options: resize the text box, make the text smaller, or spill the text into an empty text frame (click the Overflow button and click inside an empty text frame).

➤ To replace an image, double-click the existing image and select a different clip art image.

➤ To insert a new picture, text, table, or WordArt frame, click the button for the desired object in the left toolbar. Position the mouse pointer over the page where you want the upper-left corner of the object placed and then drag down and to the right. Release the mouse button.

➤ You can lay frames on top of each other, sort of like a stack of pancakes. However, selecting the frame at the bottom is as difficult as eating the pancake at the bottom of the stack without disturbing the stack. To dig up a buried frame, click the frame that's lying on top of it, and press **Alt+Shift+F6** (or click **Arrange, Order, Send to Back**).

Insider Tip

Destacking Frames

Another way to dig a frame out of a pile is to drag frames to the gray area surrounding the page. This is the *scratch area*. When you decide where you want to place the frame, drag it back over the page and drop it into place.

Figure 28.5

If you can manage frames, you know most of what you need to know to customize your publication.

Picture   WordArt   Handles

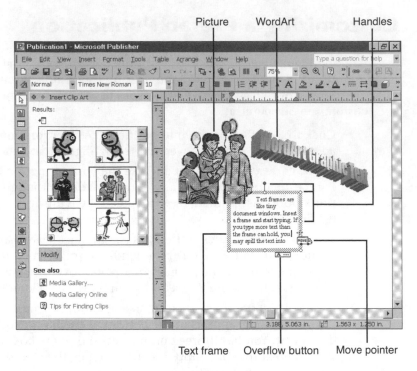

Text frame   Overflow button   Move pointer

Sure, there's much more you can do to customize your publication, but you want to get that résumé out in a hurry. Be sure to proofread it before you send it. And good luck!

Insider Tip

E-mail Right from Publisher

To e-mail your publication to someone, open the **File** menu and point to **Send To**. To send the publication as an HTML-formatted e-mail message (that anyone can open and view with an e-mail program), click **Mail Recipient**. To send the publication as a Publisher file, select **Mail Recipient (as Attachment)**. Address the message and send it as you normally would. (If you are e-mailing a multipage publication that contains a great deal of artwork, sending the publication via e-mail might take several minutes.)

Page Layout Tools You Can't Live Without

I mentioned the blue and pink dotted lines earlier in this chapter. What are they for? The pink box indicates the page margins. Try to stay within the margins, so your objects won't stretch out to an area that your printer can't print on. The blue lines are gridlines that help you position frames more precisely on a page. When you drag the edge of an object near a gridline, the edge snaps to the gridline, as though the gridline were magnetic.

To adjust the margins and turn on gridlines, open the **Arrange** menu and select **Layout Guides**. Enter the desired page margins (in inches), select the number of columns and rows you want to use in the grid, and click **OK**.

To move a gridline, open the **View** menu and select **Master Page** or press **Ctrl+M**. This displays the margins and gridlines. Hold down the **Shift** key, and move the mouse pointer over a gridline (or margin line) so the pointer displays "Adjust." Drag the gridline to the desired position. As you drag, a light gray line appears in the ruler at the top or left side of the viewing area, showing you the exact position of the line. Release the mouse button and Shift key. (To return to the foreground, press **Ctrl+M** or select **View**, **Master Page**.)

Although those sticky gridlines sure help when it comes to aligning objects, they can also get on your nerves. To turn off the snap-to feature, open the **Arrange** menu, point to **Snap**, and select **To Ruler Marks** or **To Guides** to remove the check mark next to the option. To hide the margin and layout guides altogether, open the **View** menu and select **Boundaries and Guides** or press **Ctrl+Shift+O**.

Printing Professional-Looking Publications

Modern desktop printers are capable of generating high-quality publications economically, and they give you complete control over the printing schedule. When you need a publication in a hurry, there's no better way to produce it than by printing it. However, if you need to print large quantities of full-color catalogs, three-fold brochures, menus, or other professional publications, a full-service printing shop is much better equipped to handle the job.

But where do you start? What are your options? The following sections provide the information you need to print your publications yourself and prepare your publications to have a professional printer produce them.

Checking Out Your Printing Options

Faced with the decision of how to mass produce your publications, you should consider two things—cost and quality—and try to balance these two considerations to make the best business decision. Before you decide, read through the following list of printing options:

➤ **Strict budget**—Choose grayscale, medium resolution (600dpi). Grayscale is sort of like black-and-white TV, which uses black, white, and various grades of shading to display images. (To add color cheaply, print on colored paper.)

➤ **Colorful, but a little pricey**—Choose full-color, continuous tone printing at low to medium resolution (300dpi–600dpi), assuming the printing shop offers this option. This isn't the best option for printing full-color photos, but it's great for printing text and computer graphics using a desktop printer.

➤ **Money is no object**—Choose full-color, high-end printing at resolutions of 1200dpi. If your publication includes crisp color photos and you need high-quality print, high-end printing is the only way to go. This option requires that you send the publication to the printing shop on disk or via modem.

➤ **Compromise solution**—To stay within budget and yet create high-quality publications, use *spot-printing* (or *two-color*) output. With spot-printing, most text and graphics are printed in grayscale, but another color is used for headings or other objects, such as sidebars. Because you are using only one additional color, spot-printing is much less expensive than full-color.

Do It Yourself with Your Desktop Printer

Your printer can handle most of your publication needs and should be able to produce fairly high-quality printouts, assuming you use high-quality paper. Load the paper into your printer, turn it on, and select **File**, **Print**. Enter your printing preferences and click the **OK** button.

Two-Color Output for the Budget Conscious

An inexpensive way to add color to a document is to use spot-color (also called two-color) printing. To print a publication that uses spot color, the printer must create two sets of printer plates for each page. One plate prints everything that appears black (typically the running text), and the other plate applies the color (typically for headings, lines, and some graphics).

In most cases, the imagesetter will create the actual color separations and output them on film for application to the printing plates. However, you must format the objects you want to appear in the second color. Take the following steps:

1. Open your publication.
2. Open the **Tools** menu, point to **Commercial Printing Tools**, and click **Color Printing**.
3. Click **Spot Color(s)**.
4. In the list of spot colors, select **Spot Color 2** and click the **Modify** button. (Black will be used as Color 1.)

5. Select the color you want to use for the second color and click **OK**. (You can specify a different color at the printing shop, but try to pick something close.)

6. Click **OK** to save your changes. Publisher automatically applies the second color to some of the objects in your publication.

7. To have a frame's background print in the second color, select the frame, click the down arrow to the right of the **Fill Color** button, and select the second color or a shade of it. (In spot-color publications, the available colors are limited to black, shades of gray, the specified second color, and shades of the specified color.)

8. To make a picture, text, or WordArt object print in the second color, take one of the following steps:

   ➤ **Picture**—Right-click the picture, click **Format Picture**, select the **Picture** tab, and click the **Recolor** button. Open the **Color** list, select the desired shade of the second color and click **OK**. Click **OK** to save your changes and close the Format Picture dialog box.

   ➤ **WordArt**—Click the WordArt object and click the **Format WordArt** button in the toolbar that appears. Click the **Colors and Lines** tab if it is not already up front, and then open the **Color** list and select the desired shade of the second color. Click **OK** to save your changes.

   ➤ **Text**—Highlight the text, click the down arrow to the right of the **Font Color** button, and select the desired second color or shading.

To print your document, select **File**, **Print**, select **Print Separations**, and then click **OK**. Publisher prints each page as two pages: one containing all the grayscale text and objects and a second page containing all the color text and objects. When the printing shop returns a proof of your publication, match it against your proof to verify the color separations before you give your approval for the final printing.

Printing to a File for Outside Printing

If you're outputting your publication to a file to send it to the printing shop on a floppy disk or via modem, the process is a little complicated. First, find out from the printing shop which printer you should use. You might have to install another Windows printer driver (**Start**, **Settings**, **Printers**, **Add Printer**).

When you have the correct printer installed, you can use the Pack and Go Wizard to print your publication to a file on your hard drive or transfer your publication to a set of floppy disks. Here's what you do:

1. Save your publication as you normally save a document.

2. Open the **File** menu, point to **Pack and Go**, and select **Take to a Commercial Printing Service**. The first Pack and Go Wizard dialog box appears, describing what the wizard can do.

3. Click **Next**.

4. Select the drive and folder in which you want the output stored. (If you are transferring the publication to a set of floppy disks, be sure you have several freshly formatted disks on hand.) Click **Next**.

5. Select the desired options for embedding fonts and graphics in your publication and click **Next**.

6. Click **Finish**. The Pack and Go Wizard transfers your publication into a file or set of files and includes a file called `Unpack.exe`, which you run to extract the file(s) that make up your publication.

The Least You Need to Know

With Publisher's publication wizards, task panes, and well-stocked toolbars, you don't need to know much to create and print custom greeting cards, newsletters, brochures, catalogs, and other publications. Just keep the following basics in mind:

➤ When you start Publisher, it displays the New from Existing Publication task pane, which provides a list of predesigned publication types.

➤ You can display the New from Existing Publication task pane at any time by opening the **File** menu and selecting **New**.

➤ In the New from Existing Publication task pane, select the desired publication type: **Quick Publications**, **Newsletters**, **Brochures**, and so on.

➤ After selecting a publication type, click the sample you want to start with.

➤ After you select a sample publication, use the task pane (on the left) to enter you preferences.

➤ To zoom in, open the **Zoom** drop-down list (on the Standard toolbar) and select the desired zoom percentage.

➤ The page buttons, which appear below the publication viewing area, allow you to flip from one page to another.

➤ To insert a new page in your publication, open the **Insert** menu and select **Page**, or press **Ctrl+N**.

➤ To move a frame, drag its border when the mouse pointer appears as a moving van. To resize a frame, drag its handle.

➤ To print your publication, open the **File** menu, select **Print**, enter your preferences, and click **OK**.

Speak Like a Geek: The Complete Archive

absolute cell reference   In an Excel worksheet formula, a cell address that does not change when you move or copy the formula. (See also *relative cell reference*.)

Access   The database application included with Microsoft Office. Access enables you to create forms, use the forms to enter data, and create reports that present data in a meaningful format.

action button   On a PowerPoint slide, a button that appears on the slide and enables the person viewing the slide show to perform some action, such as advancing to the next slide.

address   A combination of a column letter and row number that specifies the location of a cell in an Excel worksheet. For example, the address of the cell in the upper-left corner of the worksheet is A1. Addresses are commonly used in formulas to pull values into the calculation.

appointment   In Outlook, a scheduled time at which you need to do something but that does not require the time of another co-worker (for example, lunch with your spouse or a dentist appointment). Contrast to *meeting*.

argument   The part of a function statement in an Excel worksheet that tells the function which values to use in the calculations. For example, in =AVERAGE(A1..K15), AVERAGE is the function and (A1..K15) is the argument.

AutoContent Wizard   In PowerPoint, a series of dialog boxes that creates a prefab presentation for advertising a product, presenting a sales pitch, training new employees, and so on.

AutoCorrect   A feature that automatically corrects typos and misspellings as you type.

AutoFit   An Excel feature that makes a column wide enough to fit the widest entry in that column. Think of AutoFit as spandex for spreadsheets.

AutoFormat   An Excel feature that beautifies your worksheets without making you do too much. AutoFormat adds shading, cell borders, and other fancy formatting to your worksheet. Word has this feature, too, for use on tables.

AutoText   A feature that enables you to create shorthand entries for text you commonly type. For example, you can create an AutoText entry that inserts "Microsoft Office Shortcut Bar" whenever you type MOSB and press Enter or the F3 key.

bookmark   1. A Word feature that inserts a tag in your document so you can quickly jump back to that spot later. 2. In a Web page, a code that allows you to point a link to a specific location on the page.

border   A box around text, a picture, or some other object. You can change the color, thickness, and style of borders to give them a different look.

browser   See *Web browser*.

build   An animated effect in a slide show that introduces elements on a slide one at a time. You can create a build, for example, that assembles a bulleted list one bullet at a time.

cell   The rectangle formed by the intersection of a column and a row in an Excel worksheet. You type text labels, values, and formulas in cells to create a worksheet.

chart   A graphical representation of numerical data. Charts put numbers in perspective. For example, the federal government might use a pie chart to illustrate the percentage of taxes allocated to various programs, such as defense, social security, and education. Charts are also called *graphs*.

circular reference   In a worksheet, a formula that references the same cell that contains the formula. This results in an error; Excel slaps your hand and displays a dialog box saying you can't do that.

client   A program that receives copied, linked, or embedded data from other programs. The term *client* is also used to describe your computer when you are connecting to a server computer on a network or on the Internet.

clip art   A collection of predrawn images you can use to decorate your documents even if you have no artistic talent.

Clipboard   A Windows storage area in which data temporarily is stored when you cut or copy it.

collapse   A Word outlining feature that enables you to hide the text that appears below the headings to view and rearrange headings in the outline. (See also *expand*.)

column   In a table or worksheet, a vertical arrangement of data. Columns intersect with rows to form boxes, called *cells*, into which you type entries. (See also *newspaper columns*.)

conditional formatting   A cell-formatting option in Excel that changes the way a cell or its content appears based on the value in that cell. For example, you can format a cell so that it displays the value in green when the value is positive or shades the cell red when the value is negative. Conditional formatting is also available in Outlook to highlight appointments.

contiguous   A fancy term for neighboring. On a worksheet, for example, all cells that are next to each other are said to be contiguous.

control   A graphical object on an Access form or report that enables a user to enter data, execute a command, or display data. Common controls include text boxes, option buttons, and check boxes.

control source   The field from which a control on a form or report obtains data entries. For example, you can place a Product Name field on your report that extracts data from a source, such as the Product Name field in the Products table.

cursor   Another name for the vertical line that indicates where text is inserted when you start typing. The preferred name is *insertion point*.

data   Information a computer stores and works with.

data source   A file from which you extract data entries. If you create a form letter in Word that extracts names and addresses from an address book, for example, the address book is the data source. (See also *main document*.)

database   A computer program used for storing, organizing, and retrieving information. The term is also used to describe any collection of data.

datasheet   A mini-worksheet/table that makes entering data that you want to graph or include in a database easy. In Access, you can view a table or form in Datasheet view for quicker data entry.

desktop   The area on your Windows computer screen from which you can open programs, remove files with the Recycle Bin, and view or manage other resources.

destination document   The file into which you paste data that has been cut or copied from another document.

dialog box   A typically small window that an application displays when it needs more information to perform a required task.

document   The file you create when you work in any of the Office applications. These files include Word documents, Excel workbooks, PowerPoint presentations, and Access databases.

drag and drop   To copy or move data simply by selecting it and dragging it with the mouse from one place to another in the same document or in different documents.

e-mail   Short for electronic mail, it's a system that enables users to exchange messages and files over network connections, over the Internet, or via modem.

embed   To copy data from a document in one application and paste it into a document created with another application, while retaining a link to the application in which the data was created. If you embed an Excel worksheet into a Word document, for example, you can double-click the worksheet in the Word document to run Excel and edit the worksheet.

event   In Outlook, an activity that takes one or more days as opposed to a block of time during one day.

Excel   A spreadsheet program made by Microsoft. You can use Excel to organize numbers and other data, perform complex mathematical operations, and much more.

expand   A Word outlining feature that enables you to bring text back into view after you collapse an outline. (See also *collapse*.)

field   On a fill-in-the-blank form, the blank. In a database, you create forms for entering data. Each form has one or more fields into which you type data. A collection of field entries makes up a record.

field code   A tag that Word inserts in a document to extract data from another source. For example, the date field code inserts the date from your computer's internal clock. Word also uses field codes to pull information into a form letter, generate a table of contents, and create numbered lists.

file   A collection of data saved to disk under a specific name. Whenever you save a document, the application stores it in a file on a floppy disk, a hard disk, or a network drive.

fill   The background color used for a cell in a Word table or an Excel worksheet, or for a drawing object.

fill handle   A little black box that appears just outside the lower-right corner of a selected Excel worksheet cell. You can drag the fill handle to copy the entry from the selected cell into a string of neighboring cells.

fill series   A string of related values that you can quickly insert into neighboring cells in an Excel worksheet. For example, Excel has a fill series that consists of the names of the week. To insert the names into a series of cells, all you have to do is type **Monday** in the first cell, and then drag the fill handle on the cell over six neighboring cells. When you release the mouse button, Excel inserts the names of the remaining six days of the week.

filter   To extract related records from a database. If you had a phone book full of names and addresses, for example, you could use a filter to pull out the records Smith through Smythe.

font   A set of characters sharing the same design.

foreign key   An access field that establishes a relationship to another table. In most cases, the two tables have fields of the same name. The *primary key* in one table supplies information to the foreign key field in the other table. For example, you might have a Customer table that supplies the Customer ID to the Orders table. (See also *primary key*.)

form   A fill-in-the-blanks page common on Web pages and in Excel and Access databases. In databases you fill out a form to enter a record. (See also *record*.)

formatting   Changing the appearance or layout of a page or of selected text. Formatting includes changing margins, choosing different font styles, changing line spacing, and selecting text colors.

formula   A mathematical statement in a table or worksheet that tells the application how to perform calculations on a set of values. Formulas typically consist of cell addresses that pull values from specific cells and mathematical operators that specify which operations to perform. For example, =(C1+C2+C3)/3 determines the average of the values in cells C1–C3.

function   A ready-made formula that performs a mathematical operation on a set of values. The simple function SUM, for example, determines the total of a set of values. A more complicated function might determine a payment on a loan given the loan amount, the term, and the interest rate.

grammar checker   An editing tool built into most word processors that highlights words and phrases that are grammatically incorrect or questionable.

graph   See *chart*. Although most people call them graphs, Microsoft insists on calling them *charts*.

graphics   Electronic art and pictures. A graphic can be a drawing created on the computer; an image scanned in for digital manipulation (clip art); or various shapes, lines, and boxes created with the computer.

gridlines   Nonprinting lines in a table or worksheet that display the boundaries of cells. Not to be confused with *borders*, which actually do appear in print.

group   To select and treat a collection of graphic objects as a single object. If you have several drawn objects that compose a single graphic, grouping is useful for moving and resizing the objects as a unit. (See also *ungroup*.)

handles   Tiny squares that surround a selected graphic object or text box. You can easily change the size or dimensions of an object by dragging one of its handles.

handouts   PowerPoint pages you can print for distribution to your audience.

header   Text and small graphics (such as logos) that print at the top of every document page. Headers typically include the document's title, section title, the date the document was printed, and page numbers.

359

home page   1. The Web page your Web browser loads whenever it starts. 2. The opening page at a Web site. A home page typically contains a brief introduction to the site, along with links to other pages at the site.

HTML   Short for Hypertext Markup Language, a set of codes (called *tags*) that insert graphics, links, audio clips, and other objects on a Web page and tell your Web browser how to display the page. You don't actually see these codes when you view a Web page, unless the Web page creator didn't know what he was doing.

hyperlink   Text, graphics, icons, or other items in a document that link to other areas in the document or to pages, files, and other resources outside a document. Hyperlinks commonly are used on Web pages to link one Web page to another.

IM   See *instant message*.

insertion point   A blinking vertical line that indicates where text will appear when you start typing or where an object will be inserted.

instant message   A typed message you can send over the Internet to another person who is connected to the Internet and is using a compatible instant messaging program. The message pops up on the recipient's screen and enables the recipient to automatically reply.

IntelliMouse   A three-button pointing device from Microsoft. The middle button on the IntelliMouse is a little gray wheel you can spin to scroll through a document. You can use this button for other tasks, as explained in Chapter 1, "Up and Running with Office XP."

Internet   A global system of interconnected networks that enables anyone with a computer and a modem or other network connection to open multimedia Web pages, exchange e-mail, chat, and much more.

Internet Explorer   A popular Web browser included with most Microsoft products, including Windows and Office. (See also *Web browser*.)

intranet   An internal network (in a corporation, university, or other institution) that uses Internet technologies to make it easier to navigate the network. Intranets are typically for internal use only; access from the Internet generally is prohibited.

journal   In Outlook, a diary that keeps track of your work, including the documents you create and e-mail messages you send and receive. You can also enter information about important phone calls (for legal purposes) and record personal information.

labels   Entries in an Excel worksheet that typically are used to indicate the meaning of other entries, such as values. Labels usually appear at the tops of columns and to the left of rows.

leader   A string of characters that leads up to the text at the tab stop. Like this:

Chapter 14 157

legend   A little box that displays color codes for your charts (graphs). On road maps you've no doubt seen legends that show the mileage scale and differentiate between side roads and main drags.

link   1. To copy data from a source document and paste it into a destination document while retaining a live connection between the two documents. Whenever you edit the data in the source document, the changes appear automatically in the destination document. For example, if you paste an Excel worksheet as a link into a PowerPoint presentation, whenever you edit the worksheet the changes appear in your presentation. 2. On a Web page, highlighted text or icons that you click to open associated Web pages. (See also *hyperlink*.)

link bar   A horizontal or vertical banner on a Web page that contains highlighted text a user can click to navigate the page, open other Web pages, or jump to other Web sites.

macro   A series of recorded commands, keystrokes, and mouse moves you can play back by entering the macro's name, clicking a button, or pressing a special key combination.

mail merge   A feature that extracts data (such as names and addresses) from one document and automatically inserts it into another document (such as a form letter) to create a collection of unique documents.

main document   The primary document of the two documents you are merging. In a mail merge operation, the letter is the *main document* and the address book is the *data source*. (See also *mail merge*.)

maximize   To enlarge your window to fill the entire screen.

media gallery   Microsoft Office's collection of clip art, photographs, movies, and audio clips.

meeting   An event that you do with other people at your work, excluding complaining about the boss, betting on the NCAA basketball tournament, and sneaking out for a cigarette. Meetings require that you coordinate a time block with your fellow drones.

memory   The computer's electronic storage area. Memory used to be measured in kilobytes; but with the advances in operating systems and applications, it is now measured in megabytes. And your computer better have at least 16 megabytes if you want to use Office.

menu   A list of commands you can choose by clicking them with your mouse. Menus can drop down from a menu bar or pop up on your screen when you click the right mouse button. You can usually get a menu to disappear by clicking something other than the menu.

minimize   To reduce your window to a button on the taskbar.

mixed reference   In a spreadsheet formula, an absolute cell reference, such as $A3, that tells the formula to always refer to a cell in column A, but that when copying the formula to another cell, the row number can change.

narration   In a PowerPoint presentation, a voice recording that plays during the presentation.

network   A group of computers connected with high-speed data cables for the purpose of sharing hardware, software, data, and communications.

newspaper columns   A formatting option for text that causes it to display two or more columns of text on a page. The text runs from the top of the first column to the bottom and continues at the top of the next column, as in a newspaper or magazine.

Office Assistant   An animated character that pops up on your screen and offers help whenever you start an Office application or try to perform a somewhat complex task.

OLE   Short for object linking and embedding, OLE is a technology that enables different types of documents to freely share data. (See also *embed* and *link*.)

online   To be connected to another computer or network of computers.

operator   A symbol, typically used in a spreadsheet, that tells the spreadsheet which mathematical operation to perform. Operators include + (addition), - (subtraction), * (multiplication), and / (division).

order of operations   The sequence in which Excel performs a series of calculations, also called *precedence*. Excel performs all operations enclosed in parentheses first, next exponential equations, multiplication and division, and, finally, addition and subtraction.

outline level   A Word feature that enables you to specify how you want the headings in your document treated. By specifying an outline level for each heading, you can collapse the outline to view only the headings and then restructure your document simply by moving the headings.

Outlook   The personal information manager/e-mail application that comes with Office. With Outlook, you can keep track of appointments and special dates, prioritize your list of things to do, manage your e-mail, keep an address book and journal, and even write yourself personal reminder notes.

page break   A printing code that indicates where a page ends and a new page begins. Office applications automatically insert page breaks based on the margins and the paper size. You can, however, insert manual page breaks to divide pages as desired.

pane   A portion of a window that displays different data in the same document. Panes are useful if you are working in one part of the document and need to refer to information in a different part of the document.

PowerPoint   The Office slide show program. With PowerPoint, you can create onscreen presentations, transfer your presentations to 35mm slides, or print them on paper or overhead transparencies. You can even create talkies by recording a voice narration.

presentation   Fancy name for a PowerPoint slide show.

primary key   In an Access table, a field that supplies entries to a corresponding field in another table. (See also *foreign key*.)

print area   A portion of an Excel worksheet that you want to print. Because worksheets can become quite long and wide, you might want to print only a portion of the worksheet.

program   A special set of instructions written for the computer, telling it how to perform some useful task. You hear the words *program, software,* and *application* used interchangeably; they all mean the same thing.

query   A set of instructions that tells Access which data to extract from a database, how to sort the data, and how to arrange it. You use queries to pull data from one or more tables or from various databases to create reports.

range   In an Excel worksheet, a group of neighboring cells or a set of cell blocks.

recalculation   To run the formulas in a worksheet again after changing a value. By default, Excel automatically recalculates the formulas. If you turn off AutoRecalculation, you can have Excel recalculate formulas by pressing F9.

record   A collection of fields making one complete entry in a database. Think of a Rolodex as a database. Each card on that Rolodex is a record.

relational database   A computer program used for storing data and retrieving and combining information from two or more tables or databases. A relational database, such as Access, enables you to store data in smaller, more manageable tables and combine the data as needed by creating queries and reports. See also *database, query,* and *report*.

relative cell reference   In an Excel worksheet formula, a cell address that changes when you paste the formula into a different cell. Unless you specify otherwise, Excel makes all cell references in formulas relative, so that when you copy a formula into a different cell, the addresses automatically adjust to perform the calculations on a different set of data. If you don't want a cell address to change, you must mark it as an absolute cell reference.

report   An Access and Excel feature that extracts data from one or more databases or tables, arranges the data attractively on a page, and (optionally) performs calculations on the data. You typically use reports to analyze data and present it in a meaningful format.

reveal formatting   A task pane that displays the format settings that control the appearance of highlighted text.

route   To send a document to a list of reviewers to obtain input and revisions.

ruler   A ribbon, typically displayed above or to the left of the document viewing area, that you use to change margins, indent paragraphs, and set tab stop positions.

scenario   In Excel, a set of values you can plug into a worksheet to see how these values affect the end result. When you play with sets of values in this way, you are said to be playing What-if?.

scrap   Selected text, graphic, or other object that you dragged from a document and placed on the Windows desktop. Scraps enable you to quickly move and copy data from one document to another.

ScreenTip   Formerly known as a ToolTip, a ScreenTip is a brief description of an object, a button, or an option that pops up whenever you rest the mouse pointer on the object.

section   In a Word document, a part of a document that has the same format settings for headers, footers, and columns. By default, every document has one section. If you change the section formatting for part of the document, you create a new section.

selection box   An outline that appears around a cell or block of cells in an Excel worksheet when the cell(s) is selected.

server   On a network or on the Internet, the computer that your computer (the client) connects to and uses to access information, use applications, or share resources.

Shortcut bar   A strip of buttons that enable you to easily access the Office applications and perform specific tasks, such as creating a new document or recording an appointment. After you install Office, the Shortcut bar appears whenever you start your computer.

shortcut keys   Keypress combinations that enable you to bypass a menu or command sequence.

slide   A screen in a PowerPoint presentation. Slides can be shown onscreen or transferred to paper, transparencies, or 35mm slides.

slide master   A PowerPoint slide that works in the background to control the color and formatting for all the slides in a presentation. You can override the master slide settings on individual slides. (See also *title master*.)

slide transition   An animation feature that provides a graphic movement from one slide to the next in a presentation.

smart tags   Icons that automatically appear in a document to provide additional instructions, list common commands or options, or display links to related data on the Web or in other Office applications.

source document   The file from which you copy or cut data to insert into another document. If you copy data from a source document and paste it as a link into another (destination) document, whenever you edit the source document, your changes appear in the destination document.

speech recognition   Technology that enables a computer program to identify spoken commands and convert spoken words into text.

split box   A small bar, typically at the top of the vertical scrollbar or the right end of the horizontal scrollbar, that enables you to divide a document window into two panes. (See also *pane*.)

spool   A printing technology that sends print instructions to the hard disk and then feeds the instructions to the printer so you can continue working while the printer prints your document.

spreadsheet   A program made to imitate a ledger's rows and columns that you use to organize and display data. You can use spreadsheets to arrange data in rows and columns, to perform calculations on numerical entries, and to analyze data through charts.

status bar   A bar at the bottom of a program window that contains information about the currently active document. A status bar typically displays the location of the insertion point and the typing mode (for example, insert or overtype, recording a macro, or selecting text).

style   A collection of format settings you can apply to a paragraph or to selected text. If you change one or more format settings in a style, the changes affect all the text you formatted with that style.

subscription   An Office installation option that allows you to use one or more applications for a set period of time at a reduced price.

syntax   The taxes levied on cigarettes, alcohol, and other items that the government deems harmful to your health or moral well-being. Also, the format in which you must enter a formula or function for it to work properly. Think of it as grammar for numerical sentences.

table   A structure that organizes data in rows and columns. Tables commonly are used in Word documents and on Web pages to help align text without having to enter awkward tab settings.

task pane   A window frame that appears on the left or right side of the screen and presents options for the task you are currently performing. If you select **Insert**, **Picture**, **Clip Art**, for instance, the Insert Clip Art task pane provides options for searching through the Office clip art collection and inserting an image.

taskbar   The bar at the bottom of your Windows desktop that enables you to switch back and forth between applications or launch new programs with the Start button.

template   A pattern for a document that controls fonts, sizes, and other format settings.

text box   1. A blank space in a dialog box into which you can type a setting, such as the margin width. 2. A rectangular area on a page into which you can type text. Text boxes are excellent for newsletters and for adding sidebars and other chunks of text that do not fit in the normal flow of your document.

text-to-speech   A technology that enables a computer program to convert text into audible words. Excel's text-to-speech feature can "read" entries aloud.

timings   A PowerPoint feature that enables you to control the amount of time each slide remains onscreen during an online presentation.

title master   A PowerPoint slide that works in the background to control the formatting for the titles and subtitles on each slide in the presentation. (See also *slide master*.)

toolbar   A strip of buttons that usually appears at the top of an application's window just below the menu bar. With a toolbar, you can bypass the pull-down menu commands by clicking a button.

ungroup   To separate several drawing objects that you have grouped together to act as a single object. To delete or modify a single object, you must first ungroup the objects. (See also *group*.)

URL   Short for Uniform Resource Locator, an address that tells a Web browser where a Web page lives. You enter URLs in a Web browser to specify the location of a Web page you want the browser to open.

values   Numerical entries in a worksheet—as opposed to *labels*, which are text entries.

voice recognition   See *speech recognition*.

Web   Short for the World Wide Web, a collection of pages that are stored on computers all over the world and are linked to one another with hyperlinks. Your Office applications offer many new features that help you create your own pages for publication on the Web or download new features or updates online.

Web browser   An application that opens and displays pages on the World Wide Web. In addition to displaying the text that makes up those pages, most Web browsers can display graphics and play audio clips. Microsoft's Internet Explorer is a popular Web browser.

Web query   A set of instructions in Access or Excel that extracts data from a source on the Web. (See also *query*.)

wizard   A series of dialog boxes that leads you through the process of performing a complicated task. Office applications offer wizards as a quick way of creating documents. The Letter Wizard in Word, for example, can help you create a properly formatted business letter.

Word   The Office word processor.

word processor   An application that enables you to slice, dice, and mince your words and phrases; add graphics to your pages; and perform all other tasks required to create a printed publication.

word wrap   A feature in all word-processing programs that automatically moves the insertion point to the next line when you reach the end of the current line. Word wrap distinguishes a word-processing program from a typewriter, on which you must hit the carriage return to start a new line.

workbook   A collection of Excel worksheets. Each file you create in Excel is a workbook.

worksheet   A page in an Excel workbook on which you enter data.

wrap   See *word wrap*.

Index

C

Move to Folder button, 276
New button, 275
Organize button, 276
Print button, 275
Programs, 11
QuickShelf, 11
Reviewing, 311
Slide Master View, 207
Slide Sorter, 221
Hide Slide button, 221
Rehearse Timings button, 221
Speaker Notes button, 221
Summary Slide button, 221
Transition button, 221
Standard, 155, 176
Stop Recording, 337
Text Box, 67
tools, database (Excel), 147-148
totals, calculating (reports), 267 269
Track Changes button, 311
transforming
documents into Web pages, 314
Word documents into presentations, 307
Transition button, 221
transitions, animating (presentations), 222-223
Translate task pane, 108
translating foreign languages, 107-108
lengthy text, 108
troubleshooting, hardware problems, 32
Type drop-down list, 82
typing
Excel formulas, 153
error messages, 153

Microsoft Word documents, 47
Find and Replace command, 54
newspaper columns, 73-75
scrollbar methods, 48
Table feature, 75-77
text, moving, 52
text, selecting, 50-51
Undo feature, 55
views, zooming, 49-50

U

Undo button, 55, 169
uploading files to FTP servers, 324
usernames (Outlook), 293-296
users, multiple
Outlook, 296
speech recognition features, 35

V

values
Excel, 137
numbers as date/time, 140
numbers as text, 140
functions, 154
AutoSum, 155-156
Insert Function feature, 156-157
investments, 158-159
Vertical Alignment drop-down list, 114
video presentations, 218
video clips, 85-87
View bar (FrontPage), 325
View drop-down list, 260

View menu, 207, 237, 260
views
Calendar (Outlook), 278
Datasheet, 237-238
Design, 237-238
queries, sorting, 258
reports, 265-269
Master, 206-208
PowerPoint, 201
Form Design, 242
Normal, 201
Notes Page, 201
Slide Show, 201
Slide Sorter, 201, 221
tables, customizing, 237-238
Word documents, 49-50
Voice Command button, 37
Voice Training Wizard, 34

W-Z

watermarks, 92
Web
copying and pasting from, 144
folders, creating, 322-323
help, 26
PowerPoint presentations on, 227
reports placed on, 270
Web Component button, 328
Web folders, creating, 322-323
Web Page Wizard, 314-315
Web pages
adding, 348
formatting, 316
frames, 319-320
FrontPage, 325
creating, 327-328
customizing, 325
editing, 326